Give us this day...

A report on
the world
food crisis

Give us this day...

By the Staff of
The New York Times

ARNO PRESS

A New York Times Company

NEW YORK · 1975

Library of Congress Cataloging in Publication Data
Main entry under title:

Give us this day . . . : a report on the world food crisis.

          Articles originally published in the New York times.
          1. Food supply—Addresses, essays, lectures.
I. New York times.
HD9000.5.G57   338.1'9'08   75-1038
ISBN 0-405-06644-9

CONTENTS

INTRODUCTION

For some time scholars, commentators and others have been preoccupied by a concatenation of crises so deep-going and pervasive that they raise the most fundamental questions about government policies, the future of democratic institutions and, indeed, about human capacities to subdue the interlocking furies. Even in the United States, the most prosperous of societies, the trauma of Vietnam has been followed by the traumas of Watergate, acute fuel shortages, double-digit inflation, and economic recession.

This, however, is no time for hand-wringing despair. It is a time for problem-facing and problem-solving. And within this context, the press has an extra duty to perform in discharging its responsibilities of public service. It is important to unearth and expose corruption and injustice. But as an adjunct to what newspapers do all the time — namely, report on happenings considered important — the exposé, by itself, is no longer sufficient. There is also the responsibility of coming to grips with the so-called "big issues" — of identifying them, of digging to the core of their anatomy, and of reporting the findings to the public with some indications from the specialists in a given field of the options available for dealing with the problems.

Of the "big issues" confronting us, none is more basic than the world food crisis, which touches and affects virtually all of us. Yet surprisingly, this major problem had not left much impact on public awareness outside the areas where people were actually starving. It was not that the news had gone unreported. Newspapers, television and radio had all reported on food shortages in different parts of the world, but somehow the total "feel" and significance of the story had not stuck to the ribs.

Thus, last spring, *The New York Times* embarked on an intensive and sustained examination of the fundamentals of the world food situation. It decided to look into the key aspects of the story — human, scientific, political, economic and social — and report the findings to its readers as one of the most important news developments of our time.

This volume is the result of the inquiry thus far. Except for minor editing changes, the content is reproduced from articles published by *The New York Times*. These articles have been rearranged in sequence, but no attempt was made to update particular news events that were still evolving at the time the reports were published in *The Times*.

From June 21, 1974, to November 5, 1974, when the World Food Conference opened in Rome, *The Times* published 26 special articles on the food crisis in a continuing series and about 150 supplementary articles on particular aspects of the general food problem in New York, in the United States, and abroad. Altogether, about 50 reporters, not to mention editors, photographers and artists, worked on the food story at one time or another during this period.

Staff correspondents stationed at posts in the United States and in foreign countries moved from their bases to places where the food story was unfolding. Henry Kamm went from Europe for a long look at the African Sahel; Bernard Weinraub toured hunger-sectors of India while Kasturi Rangan reported on starvation in Bangladesh; Joseph Lelyveld proceeded from Hong Kong to Java for a story on hunger amid overpopulation and plenty; Juan de Onis investigated the food plans of the oil-rich Middle East; and William Robbins went from Washington to the Ozarks to write about the face of hunger in the United States.

The politics of food was examined by Leslie H. Gelb and Mr. Robbins in Washington, and subsequently by the latter and Clyde H. Farnsworth at the World Food Conference in Rome. H. L. Maidenberg probed the grain markets of the United States in an examination of how food is bought, transported and marketed.

In addition, technical aspects of the food story were explored in detail by five members of *The Times'* science staff — Science Editor Walter Sullivan, Harold M. Schmeck Jr., Jane E. Brody, Boyce Rensberger and Victor K. McElheny. Mr. Rensberger traveled to the International Corn and Wheat Improvement Center near Mexico City, where the "green revolution" began, and Mr. McElheny went to the International Rice Research Institute in the Philippines, and from there to other laboratories in Taiwan and India.

Like other "big issue" situations, the food crisis turned out to be a complex phenomenon involving the interconnectedness of many things. But although the issue was complex, a number of elements emerged in sharp focus.

There was, indeed, a food crisis. Far from being just talk, it was already exacting a toll of millions of lives either snuffed out by starvation or maimed by malnutrition. Nor were the well-to-do immune to food dislocations in remote parts of the world. The monsoon rains in India or a sugarbeet crop failure in the Soviet Union had an effect on prices in the United States. Moreover, all the evidence pointed not merely to a transient phenomenon, but to a chronic condition bound up with rising populations, limitations on resources, growing demands along with continuing poverty, and a host of other political, economic and climatic factors.

The scope of the world food crisis and its interrelationships are such that the world's peoples, whatever their divisions, are linked in a single food-sharing community.

As for the United States, its surplus food position and its bountiful family larders do not weigh lightly on the national conscience at a time when millions in other parts of the world go hungry. But, as Mr. Rensberger points out, individual forays into self-denial are not readily convertible to a meal for a starving Sahelian or Indian without larger and more systematic adjustments in the world production-and-distribution process.

Along with other "big issue" situations, the world food crisis poses for Americans the knotty and frustrating problem of formulating a national policy with the assent of a majority of the electorate. It is not for the news departments of newspapers to formulate national policies. It is their function, however, to provide information that can be helpful to both policy-makers and ordinary citizens as they make up their minds.

HENRY R. LIEBERMAN
Director of Science News
The New York Times

1 DIMENSIONS OF THE CRISIS

Wide World Photos

BOYCE RENSBERGER | # Early Warnings

From drought-besieged Africa to the jittery Chicago grain market, from worried Government offices in Washington to the under-filled granaries of teeming India, the long-predicted world food crisis is beginning to take shape as one of the greatest peacetime problems the world has had to face in modern times.

With growing frequency, a variety of leading individual experts and relevant organizations are coming forth to warn that a major global food shortage is developing.

They say it is almost certain to threaten the lives of many millions of people in the next year or two, and they urge international action to prevent a short-term crisis from becoming a chronic condition.

While there have always been famines and warnings of famine, food experts generally agree that the situation now is substantially different for these reasons:

• World population is expanding by larger numbers each year, especially in the poor countries that are most susceptible of famine. Last year, the population increased by 76 million, the largest increase ever. The number of mouths to feed throughout the world has almost doubled since the end of World War II.

• While agricultural production has generally kept pace, it has done so by increasing reliance on new, high-technology forms of farming that are now threatened by shortages of fertilizer and energy and soaring prices of raw materials.

• The grain reserves that once made it possible to send emergency food to stricken areas are now largely depleted. The

3

huge American farm "surpluses" that were such an item of controversy in the nineteen-sixties have long since been given away or sold and eaten. The world stockpile of grain that, in 1961, was equivalent to 95 days of world consumption has fallen to less than a 26-day supply now.

As the Arab oil embargo hastened the beginning of the energy crisis, so a major global shortage of fertilizer, precipitated by the oil squeeze, is cutting into this year's agricultural productivity in several populous countries.

The lack of fertilizer and rain and the untimely arrival of rains in some areas, are, in the view of many international food authorities, bringing the world to a food crisis sooner than had been expected a year or two ago.

The fertilizer shortage has already stunted the latest wheat crop in India and will likely reduce the succeeding crops so severely that by this autumn India could be experiencing a famine of sizeable proportions. Unless massive international aid is forthcoming, Norman Borlaug, the Nobel Prize-winning developer of high-yielding wheat, has forecast, from 10 million to 50 million persons could starve to death in India in the next 12 months.

His forecast is based on the calculated number of people the wheat shortfall would have fed plus a factor for the shortfalls expected in crops not yet harvested but lacking fertilizer and rain.

In other parts of Asia and in Latin America where supply has long barely met and sometimes failed to meet demand, people are beginning to experience unusually severe food shortages. The food that is available has become so costly that the meagerest of meals for millions of poor families take from 80 to 100 per cent of their incomes.

And in Africa the long drought may resume. International relief agencies forecast that the effects in coming months could be more severe than ever because the people have been weakened by previous years of deprivation.

By the start of 1975, many food experts fear, the soaring curve of food consumption will have overtaken the gentler slope of food production for the vast majority of the world's people, bringing more of mankind to hunger than ever before.

Many food and international relief experts say privately that they are not optimistic about how fast the rich countries will respond to a large famine. "It may take 50 or 100 million deaths before people are moved to find some kind of effective, long-term solution," one foundation official said.

A number of experts believe that the crisis may try the humanitarian potential of the American people — who control the world's largest source of food — as never before. Increasing social and political pressures within affected countries and growing stresses on "business as usual" international trading practices may test to the limit the ability of world leaders to cooperate.

Addeke Boerma, director general of the United Nations' Food and Agriculture Organization, said that the international community must soon come to terms with "the stark realities facing the people of this planet."

"Remember," Mr. Boerma said, "that, for one thing, prolonged deprivation leads people to desperation. Desperation often leads them to violence. And violence, as we all know, thrives on enlarged prospects of breaking down restraints including those of national frontiers."

Norman Borlaug often warns of the same thing when he says, "You can't build peace on empty stomachs."

The growing food shortage began to become critical in 1972, when a lack of rain in many countries led to poor crops. World grain production fell 4 per cent, a significant drop because the demand for food grows by 2 per cent each year. Drought in the Soviet Union caused that country to buy in 1973 one-fourth of the United States wheat crop.

"This small change was enough to cause violent responses in prices and shifting of foreign exchange expenditure and human suffering," said Lowell Hardin, head of agricultural programs for the Ford Foundation, a major supporter of agricultural research.

Poor weather in 1974, coupled with the fertilizer shortage, did much to limit crop yields in many countries. The effects will, of course, be felt most severely in countries where the nutrition levels are already inadequate.

Although areas of malnutrition exists in virtually all underdeveloped countries, by far the greatest food problems now exist among the 700 million people of India, Pakistan and Bangladesh. Other large problem areas are in the drought-stricken regions of Africa, in northeastern Brazil, among the Andean Indians, and in the poorer parts of Mexico and Central America.

The Overseas Development Council, a private "think tank" that studies the world food situation, estimates that one billion people suffer serious hunger at least part of the year. The F.A.O. estimates that 400 million people are malnourished but adds that "a less conservative definition [of malnutrition] might double the figure."

According to the World Health Organization, ten million children under the age of 5 are now chronically and severely malnourished, and 90 million more are moderately affected. While undernourished children may remain alive for a while, they are extremely vulnerable to minor infectious diseases.

"Where death certificates are issued for preschool infants in the poor countries, death is generally attributed to measles, pneumonia, dysentery or some other disease when, in fact, these children were probably victims of malnutrition," said Lester Brown, senior fellow of the Overseas Development Council.

W.H.O. figures show that of all the deaths in the poor countries, more than half occur among children under five, and that the vast majority of these deaths, perhaps as many as 75 per cent, are due to malnutrition complicated by infection.

While most people recognize that protein deficiency is a major problem, few appreciate that many people also suffer from a lack of starchy foods, which supply calories for energy.

"Average calorie intake in countries containing close to two-thirds of the world's people is below the nutritional minimum required for normal growth and activity," Dr. Brown said.

Even in countries where protein and calorie intake may be adequate, there can still be malnutrition due to deficiencies in one or more trace nutrients. W.H.O. authorities estimate that 700 million people now suffer iron deficiency anemia severely enough to impair their ability to work.

Every year hundreds of thousands of children, especially in Southeast Asia, go blind due to a lack of the leafy green or yellow vegetables that supply vitamin A.

Perhaps the most widely publicized recent hope for improving world food production is the controversial "Green Revolution," the use of new seed varieties that respond to irrigation and fertilizer with vastly increased crop yields.

Although the new, high-yielding strains involve mainly only two kinds of crops, wheat and rice, the potential benefits are significant because each of these grains supplies one-fifth of the world's food, more than any other source, plant or animal.

In Asia, where the situation is most critical, cereal grains, meaning wheat and rice almost exclusively, supply 74 per cent of the calories consumed. In North America, cereal grains supply only 24 per cent of the caloric intake. The difference is that North Americans and, increasingly Europeans and Japanese, consume large quantities of meat, milk and vegetables.

However, because much of the meat and dairy products consumed in the United States require grain for their production, the average American diet requires about five times as much grain to be grown as does the average Indian diet.

The Green Revolution has been criticized as giving all the advantages to large-scale high-technology farmers who then squeeze out their smaller competitors. Because most of the world's farmers have been too poor to buy irrigating equipment and fertilizer and too isolated to get the needed technical advice, they have not taken advantage of the new farming methods as readily as have wealthier farmers.

For these and other reasons, Green Revolution farming has not been practiced on one-half the arable land in any developing country, and in most of those countries it has been used on less than one-tenth the farmland.

Thus, agricultural researchers like Dr. Borlaug note, the full gains to be made through the Green Revolution have yet to be realized. Efforts are now under way through many agencies to develop credit mechanisms for small farmers to enable them to invest in higher yields and to improve the teaching of new farming methods to small farmers.

In small countries where this has been done, such as Taiwan, where the average farm size is 2½ acres, it has been found that small farms outproduce the huge "agri-business" farms of the United States. American farms yield an average of 3,050 pounds of grain per acre per year, Taiwanese farmers get 3,320 pounds.

While a long-term solution of the world food crisis depends on fundamental changes in the policies and practices of most small countries, the short-term solutions, many authorities feel, depend more on United States policy.

From the mid-nineteen-fifties to the nineteen-seventies, while the United States Government was buying surplus grain to keep market prices up, much of the developing world relied on this excess production to prevent famine. Through a change in Department of Agriculture policy, American grain reserves have now been largely eliminated.

To an extent greater than many people realized, it was American surpluses that stood as the world's buffer between enough to eat and famine. Now there is considerable controversy over whether the United States should re-establish large grain reserves or, as an alternative, contribute to a proposed world granary that famine-stricken nations could draw upon.

The debate includes concern over the impact of an American reserve on domestic prices, with the perennial conflict between farmers who want to sell for high prices and consumers who want to buy for low.

Although many food experts see a world grain reserve as essential in dealing with sporadic famines, most agree that, for the long range, even the vast productivity of American farms cannot forever make up the world's food deficits. Population is growing too large.

While every country produces all or most of the food it consumes only a handful produce much more than enough for domestic needs, thus providing large quantities for export. Besides the United States, the major food exporters include Canada, Australia and Argentina.

For the long-term solutions, few experts see any realistic solution other than to intensify the agriculture within the developing countries, trying to make each country as nearly self sufficient as possible. The agronomists note that because agriculture in the United States and other developed countries is already operating near the limits of presently available technology, whatever gains that can be expected must come from improvement in the countries where agriculture remains poor.

However, the experts note, upgrading agriculture in the poor countries will not be easy, because that effort would depend on ample supplies of fertilizer (and the petroleum from which much fertilizer is made), irrigation equipment and know-how, new credit mechanisms and continuing plant-breeding programs to adapt the better strains to local climatic conditions.

Much of this effort is becoming increasingly costly in a world of scarce resources and tight markets.

Many experts, such as George Harrar, a pioneer in breeding better food plants and a former president of the Rockefeller Foundation, see difficult conflicts between the humanitarian desire to rescue famine victims with food handouts and the need to increase incentives for poor countries to become more self-reliant in food.

"Why should we feed countries that won't feed themselves," Dr. Harrar often challenges.

While no one advocates abandoning innocent famine victims, many agree with Dr. Harrar that ways must be found to end the history of dependence on the United States for food that many small countries have had.

Because of the great complexity of the food problem, and because of the increasing interdependence of nations in matters of food, fertilizer, energy and raw materials, many authorities see a need to develop new world institutions to deal effectively with the problems.

Even then, most experts are not sanguine, for there remains the problem of population growth.

"I don't think there's any solution to the world food situation unless we get population stabilized," said Sterling Wortman, vice president of the Rockefeller Foundation. "Those of us who have been working to increase the food supply have never assumed we were doing any more than buying time."

2 FACES OF HUNGER

The New York Times / Raghubir Singh

Bankura: The Spread of Anguish

A woman feeds her emaciated child in an eerily quiet outdoor Government food kitchen. An old man, sitting on the ground, bites his knuckles and stares vacantly at the line of hungry families. A young man who holds a small boy in his arms begins to cry.

"No food for two days, no food for two days," he says in Bengali. His wife, clinging to an infant, groans, then lifts the child and shrieks that it will die.

Anguished scenes are unfolding in northern and eastern India. Famished children are digging grass and eating leaves or bark or rats to stay alive. Adults have left their villages to hunt for jobs, leaving terrified old people and children behind. Parents are selling children in Madhya Pradesh.

Mihir Dey, a laborer, stands in line each morning here in Bankura and gets a free pot of rice gruel that he shares with his wife, his aged mother and his two children. "The children are ill. We are hungry."

The food shortages that grip West Bengal, Madhya Pradesh, Orissa, Rajasthan and Bihar are a result of spring and summer drought, floods, the inexorable population spiral, Government bungling, and hoarding and black-marketing. The Indian Government has conceded in recent weeks that the situation is difficult," but it has denied that starvation deaths are taking place and has even predicted that the nation will reach self-reliance in food shortly.

But a visit to drought stricken areas in Rajasthan and Bihar and in West Bengal — one of the poorest states and probably

13

the most desperate — and reports from elsewhere underline the wrenching plight of hundreds of thousands, possibly millions.

Officials and relief workers are now saying privately that a tacit decision has been made to deal with the crisis by feeding the tense cities at the expense of the rural districts.

Rice is available at markets in the stricken states, especially West Bengal, but most hungry peasants cannot afford it. Since last year market prices have doubled and the ration system has proved chaotic. Wages for landless laborers are static — often as little as 35 cents a day — and families must scavenge for food.

"It's not a typical famine situation — some people are doing just fine and others are starving," said Bob Holson, the CARE representative in Calcutta, whose territory is West Bengal. "It's mostly the old people and the babies, the physiologically weakest, who are affected. You see children who will only live for 48 hours."

There are moments of terrible heartbreak. At the railway station in the Burdwan District of West Bengal, a woman whose 6-month-old daughter has died cries into the child's ear and shakes her. A crowd gathers and someone offers the woman five rupees, or 70 cents. She screams in Bengal: "What will I do with it?"

At the gruel kitchen in Bankura, where hundreds wait in line for a watery mixture of cracked wheat and lentils, Shanti Das stands trembling with her two sons, age 5 and 3. "My husband is a weaver and he's gone blind," she said. "What am I going to do?"

In villages near the Orissa border women call to passers-by: "We want work! We want food! Our children are dying!"

So far the only states where people are known to have died of starvation are Assam and West Bengal. Relief workers also report deaths in Madhya Pradesh and Bihar as a result of prolonged malnutrition from eating wild fruits, poor food grains and grass.

Politicians and relief workers in West Bengal say that at least 1,000 people died of starvation — some estimates run as high as 3,000 — in the district of Cooch Behar, a former princely state where the bodies of the victims are abandoned

The New York Times / Bernard Weinraub

A woman, who fled with her four children from a village where they could get nothing to eat, tends her ailing daughter on a street in Calcutta. They sleep on the pavement.

even on school verandas. Children with gastroenteritis cannot move without help.

Three other districts in West Bengal are afflicted: Bankura, about 200 miles northwest of Calcutta, the state capital; Purulia, near Bankura, and Jalpaiguri, near the Nepal border. These districts, with more than seven million people, mostly landless laborers, have suffered for years from government neglect, exploitive landowners and inadequate relief.

The government is believed to be feeding 600,000 in gruel kitchens although officials have said that 15 million of the 50 million in the state are in distress, eating a meal a day or less. A portion of the feeding program has been taken over by Hindu and Roman Catholic relief organizations, CARE, charities run by Marwaris, a business caste, and chambers of commerce.

Kashi Natha Misra, a harried Congress party legislator from Bankura, estimated that at least 200 had died of starvation in the district. The lone cottage industry, the weaving of cotton, is doomed because of inflation and paltry wages.

"Middle-class people are ashamed to stay in line at the gruel kitchens and some of them stay home and just die," he said. "Women don't go out during the day because their saris are torn. We're helpless."

Sivadas Banerjee, an agricultural specialist for The Times of India, who has written a series of stinging articles about the food situation in West Bengal, said: "You travel around and you see emaciated bodies, mothers and fathers abandoning children, people leaving their dead on the street, women selling themselves."

Critics have termed the West Bengal government inept and corrupt, and district officials report that warnings reached Calcutta months ago but that pleas for emergency food were ignored. It was only after Calcutta newspapers began publishing articles and photographs that they began to act.

All across India, a nation of 580 million, food production has slumped. The total for the 1974-75 agricultural year, which runs from July to June, may barely reach the 103-million-ton yield of the previous year.

To keep her population fed, India needs 115 million to 120 million tons of food-grains. The gap this year — at least 10 or

12 million tons — can be filled only by imports. So far, India has ordered about 4.5 million tons abroad and is hoping for shipments on preferential terms from the Soviet Union and the United States.

Despite the food crisis, which has been developing for three years, India has been extremely reluctant to ask for American food because, officials indicate, it might hurt the Government's pride.

If the decision is made to supply urban areas at the expense of rural ones, it will mean keeping rice and wheat flowing where 80 million to 100 million people depend on the ration system for cheap food. If the system breaks down, officials imply, the cities, already hard hit, will explode in violence.

"The brunt of the lean months will be borne by the landless laborers in the countryside," a food expert said. "In Bihar that's 40 per cent of the work force. In West Bengal it's 28 per cent. The people work no more than 200 days a year. They earn 2 to 5 rupees a day. This year food is out of reach. Their savings are gone. They have nothing, and they are starving."

If the Indian Government is to be criticized, it is for failing to shape emergency measures to deal with the crisis, for failing to ask for international help, for failing to acknowledge, even now, the scope of the problem, for failing to take steps against farmers who have circumvented official programs to build food supplies at set prices. Instead, the farmers, many of whom are heavy contributors to the governing Congress party, have hoarded food, sold it on the black market or shipped it abroad.

"There's a lot of brave talk about food procurement, a lot of radical rhetoric, but the state government and New Delhi don't want to upset these politically powerful landowners," said a food expert in Calcutta. In West Bengal, for example, the state government has procured 156,000 tons of rice toward a goal of 500,000 tons.

In the past few weeks relief efforts have been stepped up and there are reports that New Delhi will allot about $40-million to provide emergency employment. The program — cracking rocks, widening roads, razing land — is designed to give purchasing power to the landless.

In Bankura, Bishnu Bajoria, a businessman who is secretary of the Chamber of Commerce, which is helping to feed at least 25,000 people a day, stood at the gruel kitchen and watched hungry families wait in line for their only meal of the day. Only those with cards issued by the district authorities qualify.

Those without cards wait quietly, albeit desperately, for food.

"We try to feed the people without cards also," Mr. Bajoria said. "We make extra food. This is the only food that people get, and they need it. Look at them. It's the difference between life and death."

Calcutta: On the Precipice

This is a hungry city. It is a place where thousands "survive" each day on a slice of bread or a bowl of rice, a potato or a scrap of garbage.

It is a metropolitan area of nine million people where the line between life and death seems precariously thin. Long a stricken city, it is now beset by tens of thousands of impoverished peasants who have surged in over the last few months because of hunger and drought in surrounding West Bengal and such neighboring eastern states as Bihar and Orissa.

Rice and wheat, the dietary essentials, are in short supply. Fish, chicken, vegetables and the spices that are an important part of Indian fare are out of the grasp of millions. Prices have climbed inexorably, and the lives of middle-class clerks, shopkeepers, teachers and businessmen are tormented. Food — its cost and availability, its preparation and consumption, its quality and taste — is an obsession.

Government officials and relief workers voice alarm. "We may just tide over this crisis," a senior state official said. A relief worker commented: "There's not much starvation in Calcutta, but there's so much hunger now. For a person to starve in Calcutta, he would have to be in social isolation — either a crazy person or an old and sick person who literally can't cry out for help. People are not starving, but they're at the bottom."

The New York Times / Bernard Weinraub

Hunger has always been a common problem in Calcutta, but now it is more acute than usual.

If Calcutta always seems on the precipice — it has long served as a metaphor for urban disaster — the food problem this year is especially dangerous. Like a vacuum, Calcutta sucks in thousands of tons of rice and wheat a week from state and national stocks. This year the production is dismal, reserves have dwindled and the food bins here threaten to go bare.

Akhtari Haque, a lithe, long-fingered woman, speaks with fatigue through dry lips, her eyes half-closed. She has eight children, ranging in age from 2 to 22. Her husband earns $35 a month as a tailor. The family has lived for nine years in a Calcutta bustee, a mud hut that rents for $3 a month.

In a single room 9 or 10 people cook, eat, argue, study, make love and sleep.

There are only eight ration cards for the family. It is too complicated to get cards for the younger children, Mrs. Haque said, because the clerks are nasty and the lines are too long.

The weekly ration lasts four days. There is a rice dish in the morning, mixed with a boiled vegetable, and a wheat chapati, a thin bread, at night. Mrs. Haque spends her days preparing dhal, a lentil sauce, cooking the chapati and rice, and shopping.

On the fifth day of the week the family cuts back. Last year Mrs. Haque could afford spices, bananas, biscuits, some carrots and sweets. This year prices have doubled. "We suffer through the fifth and sixth days," she said in Bengali. "We take one meal. I take the last portion, and nothing is left over now."

"There's so little we can afford, and we go without food, except for the baby," Mrs. Haque said. "Sometimes the children cry. Sometimes I cry. It is not enough. It is never enough. We are all half-starved."

Calcutta exists on a ration system that seems vulnerably simple. Although statistics are slippery, this, roughly, is the food situation:

There are 9.3 million ration-card holders in West Bengal, 8.5 million of them in the Greater Calcutta area. One day a week people line up at the 2,400 ration shops in the state to get their weekly allotments.

The rations for the city have gone steadily down. In 1972 an adult Calcuttan received nearly eight pounds of food grain weekly — then considered a reasonably adequate diet since it meant the daily consumption of at least a pound of wheat or rice (children receive half rations).

In 1973 the weekly ration was cut to between 4.6 and 4.8 pounds; this year it is 4.4 pounds, and even this seems precarious. Late in July the vital rice ration was cut by 25 per cent, but the wheat ration was increased to keep the weekly total from falling below 4.4 pounds.

The wheat ration is in the form of a coarse flour known as atta, which is pounded and baked into bread or used in stews and gruels.

Until the rice cutback wheat cost about 8 cents a pound and rice was about 10 cents. On the open market the prices were more than triple.

Calcutta receives its food from the Central Pool, the Government's supplies. Because the national procurement and distribution system is in greater disarray than ever, Calcutta officials are doubtful that they can keep the city fed.

Dr. Gopal Das Nag, the Acting Food Minister of West Bengal, said in an interview that the state was receiving a monthly supply of 50,000 tons of rice and 80,000 tons of wheat from the Government. However, other officials place the figures at 40,000 tons each.

Furthermore, some sources say that Government shipments have occasionally been even more deficient. In June only 18,000 tons of rice arrived, they say, and the flow was dismal last month.

The problem in Calcutta is intensified by the hundreds of thousands without ration cards: the 200,000 who live on the streets, where the gutter serves as a bathroom; the thousands in bustees; the floating populace of the destitute, beggars, homeless children, families. Desperate and terrified, they are all in the shadow of starvation.

Noorjehan, a frail, wide-eyed woman in her thirties, lives on the pavement on Chowringhee, the main avenue in the downtown center. She has four small children with her; her husband is dying of tuberculosis in a coastal village.

She came here six months ago because there was no food in

the village. She begs with one or two of her half-naked children, who range in age from 5 months to 5 years. The other children beg on their own and pick through refuse cans. When it rains the family sleeps beneath a park bench. She says the children are always screaming for food.

Each morning, Mrs. Noorjehan gets a bagful of chickpeas from a Roman Catholic charity. The children line up at night outside restaurants whose proprietors dole out leftovers.

"People do not have much to give any more," Mrs. Noorjehan said in Bengali. "No one has money. There are too many children beggars now. No one wants to give them anything."

The mother is illiterate and the children have no hope of going to school. Mrs. Noorjehan is trying to breast-feed her infant, which has dysentery. Her daughter is frightened of the city and has stopped talking. Her sons run wild.

"I am too ashamed to go back to the village," she said, adding: "There is no food there, nothing. Everyone is in trouble."

Although officials insist that no one has died of starvation in Calcutta recently, there are dozens — perhaps hundreds — of deaths weekly from dehydration, dysentery, cholera and tuberculosis.

At Mother Teresa's home for dying destitute people, an associate, Sister Agnes, said: "The people are suffering so much. We see it. It's hard, it's very difficult, it's getting worse. The prices have gone up. People are hungrier."

"By nutritional standards some of these people should be dead," a foreign relief worker said. "You see some children eating grass, rats, the green scum off tanks."

A survey has found that 98 per cent of the children under age 4 are undernourished and that the average Calcuttan suffers from acute vitamin deficiency.

"Everyone's hungry now," said Maj. Dudley Gardiner, a former British Army officer who runs the Salvation Army social-service center, which feeds 5,800 people a day. "Infant mortality is very high, but if they survive the first 12 months in all of this filth, they get robust. They seem to thrive."

"Even my supply is down and I begin to worry about the shipments coming in," he added.

CARE, the Salvation Army, Mother Teresa and other charities maintain daily feeding programs. The state provides three slices of bread for 40,000 children daily.

"These children will get the bread, squirrel it in their shirt and run home," a relief worker said. "Everybody is so close to the borderline."

The most searing scenes are visible. A child watches another eat an ice-cream stick. When the ice cream is finished and the wooden stick tossed in the gutter the watcher picks it up and sucks it. On the Howrah Bridge a woman squats in the center of the crowded road and picks up grains of rice that have fallen from trucks.

Mrs. Dorothy Henderson, whose grandfather was English, and her friend, Mani, also an Anglo-Indian, go to the Salvation Army every day at 12:30 P.M. for their only meal of the day — a curry of vegetables, flour, tomato sauce, apples and soya bean soup. They eat in silence and then lift their bowls and lick the remaining drops of gravy.

It is only in the last two months that the two women have gone to the Salvation Army. "I take tea in the morning," Mrs. Henderson said, "and this is what I have during the day."

"I've got nothing and no one," she went on, with a shrug. "I have some relatives in Sheffield, but I haven't heard from them in years. It's only in the last year, with the prices and all, that I couldn't make out. I'm a 60-year-old woman. I can't work. I'm scared, a bit."

Her friend said: "I had two ration cards and both were stolen. The last time a man just grabbed it at the fruit stand and ran. I went back for another ration card and the clerk called me a parasite."

Shaking her head, Mrs. Mani continued:

"My husband died 18 years ago. I wanted to leave Calcutta but I couldn't. And now look at the prices. How can you live?

"The vegetable men used to be so nice to me. They used to call me Mem-sahib. They used to give me a nice little concession, an extra fruit here and there. The older men were kind, but these young boys are rough."

"Can you imagine?" she said abruptly, referring to the official clerk. "That man called me a parasite." Her face was wet with tears. "The nerve! A parasite!" Mrs. Henderson leaned toward her and said: "Hush up!" Mrs. Mani smiled and nodded.

As the center of eastern India Calcutta was founded on a malarial swamp 285 years ago by British merchants seeking to expand trade with the heartland. The port, growing chaotically out of three marshy villages, became the headquarters of the British East India Company, which dominated trade.

Appropriately, Calcutta's deity — and its namesake — is Kali, the Hindu goddess of death, who represents, according to one commentary, "the supreme night, which swallows all that exists."

After independence from Britain and the partition of the subcontinent in 1947, the already-jammed metropolitan area was swollen by 1.5 million refugees from what had become East Pakistan, now Bangladesh. Since then the foul-smelling city's erosion and decay — its inability to cope even minimally with sanitation, water supply, transport and housing — have been exploited by politicians and journalists, overwhelmed social scientists and aid agencies and embarrassed the Indian Government.

As for the current food crisis, West Bengal — a state of 60 million that is one of the sickest in India — has received less than a third of its goal of 500,000 tons of rice. That is what the state government sought to purchase, at a fixed price, to feed the Calcutta area and hard-hit rural districts.

Affluent farmers and traders have failed to heed the state's demands, mostly because hoarding and smuggling are extraordinarily profitable. Moreover, the state has failed to take tough measures against them since they are politically powerful contributors to the governing Congress party.

"The situation would not have been as desperate as it actually is had not the Government's procurement drive been such a dismal failure," said The Hindustan Standard, a Calcutta newspaper. "Two factors were responsible. First, administrative incompetence abetted by corruption; secondly, lack of political will. And the latter perhaps is the more important factor."

Enmeshed with the political constraints are subtle but

powerful changes in West Bengal, particularly landlessness, which is increasing sharply. One estimate says that landless agricultural laborers, who were 15 per cent of the work force in 1961, were 26 per cent in 1971.

Banchu, who drives a ricksha, came to Calcutta from Barauni, a village in Bihar, about two years ago. He had three children, one of whom died in the village.

Mr. Banchu earns about 3.5 rupees a day, or nearly 50 cents. He sleeps in his ricksha, bathes outdoors and spends most of his money on food — chattu, coarse grain rolled into a pastry ball mixed with chillies and onion. He tries to send his wife a dollar a month.

Echoing others, Mr. Banchu said that no one in Calcutta had money, and his earnings had fallen. Even the rich are walking to work, and Mr. Banchu said that his friends who wash cars or watch them in parking places outside hotels and restaurants were in trouble.

Prices are frightening, he said. A dhoti, a loose cotton wraparound that cost 21 cents last year costs 40 cents now. Roasted corn cost a cent and a half last year and 4 cents now. How can a man live? asked Mr. Banchu.

Another ricksha driver, Sarjad Mohammed, a tough aggressive man who is a bachelor, said he had raised his prices. Six months ago he charged 12 cents for a 600-yard ride — from one end of Wellesley Street to the other; now he demands 16 cents. "I manage to stay alive," he said with a grin.

To officials the hopes for keeping Calcutta fed rest on increased rice production in West Bengal and in the long run, on lifting the darkness and misery in such neighboring states and Bihar and Orissa. As long as they remain at the mercy of the primitive plow and the bullock, and in the grip of large landowners, the peasants will stream into Calcutta.

"We still wait for the rain god in India," said Shyamal Ganguly, an agricultural specialist and journalist. "After 27 years of freedom we still have so little.

"We could do miracles in eastern India if we had the water, the insecticides, the fertilizer. It's not the lack of imagination and skill at the bottom — we have hard-working farmers, some of the best in the world. It's the lack of imagination and skill at the top."

Outside the Grand Hotel on Chowringhee: "Hey, mister, shine your shoes, please? Very hungry. No food today. Hungry baby. Please, mister! Shine your shoes. O.K. Tomorrow, you promise, tomorrow, tomorrow. I see you tomorrow. You promise, tomorrow. Tomorrow...."

KASTURI RANGAN | **Bangladesh**

Dacca: Famine Follows the Flood

The people who survived months of floods in Bangladesh are now facing starvation.

According to final official estimates, more than half of the country was inundated by floods affecting 35 million people, or nearly half the population. During the worst flooding in August at least 2,000 people were killed, but officials say that they do not have reports of all deaths from distant villages.

What is worrying the nation now is the specter of famine and large numbers of deaths from starvation.

Although the flood water has receded from the stricken villages and towns, the bulk of the arable land remains submerged and unfit for new sowing. Even if planting can be done in the next few weeks, harvesting will not take place before the end of December [1974].

Until then 15 million people, mostly peasants who have lost their homes, food and jobs because of the floods, will have to be looked after.

In this capital city three gruel kitchens have been opened to meet the needs of the hungry, who are pouring in by the hundreds every day. In the last two weeks the city's population of two million has been increased at least 15 per cent.

At a typical gruel kitchen at Mirpur a crowded suburb of the city, 1,000 people line up for one piece of roti, or unleavened bread, made of wheat flour. The ration is supplemented by one protein biscuit and three ounces of milk donated by the Red Cross. This food is served only once a

27

day in the afternoon. There is so much scrambling and fighting that the supervisors have used canes to keep order in the crowd, made up mainly of old men, women and children who look shockingly famished.

Hashim Moha, a 50-year-old villager from the northern Mymensingh district, said that he had come to Dacca eight days ago in search of a job but could not find one. He began begging and the policemen brought him to the feeding center.

"I've lost everything," he said. "My family is in my village waiting for money from me. What can I send them? I'm myself starving."

The feeding center here also serves as a home for destitute people. Eight hundred people live in three sheds, and many of them are sick and hungry.

Mohammed Ishaque, the Government official in charge of the center, said that eight people had died there in the last three weeks. Medical care is poor, although the destitute people have been inoculated against cholera and smallpox.

Many of the indigent wander around the city begging. According to reports in the local Bengali newspapers, municipal authorities and Moslem social welfare organizations in Dacca pick up at least 25 bodies from the streets daily. The three burial grounds in the city area are already full.

The condition of the destitutes in places just outside the city is much worse.

In Munshiganj, 15 miles southeast of here, there are thousands of people too poor to pay for the boat that they must take to cross the wide Burhganga River to reach Dacca.

Eighty persons have died of starvation there in the last two weeks, according to local authorities. Only one of the two gruel kitchens there is functioning and grain supplies are erratic and inadequate.

Even the kitchen that serves food gets enough wheat flour to make only 500 rotis, but there always are more than 1,000 persons in the queue.

The destitutes begin coming to the feeding center in the early morning for half a piece of roti that will be handed out in the late afternoon. No milk or lentils are supplied.

"For every person coming here there are at least three or four left at home," said Mohammed Jehuruddin, who is

United Press International

Members of a family in Dacca, where they went, with throngs of other people, to find food. The couple's other children help by begging in the streets.

supervising the distribution. "They are all old people or children too young to come."

"There are 25,000 people in this place," he said. "At least 10,000 are starving. Half of them will die."

As road and rail communications have been opened, hundreds of thousands of hungry people have begun to move from the villages to the towns seeking jobs and food. Many others are too weak or diseased to travel.

"People are dying in dozens," said Dr. E. S. Hain, the acting chief of the World Health Organization in Dacca. "Cholera has broken out in epidemic form in many places. After two months of isolation and hunger, the poor villagers are left with no resistance to infection."

He said it would not be an overestimate to say that at least 100,000 people would have died before December [1974]. However, he conceded there was no way of supporting any such figures because no proper official information was available.

"It will be difficult for people outside the country to comprehend the situation here," Dr. Hain said, "The tragedy here is not going to be as dramatic as a typhoon or an earthquake."

Food Minister Abdul Momen has estimated that starvation deaths so far are fewer than 5,000. He has pledged that the Government will "spare no efforts" to prevent further deaths from lack of food.

But the efforts are hampered by huge problems. The Government needs 600,000 tons of food in the next two months to meet a feeding program begun only recently. More than 3,000 gruel kitchens or feeding centers have been opened throughout the country but grain stocks are insufficient to supply even half.

Another 15 million people have to be supplied with grain through fair-price shops, because the price of rice and wheat has increased so much in the open market that the average family cannot afford to buy grain.

"I wish friendly countries who want to help us now had responded to our appeals more urgently and more generously," said Food Secretary A.M. Khan.

Under an agreement signed here last week [Oct. 1974], the U.S. has offered 150,000 tons of wheat and rice on concessional terms. Pledges from other nations, including a gift of 5,000 tons each from Pakistan and Communist China, and purchases from the Government's own resources will total 900,000 tons. This will still leave a gap of 1.2-million tons this year.

Mr. Khan said the Government was hopeful that the United States would fill a substantial part of this gap, especially after the visit of Secretary of State Kissinger to Bangladesh scheduled for the end of this month.

"But what are we going to do for our immediate needs?" asked Mr. Khan. He said that some nations such as Saudi Arabia and Iraq had pledged cash grants for the purchase of food. But such purchases, even if they are made immediately, will take weeks or months to reach Bangladesh because of shipping and communications problems, Mr. Khan said.

By all indications the Government appears to be resigned to the inevitability of large-scale starvation deaths.

Dacca: The Future Seems Hopeless

The fear of widespread famine that haunted Bangladesh a few weeks ago [Nov. 1974] has become reality.

Officials here concede that they were not prepared for the widespread devastation that has occurred despite a substantial flow of foreign food and economic aid.

An official of the nation's planning commission said that several thousand people may already have died and that many thousands might die in the next few weeks because of malnutrition.

"The maximum damage has been done," the official said. "The future seems hopeless."

He compared the present famine conditions with the situation during the great famine of Bengal in 1943, when hundreds of thousands died of starvation.

"The difference today," he said, "is that we have been able to save five million lives." He said that 6,000 gruel kitchens, or feeding centers, set up by the Government throughout Bangladesh were keeping that many people alive.

Government planning has been upset because the number

of persons made destitute by the famine has been at least three times more than the total anticipated. In August, when the Government made its plans to open gruel kitchens, it was thought that about 4,000 feeding centers would be sufficient to feed an anticipated two million persons.

Until the end of September, fewer than 3,000 kitchens were functioning and most of these were not receiving regular supplies. The Government had no stocks of food, and imports were at a low level. For the whole of September, a most critical period, only 20,000 tons of food grains reached the ports. This compares with more than 250,000 tons expected during this month and next.

Because there now are more gruel kitchens, even these large imports are insufficient. Demand from the kitchens has substantially affected supplies to the regular rationing outlets, on which the bulk of the working population in this country of 75 million depends. Prices of rice and wheat in the open market are so high that most of the population cannot afford them.

The result is a nightmarish situation in which perpetually hungry people survive solely on Government dole. Even the ration available in the kitchens is less than a marginal diet. Each of the 1,000 or more people who crowd around a feeding center once a day is served one roti (unleavened bread) or four ounces of a porridge made from rice and lentils. In some places the ration consists only of "survival biscuits," mostly donated by the United States.

Although harvesting of the autumn crop has begun and some of the destitute have begun leaving the cities in the hope of finding employment and food in their villages, officials believe the kitchens will have to be maintained at least until the end of the year. Many of the destitute lost everything — their homes, jobs and property — during the recent floods, and there is nothing for them to return to.

In Tangail, 60 miles northwest of here, 2,000 persons are being fed at a large gruel kitchen. Most of them have come from northern districts, which were the worst hit by the floods.

Tara Banu, a 30-year-old widow from the northern district of Rangpur, has existed on gruel-kitchen rations for the last

Children waiting in line for powdered milk at a school at Baidyer, Bangladesh.

two months. Her husband died in the floods and two of her children died of malnutrition last month. She is left with only a 3-year-old girl, and their home is a sidewalk in the bazaar.

"I have nothing at home," she said. "If the kitchen is closed I will have to beg — else I will die. But I want to live for the sake of my daughter."

It is evident that there are many destitutes in the same situation as Tara Banu. They have no hope of living for a long time.

Government officials, who have become reconciled to large-scale deaths from starvation, are now worried about future food prospects. The flooding and famine have helped Bangladesh win international attention. Although more than 20 countries have offered food shipments, the Government is left with a deficit of one million tons for the year that began in July, 1974.

The floods in July and August washed out the bulk of the summer crop and late sowing has cut the autumn output. Officials say that a shortage of fertilizers and seeds will reduce the winter crops, which also depend on the timely arrival of the rains.

The incoming shipments of food supplies "have certainly improved the food position now," said A. M. Khan, the Food Secretary. "But the situation may start deteriorating again from February."

On the economic front the prospect is even bleaker. The situation is deteriorating so fast that officials have stopped working on development plans until the outlook for foreign aid and the food-supply situation become less uncertain.

A recent meeting of 22 nations on aid to Bangladesh reportedly agreed that the country would need about $1.2-billion in aid this year, and that each country should pledge a substantial amount. However, many of the countries are said to have made aid conditional on a devaluation of the Bangladesh currency, which is highly overrated, and measures to increase industrial production, particularly in the jute industry.

The Government has balked at both these demands. Although devaluation might be good for the economy in the long term, it would immediately push up domestic prices, already very high because of inflation and scarcities.

A shortage of raw materials and chronic labor problems have dislocated most industrial production, and the Government has no immediate solution. Furthermore, much of the land used for growing jute now is used to produce rice.

Officials talk of a large inflow of petrodollars from Arab nations sympathetic to the plight of a sister Moslem nation.

The Government is determined to explore these sources fully before submitting to pressure for devaluation from the World Bank and Western countries.

Panchasari: Nature and the Price of Oil

The Bangladesh Glass and Metal Industries in this town 207 miles southeast of Dacca has been turned into a poorhouse. The $60,000 plant no longer makes glass or metalware. Its chimneys, billowing with thick smoke until two months ago, are [in Oct. 1974] cold.

Only five of the 1,000 workers of the factory have been kept on by the owner. They make rotis (unleavened bread) — and distribute them to the hundreds of starving destitutes who come once a day to be fed.

The plant is a mute symbol of the present state of affairs of the economy of Bangladesh, a nation that severed itself from Pakistan three years ago.

In August the plant stopped production when floodwaters invaded it for nearly a month. When the water receded the factory could not start up again because the fuel supply, furnace oil in this case, had not arrived from Dacca. Other raw materials, silica and chemicals, also became unavailable.

"I managed somehow to get the raw materials," said Ansar Ali, the owner. "But I could not get furnace oil anywhere. The Government imports very little and most of it disappears in the black market."

Mr. Ali said he wanted to keep the plant running so that the employes could continue to earn and feed their dependents, now starving. The floods shut off other employment opportunities: Most of the workers have become destitute, living on the Government dole of half a roti a day.

"It pains me to see my own workers standing in the queue with the destitutes," Mr. Ali said. "It's little consolation that my plant serves as a feeding center for the poor."

Mr. Ali said he invested $60,000 in the plant after independence three years ago to make tumblers, bottles and hurricane lanterns, which found a ready market all over Bangladesh. Like Mr. Ali, many other entrepreneurs, spurred by a sense of patriotism, invested in new industries, hoping the nation would prosper. But the troubles started last year with the steep increase in oil prices that forced the Government to reduce imports.

This has led all the new manufacturing establishments

either to reduce production or shut down. According to official sources in Dacca, 75 per cent of the small industries in Bangladesh have stopped production. Major industries such as jute, textile and saltmaking plants also reduced output.

Millions of workers have been laid off, joining the vast army of hungry, landless people who lost everything during the floods.

But officials in Dacca are optimistic about the future. They say that foreign aid has started coming, and that in the next few months Bangladesh will be able to revive her industries.

The Prime Minister, Sheik Mujibur Rahman, told his nation on his return from the United Nations on Oct. 7 that he had been assured of foreign aid and the present difficulties were only a temporary phase.

The United States, which has already given $500-million since independence, is expected to multiply that aid threefold or fourfold in the next few years. Other Western nations are joining in the aid program.

The World Bank has scheduled a meeting of donor nations in Paris on Oct. 24 to form a consortium of aid to Bangladesh. A significant feature is that three oil-producing nations — Iran, Kuwait and Abu Dhabi — are expected to join that consortium.

Last week, during Sheik Mujib's visit to Iraq, he got a pledge of $51-million. Saudi Arabia had earlier granted $10-million for flood relief.

Foreign observers contrast this generous attitude of foreign nations to that shown in the months preceding the floods. At that time, Bangladesh had a hard time persuading the World Bank to raise a commodity-import loan by a mere $10-million to $50-million.

"People in this country live with and live on the floods," said a foreign diplomat, contending that the floods were a blessing in disguise. "True, thousands of people may die of starvation and there is great dislocation of economic activity, but ultimately, when the waters recede, the fields will be more fertile and foreign donors will be more sympathetic."

It was not compassion alone that motivated the Western aid-givers. Along with assurances that the aid money will no longer be squandered or appropriated by corrupt officials, the Government has also announced a drastic change in policy on domestic and foreign private capital.

The ceiling for private-sector investment has been raised from $300,000 to $4-million. The Government has also declared a moratorium on nationalization of industries for 15 years. And to attract foreign investment, the Government has provided for liberal repatriation of profits and salaries.

By all indications, the future state of the economy in Bangladesh does not look as depressing as it did a few weeks ago. However, for people like Mr. Ali of Bangladesh Glass and Metal Industries, it is going to be a long wait. It is hard to convince him that his problems will be over soon.

"All I want is a barrel of furnace oil every week," Mr. Ali said. "I need it right now, not one month or two months later. I'll be broke by then. I can't believe the Government needs foreign assistance to supply a barrel of oil."

THOMAS A. JOHNSON | # The Sahel

Dakar, Senegal: A Time to Suffer

The loss of two young children and 45 head of cattle to the six-year drought in the southern Sahara was recently [March 1974] described by a Fulani herdsman with a single word: "Soudure."

The herdsman, Ibrihima Sow, spoke while sitting under a tent of animal skins, canvas patches and grain sacks near the desert town of Dori, in Upper Volta. With the single word he pointed up a vital aspect of the region's way of life and the state of mind of many of its farmers and herdsmen.

"Soudure" is the French word for "solder," and in the southern reaches of the Sahara it carries the connotation of fingers welded together so that one is helpless to feed himself.

It is synonymous with the annual ritual of suffering that begins in late spring, after food supplies are exhausted and grazing lands disappear, and it lasts through the summer·rains that renew the pastures and bring a single harvest of millet, sorghum and peanuts in the fall.

This yearly period of suffering is expected and accepted. The pattern has continued for centuries and is so predictable that farmers, herdsmen and Government officials were initially and mistakenly inclined to look upon the killing drought of 1973 as just another bad, but temporary condition.

Generally, the region's farmers and herdsmen did not expect help. Generally, they did not ask for any. Mr. Sow, who had lived in a sprawling desert refugee camp for almost a year with no plans for the future, heard that food was available in the town, but he moved only after the last of his animals had died.

"When suffering is a way of life, who will think to make a special plea to relieve it?" a Malian relief official recently asked.

Other African relief workers have suggested that it was primarily the conditioning of people in the region to hard times that delayed requests for outside assistance.

Africans throughout the desert and savanna regions of Chad, Mali, Mauritania, Niger, Senegal and Upper Volta have come to live with a regular pattern of hard times. Immediately after the harvest, the harmattan winds — hot and desiccating — engulf the region. Herdsmen wander in search of new pasture lands. Young farmers trek to distant cities to work as water carriers or watchmen. Many of those left resort to demolishing anthills to steal the few wild grain seeds stored inside, and they cook the leaves, roots, bulbs and berries that are ignored during better times.

The delivery of relief food to the southern Sahara was complicated by factors other than the Africans' stoicism. Some governments feared that they would be blamed for the seriousness of the drought and tried to keep things quiet. Communication was poor, distances great, and there were few roads.

All areas affected had far more people than the official records showed because many sought to avoid paying taxes by not registering in their communities.

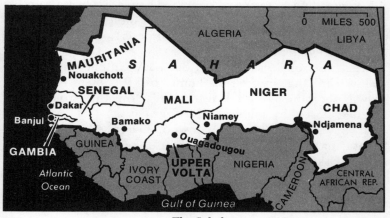

The Sahel

No country involved efficiently handled the shipping, trucking and rail movement of large grain shipments.

As a result of the continuing international relief operations, anyone reaching a permanent town, village or oasis could be fed.

Even so, refugee stations continued to report the deaths from starvation, malnutrition or disease of people who waited too long to seek help.

Relief workers are less concerned with traditional diets than with keeping people alive. An African official north of Agadez, Niger, pointed out some of the problems this causes:

"Some people have complained that sorghum had made nomads sick because they were used to mostly milk and cheeses. We don't worry about that."

He explained also that pounding grain into flour was women's work and often, when men attempted it in refugee camps, they did not do a thorough job, or they tried to eat the grain whole, and could not digest it.

"We don't worry about that at all," he said, "because those nomads who got sick are still alive. In the soudure the important thing is to stay alive."

Dori, Upper Volta: The Plight of the Tuaregs

A ragged line of men was stretched beneath a brutal sun for a quarter of a mile alongside a brown mud wall and several poorly stocked market stalls made of desert palm fronds atop gnarled wooden poles.

Near the front was Mamadi Saw. He clutched a wrinkled yellow card that insured his family of 19 enough American-grown sorghum — stacked carefully on the ground and guarded closely by soldiers — for four days.

Mr. Saw, a Tuareg tribesman who once raised camels in the Sahara, had no plans other than to take the food to a tent made of skins, canvas and grain sacks outside this village and then come back after four days.

"We cannot go back to the desert near Kidal because we have no animals," Mr. Saw said [in April 1974], referring to his home in Mali. His clan had lost all its camels, cattle, sheep and goats in six years of famine and drought here along the southern border of the Sahara.

In this desolate and inhospitable pocket of the region, it is the Tuaregs, a distinct minority, for whom the future is most uncertain. A Hamitic people, although many show varying mixtures of black African blood, the desert-dwelling Tuaregs have spurned contacts with and allegiance to the independent Governments of Mali, Niger and Upper Volta. Many remained in small clans at remote water holes until people and animals died of starvation, malnutrition and disease.

"The French had promised the Tuaregs a nation of our own when they left," Mr. Saw said. "Because of this promise many Tuaregs here fought in Indochina for France because they thought they would have a country of their own."

Tuaregs in Mali, claiming autonomy, took up arms against the army some years ago but were defeated. The army still maintains forces in the Tuareg region.

Historical antagonisms are common between peoples in this region. Travelers have particularly noted reciprocal suspicion, fear and contempt between sedentary farming peoples and the Tuaregs.

Since 1973 Tuareg refugees living in Mali and in neighboring Upper Volta and Niger have maintained that the three black African Governments are using the drought to exterminate the Tuaregs. A French newspaper recently repeated this charge against the Government of Mali, which has denied it, as have the two other Governments. International relief workers have also denied it.

"The charge is completely false," said Dr. Ibrahima Konate, a Malian who is coordinator of the six sub-Saharan nations' committee that handles relief operations and long-range rehabilitation. "The fact is we have special instructions from Mali, Niger and Upper Volta to make certain that the Tuaregs are not treated unfairly because of the historical conflicts."

Moise Mensah, the West African regional director for the United Nations Food and Agriculture Organization, declared: "The people handling relief supplies in these countries are doing their best to get food to everyone in need and under very difficult conditions. Such charges have long been completely disproved."

A period of drought that began more than seven years ago has been taking a grievous toll in countries of sub-Sahara Africa. This is a scene in Senegal where an oasis simply disappeared.

Western journalists who have traveled extensively through the region tend to agree with Mr. Mensah.

"We do not pity the Tuaregs," said the chief of a millet-farming community near Ouagadougou, Upper Volta, to a recent visitor, "because they are being fed free while we must work and work for everything we get."

It was evident that the Tuaregs' history as raiders of farming tribes and their incorporation of some of the tribesmen into their way of life as "slaves" were his principal reasons for disliking them.

Following a pattern observed in several African regions, the captured people became laborers in the Tuareg camps. They are also the artisans and craftsmen in clans whose chieftains have decreed that religious leaders must be the sons of slaves — a move aimed at limiting the religious leaders' powers.

The slaves have become a power of their own among their captors. Since the subject peoples, often called bouzous or bella bellas, are free to leave when they choose — many thousands have left during the drought — the system is not considered slavery in the legal sense.

In the equalizing effects of the drought, Tuareg noblemen and bouzou craftsmen join the same ragged line for food. On the same line are farmers from the Mossi tribe, whose millet crops failed last fall for lack of rain.

Fulanis, whose vast cattle herds have been taken farther south or have perished in the hot sands, stood in the same line.

Mr. Saw said he would remain here and try to keep his family together. They sold their swords, daggers and jewelry some months ago. He recently refused to let his young sisters travel to Niamey, Niger, to seek jobs in nightclubs as "hostesses."

HENRY KAMM | # The Sahel

Dakoro, Niger: The Rains Come

Fields of millet, taller than a man and heavy with ripening grain surround the large camp of nomad herdsmen and their families who were driven to this southern region of Niger by drought and famine in 1973.

Here at last, and along a 500-mile drive eastward from Niamey, the national capital, it looks [in Sept. 1974] as though the drought is over. The rains have been plentiful and timely since the beginning of the wet season in late June.

Heavy monsoon clouds still hang over the greening landscape, indicating that more rain may fall before harvesting can begin in earnest later this month. The villagers who live in the south as well as the nomads who fled as the Sahara advanced southward in the drought are cheerful.

But, even with a good harvest, Niger will not be able to feed herself this year. The untold damage of the drought, which began slowly six years ago before becoming a disaster along a broad belt between the desert and the lush tropical coastal lands, will be difficult to repair.

Experts of the many nations and international groups that have contributed to the relief effort know that much work remains to be done and continuing help is needed.

Paradoxically, the rains that are bringing so much hope are also bringing problems. Flooding has washed out roads on which food supplies must be carried.

The countries of The Sahel — the Arabic name meaning "fringe" that describes the sub-Sahara region — are some of the world's poorest. The scarceness of all-weather roads is one of the indices of their poverty.

44

The 75-mile dirt road leading here from the principal east-west highway — also only partly surfaced — has been able to bear a steady flow of relief food northward to Dakoro. Earlier this year, the road was one of the tragic scenes for many of the moving photographs of starving children and dead cattle.

Two thousand to 3,000 persons remain in the camp at the edge of this way station, which lacks only the Foreign Legion fort to be a perfect setting for a remake of "Beau Geste."

"We need only two more weeks of rain," said Tahirou Moussa, the tall and elderly, robe-clad subprefect, in a conversation in the cool, colonial-style house that belonged to his French predecessor before independence in 1960. "The nomads will leave here then, when the millet is ready."

Asked how the Tuareg and Fulani tribesmen, traditional cattle, camel and goat herders, would fare on their own after having lost so many animals, Mr. Moussa shrugged and replied in French:

"That will be a little difficult. But what can we do? It happened, and that's that."

The millet fields that surround the camp do not belong to the refugees but to the villagers. The Government's eagerness to see the nomads head northward once more stems in large measure from traditional suspicion between the sedentary and the nomad.

The herdsmen seem as eager to leave as the villagers are to be rid of them. The scarceness of men in the camp is believed to indicate that some have stayed with at least part of their herds and found grazing land across the border in Nigeria and others have more recently gone to join the herders to help them drive the livestock northward.

The town of Maradi, on the main highway, after having been swollen to double its size of 40,000 with nomads, is now almost empty of outsiders. The refugees, mainly Tuaregs, were rounded up and trucked northward last May. Many left the certainty of regular feeding with reluctance.

Feeding the nomads on their northward trek will remain a relief operation until they can reconstitute viable herds. There remains also the results of the famine on many of those who survived it.

A Fulani woman, walking about with her suckling baby, squeezed her thin breast and shook her head, to indicate she had not enough milk. The baby squalled. No signs of extreme hunger were evident, but many women offered their traditional necklaces, bracelets and earrings for sale to raise money for food.

Tuaregs and Fulanis, people of limited commercial ambitions, put their wealth into herds and into jewelry for their women.

Malnutrition is a serious problem also among the villagers. Although their plight has been less dramatic than that of the herdsmen, because they did not have to trek southward to find relief, they have also been hard hit by the drought and have lived largely on the dole.

"Right now they are picking head by head the millet that is ripe," said Dr. Burt Long, an American who runs the hospital of the Sudan Interior Mission near the village of Galmi.

"And I'm afraid they're picking some before it's ripe."

Dr. Long, who has been at Galmi for 24 years, said the famine had greatly reduced the life expectancy of a people who even in years considered good suffer from malnutrition.

"They have no reserves," Dr. Long said.

"If this year's crop breaks the famine," the doctor continued, "we will see for five years to come a much higher rate of deaths and then five more years of more deaths than is normal."

Ayorou, Niger: Red Cross at the Scene

Timidly, speaking a halting pidgin French, a youngish man in a ragged cloak that once was white told the nurse that his baby was ill. He pointed to his wife standing behind him, and she turned to display the baby, carried in a sling low on her back. The mother looked frightened, the baby wan.

"You must take her to the dispensary," said the nurse.

A Tuareg feeding his child powdered milk, which was flown to Niger from Europe during the drought.

The man repeated the words softly and left, followed by his wife. The nurse, a Dane, allowing her voice to regain its normal gentleness, said almost to herself: "That's the worst part of it — sending the sick ones away."

"But if we start trying to take care of all of them, they will all start coming, and we'll never do our work," she explained. "We just can't do anything but send them to the dispensary."

The dispensary, which is run by a local male nurse since Niger has 16 physicians for a population of 4.2 million, is in the camp at the edge of this primitive market town near the border of Mali. The camp houses [in Sept. 1974] about 600 victims of the drought and famine that devastated the region south of the Sahara.

The Danish nurse, Anne Lise Timmermann, is a member of a medical-nutritional team of the League of Red Cross Societies that is trying to repair the damage of the famine among the most vulnerable groups: children, pregnant women and nursing mothers.

Living in a house of mud bricks and thatch without electricity, eating the local food and working nearly around the clock, the team of five Europeans and Canadians takes care of about 20 nomad camps and destitute villages as far as 60 miles away. There is not an inch of paved road in the region.

Visiting a village, the team applies the simplest test for malnutrition: It measures the upper-arm circumference of the younger children with a plastic strip with a red line at 12.5 centimeters (almost five inches). Those who fall short — 5 to 10 per cent in every village — are put on high-protein diets of corn-soya-milk powder and fishmeal.

The method is intentionally simple because the goal is to teach nutritional habits that will persist after the nine teams working in Niger have left.

Boiling river water for drinking is another new practice that is stressed. The teams, which realize how difficult their campaign is in the face of tradition and grinding poverty, know that firewood, the only heating material in use, is not plentiful and is expensive, so it is unlikely to be "squandered" for boiling.

"We can show them while we are here," said Marthe

Ouellet, a Canadian dietician, "but this is a matter of their own civilization."

Henry Gates, another Canadian, said that malnutrition was higher in the nomad camps than in the villages, where increasing quantities of homegrown staples are being eaten now that an abundant rainy season is ending.

The camp here remains at the edge of misery. Miss Timmermann, who has been here for three months, said it looked good now compared with then and the state of health was much better.

As she drove her Land-Rover into the shade of one of the few trees on the parched camp ground and stepped out, there were calls from many of the huts.

A laughing woman grabbed Miss Timmermann by the arm and led her into a hut. Stooping through the low entrance, she exclaimed, "A newborn baby!" The young mother giggled. "It looks healthy," the nurse said, pinching the mother's cheek in congratulation, and ducked out.

In another hut a young man, obviously ill, was lying on a mat, his mother fussing over him. Touching his forehead, Miss Timmermann said, "Malaria — nothing we can do." "Boil his water," she said to the mother in English, explaining with gestures.

Miss Timmermann explained that people continued to arrive in the camps in an advanced state of malnutrition.

They come and they go, and no one knows whence or whither. The aid teams have given up trying to fathom the nomads' ways.

Except for those acutely ill, the camp people display a cheerfulness that defies explanation. They have lost their only sustenance, their herds. After a long period of hunger and of harrowing treks through the desert in which every family must have lost close kin, they are subsisting idly on meager handouts of unaccustomed foods, living in a confined and ugly place a world away from the freedom to which they are accustomed.

If they think about the future they do not confide their thoughts to strangers. And their compatriots who live in a sedentary style are as much strangers as the Danes and Canadians. But the Danes and Canadians have come a long way to help, while the villagers and nomads of different tribes do not think those who suffer are their concern.

Niamey, Niger: Rebuilding the Country

An extensive international relief effort has substantially ended the famine in Niger, one of the countries most tragically afflicted by the catastrophic drought of 1973 that spanned the African continent immediately below the Sahara.

This rainy season, now drawing to an end [in Oct. 1974] gives hope for a good harvest. But for years to come, even with continuing good harvests, Niger will need help in feeding her population of about 4.2 million and in overcoming the long-term effects of the drought.

Many people are presumed to have died of starvation or of illnesses fatal only because of the hunger-weakened state of the victims. Mortality was highest among young children, who will also suffer most from the long-term effects of malnutrition. But in a region where even the number of the living is a far-from-precise statistic, it is impossible to know how many died.

Both President Seyni Kountche and the Public Health Minister, Moussa Sala, said in interviews that they could not estimate the number of dead. They said that the international rescue effort averted the worst. Certainly the gloomiest predictions of last year, forecasting mortal danger to millions in the sub-Sahara region, proved excessive.

But even fewer might have died or suffered grievously if relief had arrived faster and more nations had helped.

Although a study mission prepared an accurate blueprint of Niger's needs in October [1973], it was March before the flow of food began in earnest.

Taking into account port and road transport facilities an optimum goal of 25,000 tons a month, beginning in January, was set for the arrival of food supplies. But by mid-March, no more than 10,000 tons had reached Niger.

The optimum flow, which would have adequately stocked forward distribution centers before the summer rains made much of the country inaccessible, became instead an unman-ageable flood of 50,000 to 60,000 tons a month through Nigerian and Dahomeyan ports in April, May and June.

The United States provided more than half of the nearly 200,000 tons of food, mainly sorghum, that pulled Niger through. The European Economic Community, as well as West Germany, France, Belgium and Canada, and the United Nations World Food Program, were the other major contributors.

Others capable of helping have been more reticent.

The assistance from Arab countries to this Moslem nation was "infinitesimal," President Kountche said.

Kuwait and Algeria each sent about 1,000 tons of wheat and Iraq 850 tons of dates. President Kountche, a devout supporter of Moslem unity, said that since he seized power in a military coup April 15, Libya and Algeria had provided some help.

In a recent [Sept. 1974] statement, the head of the Saudi Arabian diplomatic mission here, Hassain al-Rachach, said that his country had contributed about $2-million. But international development experts here put the cost to Niger so far of increased fuel prices close to $9-million, or about one-fifth of the total national budget.

The Soviet Union has donated 2,412 tons of rice and five trucks. China has provided no help, unless 500 tons of rice given in the name of Prince Norodom Sihanouk, nominal head of insurgent forces in Cambodia, was of Chinese origin.

Aid missions here are at a loss to explain the three-month delay in the start of food deliveries. At the United States Embassy and at the European Economic Community and United Nations offices, distraught officials offer to show stacks of telegrams that they dispatched in the critical months importuning governments and international organizations to act.

"We felt a heavy responsibility," said Alexander H. Rotival, representative of the United Nations development program and a coordinator of the aid effort. "The people had eaten their reserves and were down to their stoic ability to resist death without food."

The slowness of bureaucracy is the reason most often ad-

vanced. The United States Ambassador, L. Douglas Heck, said he believed the decision in Washington to make the American effort as much as possible part of the international program made a slow start inevitable.

Drawing a lesson from this performance, the United States has already set aside 100,000 tons of food grains for the sub-Sahara area for the coming year. A quarter of that is destined for the stockpiles of this country.

The pressures on the White House resulting from the Mideast war and Watergate may have been responsible for the Cost-of-Living Council's one-month delay, from December to January, in approving the 400,000-ton grain program for the drought area.

The results of the delay are still being felt here in the inordinate difficulties of distributing the food to the remote regions of this thinly populated, landlocked country, which is larger than Texas and California combined.

Camel caravans have taken over where even four-wheel-drive vehicles fail. Three convoys of Algerian trucks are crossing the Sahara from Algiers, carrying 1,500 tons of American sorghum to the northern regions of Niger not reachable from the south. The United States and the United Nations Food and Agriculture Organization are sharing the transport costs.

In the most hopeful of estimates, it will take at least three years of continuously good growing seasons for Niger to regain what President Kountche called her "food equilibrium."

Ndjamena, Chad: Reaching the Hungriest

At a cost of more than $1-million, the United States is airlifting 2,000 tons of sorghum to Chad. Half is being flown to a remote desert region that has suffered only marginally from the great African drought and has little immediate need of relief.

UNICEF / NAMBIAR

The suffering that millions of Africans have endured in the drought of the past few years is etched on the faces of this father, daughter and grandchild.

The grain is being flown to Chad from Maiduguri, Nigeria, 154 miles from here, where thousands of tons of sorghum have been arriving since last March and thousands more are on their way.

Great as her food needs are, Chad has failed to absorb and distribute to the hungry most of the supplies furnished by the world community.

Of about 4,000 tons of American sorghum remaining in Maiduguri, an inspector has found 1,000 to be rotten and 700 infested with bugs.

The expensive airlift to a region of marginal need and the backlog in Maiduguri with more grain on the way illustrate the dilemma of the American relief effort to Chad. It is shared by the many other donors — governments, international organizations and private groups: The need is great, assistance has been made available but donors are powerless against Government handling of transport and distribution.

Ten days of conversations here with representatives of most of the principal donors — the United States, France, the United Nations and various affiliates, the Common Market's European Development Fund and private groups — as well as two field trips disclosed remarkable unanimity in assessments of the problem.

The Government of Ngarta Tombalbaye is believed to be mismanaging the relief effort. The principal reasons cited are incompetence, apathy and participation in or toleration of profiteering on the part of persons close to the national leadership.

It is part of the dilemma of those attempting to help the people of Chad that if they criticize the Government's performance they incur a high risk of being barred from further assistance to those stricken by drought and famine. Consequently, all persons interviewed insisted on anonymity.

"We are here to help the people of Chad, Government or no Government," an international official said.

One price exacted by President Tombalbaye for allowing his four million people to receive assistance is that all decisions are made by his Government; whatever goods and services are put at Chad's disposal, the Government decides how to use them.

The American airlift to the Sahara is an example. Last June, with the rainy season at hand, which makes most of Chad's roads unusable, the Government urged the donors to provide air delivery. The United States, mindful perhaps of the large stocks lying useless in Nigeria and with a desire to give no offense to groups at home, agreed reluctantly and at the same time said it would carry its sorghum where Chad wanted it.

The American Embassy was surprised when Public Works Minister Abdoulaye Djonouma , in charge of all drought relief, ordered 1,300 of the 2,000 tons to be delivered to northern locations. It was aware that the 70,000 nomads of the Saharan region there live in permanent drought and have for centuries coped without outside assistance. The embassy persuaded the minister to reduce the allocation to half the 2,000 tons and proceeded with the airlift.

The Prefect, or Governor of the region, said in an interview in his oasis capital, Faya-Largeau, that the people had had less food during the drought period because less arrived from the south but had survived without too much hardship. Now, he said, caravans are again arriving with millet from the first harvest of the new crop.

The American planes, a vastly more expensive form of transport, are arriving at the same time. About 700 tons have arrived so far, 15 tons at a time carried over distances of about 1,000 miles each round trip.

The Prefect, Bakary Diallo, said all but 50 tons would be stocked until April or May, when the nomads will be running out of the proceeds of this year's date crop and before next year's can be marketed. Throughout rural Africa the period before the new harvest is one when people have a difficult time making ends meet, but it is not considered an emergency.

Mr. Diallo appeared to see no paradox in carrying grain by emergency airlift only to put it in storage for seven months. The American Embassy does but feels powerless.

Aid and development officials here can only guess at the reasons motivating this surprising allocation.

One line of speculation is that Mr. Tombalbaye is sending American grain to the north because he wants to appease the nomads, who are openly disaffected and who have often rebelled against all governments trying to dominate them. Another reason offered is that grain sent so far away can be disposed of without anyone's knowing its ultimate use. A third speculation is that the grain can be used to feed Government troops sent north to keep the nomads in check.

There is no need to guess, however, at the reason for the constant backlog of relief food, which made airlifts necessary last year as well and has caused great hardship to many of the two million Chadians estimated to have been affected by the drought. The reason is the Government failure to break the monopoly of the Chadian trucking industry in this land-locked country without railroads.

Throughout the relief operations beginning last year, the donors have carried on a running fight with the Cooperative of Chadian Transporters, the truck monopoly.

"We have the monopoly and we fix the tariffs," boasted Cameron Agar, a Syrian-born Lebanese of French citizenship who founded the monopoly 20 years ago. The truck owners used it to enforce the highest ton-per-mile rate in the world and to keep the cheaper, faster and larger Nigerian trucks from carrying grain here while Chadians starved.

Mr. Agar said he gave "temporary authorization" for Nigerian truckers to come as far as this capital last May. In an interview, Public Works Minister Djonouma said the Government had ordered the lifting of the monopoly.

An international official said that the Government "could not impose its will on the truckers," and one of his colleagues called the truckers "a mafia." But a leading figure in the trucking industry said that most members of the Government had an interest in truck ownership through close relatives, including President Tombalbaye's wife.

A shipment of grain sorghum being unloaded in Africa.

Timbuktu, Mali: Charm After Horror

Timbuktu is the beautiful, changeless desert city of old once more, now that the drought is over and its victims have either left or died.

On the feast day yesterday that marked the end of the one-month fast of Ramadan, sumptuously robed dignitaries crowded into the colonial mansion of the regional military Governor to pay their respects.

They were received by the Governor, Capt. Korcissy Tall, who in honor of the day had shed his paratrooper uniform and beret for an elegant white and gold robe and cap.

Later, the turbaned elders, leaning on scepterlike staffs, joined the rest of Timbuktu's male population — few married women ever go into the street except to go to market or draw water — in an afternoon promenade on the market square of desert sand. Everyone was dressed in his finest robe.

As groups gathered, blended and dissolved, "A Thousand and One Nights" seemed to come to life in flamboyant hues.

At dark, Araby became Africa. The tomtoms began to beat in the unlighted streets of low, stark mudhouses, and dancing began. Men and women danced separately.

"Dancing together is an offense to the sense of shame," explained a young man who said he would not personally be offended.

All was quiet on the sprawling expanse of sun-baked sand at the edge of town. Last year more than 10,000 nomads camped there for handouts of grain and for medical attention for those who had barely survived the hungry trek across the grassless pastures and for more than 200 of them who lived this far to await death from starvation, measles or cholera.

Now it looks more like a scout camp.

Neatly aligned tents shelter only a few hundred nomads — old people and orphans mainly — who have no one to care for them and who have not been able to set out again to try to recreate their traditional way of life, which would depend largely on the animals they lost to the famine. No one in the camp showed signs of undernourishment.

The town has resumed its ancient ways. It is no longer inundated by once-proud Tuareg herdsmen who had lost their camels, cattle, sheep and goats and thus had been reduced to selling their swords and their wives' jewelry or to begging for money or food.

What the handful of remaining Tuaregs offer for sale now are trinkets made for the tourist trade, many smuggled in from Mauritania. The only beggars are the usual smiling children who hold out their hands and continue smiling whether something is put in their palm or not.

Most of the Tuaregs left the camp during the rainy season, which this summer brought what the name promises. Although many had lost all their animals — the average loss in this pastoral region is estimated at 85 per cent — they left toward their old grazing grounds as grass began sprouting.

They took with them, Captain Tall said, three months' supply of grain and some powdered milk and cooking oil.

Their hope is either to live off the animals that survived or to find clansmen who salvaged more of their animals and with them to reconstitute their herds and lives. In seven to ten years, experts believe, the nomads reconstituted their herds after earlier droughts, to which this region is periodically heir.

"It is an experiment," Captain Tall said. "It is bad for them to stay in the camps too long and lose the habit of work. They have to try to resume the work. But if they don't manage, we will have to see what we can do."

Informed sources reported that in a similar experiment last year, most came back to the camps. Those who did not leave voluntarily have recently been sent out by the administration to gather a kind of wild grain. It grows abundantly and is traditionally used to tide over people in the lean period, when the last year's crop is eaten up and the new crop not in yet.

Those who stay around town strongly express traditional Tuareg animosity to the blacks who govern Mali. The Tuaregs, a Berber, Caucasian people, traditionally lived from the milk and meat of their animals and the work of the black slaves they captured in frequent raids on sedentary villages.

Their attitude remains haughty to those of skin darker than theirs, and the governing powers feel little tenderness for the

Tuaregs. But diplomatic observers believe that the Government has nonetheless fairly distributed food and other available assistance to the nomads.

Whatever the victims of the drought have done to repair their lives, foreigners are above all impressed with the ability of the sedentary and nomad populations of this semiarid region to survive and work with what to outsiders seems less than the minimum daily requirements of everything — food, shelter or medicine.

Where does their strength come from? Captain Tall was asked.

"Underdevelopment," he replied laconically.

| **Indonesia**

Sawahrejo: Lush but Not Rich

The name of this hamlet in Central Java means "prosperous rice fields," and a glance at the lush landscape is enough to reach the conclusion that the word hunger ought never be uttered here.

The irrigated paddies are vivid variations on the theme of green as the grain ripens in the sun; ducks cruise the irrigation canals, evoking far-fetched comparisons to swans in an English village stream; fruit trees grow everywhere, offering a seemingly endless supply of plantain, mango and papaya, in addition to more exotic fruits with names like belimbing, jambu and nangka, whose textures and tastes are simply beyond the imagination of denizens of the Temperate Zone.

If the word hunger is rarely uttered, that is only because the Javanese — a people of elaborate politeness and reserve — regard it as unseemly to speak bluntly about their most urgent needs. In fact it soon becomes obvious that most of Sawahrejo lives on the edge of hunger.

For the fecundity of Java extends to its people, and although it has been said for decades that the saturation point had surely been reached, the population has continued to rise. Now there are about 80 million living in an area only slightly larger than the state of New York. In rural Pemalang County, where the hamlet is situated, the density is about 2,200 a square mile. If the United States had that density, its population would exceed that of the world.

In Sawahrejo 420 households — about 2,000 people in all — live on 673 acres, a little more than a square mile. The hamlet, which is divided into two clusters of houses by an irrigation canal, is neither especially well off nor especially poor by the standards of the area.

The village office and the school are set on the banks of the canal, which is crossed by a narrow bamboo bridge. Beyond the bridge is a broad path, the hamlet's main thoroughfare, which is lined on both sides by the stucco houses of the prosperous farmers and the rattan huts of those whose buildings are so small that they can be nothing more than spectators of whatever prosperity the hamlet experiences.

The first impression is of tranquility and order. Every hut on the path has a fence of some sort and all but the poorest have a gatepost with a small lantern on it. Even when the sun is directly overhead, the path is shaded by the myriad fruit trees. And at night the kerosene flames in the lanterns glimmer beguilingly.

If Sawahrejo had several hundred fewer residents or several hundred more acres, the first impression would remain the strongest. But, finally, it is statistics that describe the place most vividly. Of the households 284 farm less than an acre; 78 are classed as landless.

Consider the case of Kayin — Indonesians typically have one name — whose holding, like that of 184 other peasants in the hamlet, is a mere fifth of an acre. It is really a patch of garden rather than a farm, and because it is so small Mr. Kayin is able to lavish loving attention on every seedling, checking daily for weeds, insects and rats that might threaten his tiny harvest.

By careful cultivation he can reap nearly 500 pounds of rice in a good season — barely enough to sustain himself, his wife and their two surviving children. (Three other children died; in Java, a quarter of all deaths are of children under a year.) How barely the land sustains them can be seen in Mr. Kayin as he trudges barefoot through the fields. At about 45 — he is unsure of his exact age — he is gaunt rather than wiry, not middle-aged but old.

Mr. Kayin sells only enough rice to buy seeds for the next season and small doses of fertilizer. For his present crop, nine pounds of fertilizer, costing less than $1 even at a black-market price, was all he thought he could afford.

Not because he resists change but because he is a realist, he takes it for granted that he will never penetrate the cash economy sufficiently to be able to afford the high-yield seeds, insecticide and quantities of fertilizer that have dramatically increased the output and incomes of larger landholders in recent years. All he can hope for is opportunities to work as a day laborer in their fields at the going rate of 50 rupiahs — about 12 cents — a day, plus meals.

Such work, which he appears to find no more than 120 days in the year, provides his family with its only cash income, nearly all of which goes for cassava, the starchy root that he and other poor Javanese eat as a supplement or alternative to rice (any desirable fruit is sold). There is not much nutrition in cassava but there is bulk; when there is nothing else it staves off hunger.

Mr. Kayin does not describe himself as desperate. On the contrary, he says that he is better off than he used to be, thanks to repairs this year to an irrigation canal that flows near his field. Built in the period of Dutch colonial rule, it had silted up and fallen into disuse, leaving plots like his subject to the weather. Now, although his lack of means firmly limits his ability to increase his output, his crops are at least safe.

The condition of Wartam, a landless father of two, is much worse. For him nearly everything depends on his ability to find work, but the very pressure of population makes that a matter of chance. Even at the height of the harvest there are not enough jobs to go around.

The actual facts of Mr. Wartam's situation emerge only indirectly. Asked whether he finds work every day or whether his family has enough rice, he avoids a negative answer; a man should be able to work every day and feed his family, and Mr. Wartam does not want it to be thought that he does less than a man should.

When he works he earns 50 rupiahs. He needs 300 to buy what he deems to be an adequate amount of rice for his family. He masks the discrepancy by saying that he goes to market to buy rice whenever he is "feeling good."

That means, it develops, when he has worked for several days consecutively. "Did you work today?" he is asked.

"No, not today."
"Yesterday?"
"Not yesterday."
"This week?"
"No."

Like most of Sawahrejo's landless Mr. Wartam lives on state land on the banks of an irrigation canal, the best available property in the hamlet. Irrigation officials allow the landless to grow cassava, bananas and rice in minuscule patches there. It is a personal, extralegal, basically feudal arrangement between the landless and the officials, who periodically turn up to ask for a share of whatever rice is grown or, in lieu of that, an informal cash tithe.

Mr. Wartam does not have enough land to cultivate rice, so he feeds his family on a root called perut, which is so much less appealing even than cassava that it is never on the local market. Still, it is all Mr. Wartam has available, and he offers a plate to a foreigner who has come to call. What taste the root has is vaguely turnipy, but it is mostly cellulose and barely digestible; the sensation is that of eating paper.

"Every day there are a couple of families that have nothing to eat," says Damhurai, another landless laborer, who spends

most of the year as a sidewalk hawker of food in Jakarta, 200 miles to the west. When there is nothing, the landless say, they borrow from friends. But according to the landed that is not quite the whole story; not infrequently, they allege, they discover that their cassava plants have been uprooted or their fruit trees stripped.

Chasmin, a neighbor of Mr. Wartam's on the canal bank, does not wait for a job to turn up. When there is no prospect of work — the usual situation — he hikes four miles to a forest and picks leaves until he has enough to form two tightly packed bundles of about 20 pounds each. The next day he hauls these six miles to the nearest market, where he sells them for 150 rupiahs, about 35 cents, to traders who use the broad, sturdy leaves for packaging.

The pressure of population can be inferred from such makeshift efforts or from the fact that women in the hamlet account for about 60 per cent of its adult population. Those men who cannot scratch out a living tend to drift off to the towns, usually Jakarta, which has been proclaimed a closed city but is actually growing faster than any other in Asia.

The pressure of numbers is not simply inferred. It is palpable, and the hamlet is aware of it as something extraordinary, especially at harvest time, when 300 to 500 people may show up to cut the rice on a mere two acres.

By Javanese tradition the harvest is an occasion for sharing: Anyone can take part. The work, done by hand with a blade called an aniani, is usually assigned to women and children, who are rewarded with a fraction of whatever they cut, an eighth or a 12th.

These days the numbers looking for work are so great that it is commonplace for people to be turned away. Kambali, a relatively prosperous farmer with a holding of three and a half acres, says that if too many harvesters show up he sometimes has to delay for a day for fear of loss through careless handling, trampling or even pilferage.

What is involved is the delicate social mechanism, the bal-

The New York Times / Joseph Lelyveld

A landless family of Sawahrejo posing outside their home. There are 420 households on a little more than a square mile.

ance wheel, of the Javanese village, which has made it possible for it to absorb an ever-increasing population. Now that
mechanism is being strained, not just by rising population by
by the sudden injection of an element of dynamism into the
economy through the new agricultural technology that is
available to the minority whose holdings are large enough to
be viable.

The old sense of obligation has not died. On a recent Friday an announcement was made at the village mosque invit-
ing worshipers to the home of a landowner who was holding
a traditional ceremony called slametan, in memory of his
father, who died 1,000 days before.

After the ceremony the landowner distributed 500 boxes in
the village, each crammed with bananas, rice, dried fish and
chicken. In his own mind this was a necessary part of the
memorial to his father; for most of the recipients it was the
first good meal in days.

There are slametans before the harvest and on other important occasions such as births and marriages. But such cere-
monies are no longer enough, if they ever were, to bridge the
gulf that separates the prosperous farmers from the small
holders and the landless.

Supadi, a retired police officer, has five irrigated acres and
five and a half that are rain-fed, enough to make him one of
the three biggest landowners in the hamlet. In a three-month
season, he says, he needs to hire labor only on five days —
one day for transplanting, three for weeding and one for the
harvest.

Some prosperous farmers invest their new profits in a pil-
grimage to Mecca, which costs about $1,500. Mr. Supadi's
money has gone into the hamlet's most imposing house, a
comfortable whitewashed structure with a bricked-in terrace
where he has planted an orange tree. But he does not feel
entirely secure there.

"In the coming 20 years," he said, "the situation will get
worse and worse. If the landless and the poor have nothing to
eat, they will become robbers, they will become hoodlums."

The 185 smallest holders in the hamlet own only 5 per cent
of its land. More than half is owned by the prosperous
farmers who use the new techniques and seeds, which have
improved their yields by as much as 50 per cent.

There is little doubt, then, that Sawahrejo grows enough food to feed itself, but self-sufficiency is an abstraction as far as the hamlet is concerned. Only a minority of farmers have a surplus, and those who do naturally send it to market. If the rest are self-sufficient, that is only because they lack the means to be anything else.

On Java as a whole, rice production is expanding faster than population, and it is even arguable that per capita rice consumption is higher than it has been at any time in this century, but self-sufficiency remains a vague and ever-receding goal. Last year [1973] with the best harvests on record, Indonesia had to import 1.6 million tons, more than any other country in the region.

From the perspective of the hamlet it is apparent that increasing production has no necessary bearing on the actual food consumption of the rural poor whose foothold in the local economy seems increasingly tenuous. For those who cannot count on eating rice, per capita rice consumption is a meaningless statistic.

Insofar as the local government responds to their predicament at all, it is with slogans about modernization. It offers neither work nor rations.

In Sawahrejo local government is personified in the paternalistic figure of the village headman, an army veteran named Amin Sojitno, who was installed by the military authorities in 1965. The previous headman, now said to have been a Communist, was killed in the bloody reprisals that swept Java and Bali in the wake of an attempted Communist coup d'état.

Mr. Sojitno and his wife — she is the hamlet's kindergarten teacher and family-planning officer — have worked hard to be accepted in Sawahrejo and, by all accounts, they have succeeded. But their status is essentially that of gentry. The headman rides a Honda scooter, smokes imported Dunhill cigarettes and buys the latest cassette recordings in town. On his right hand he cultivates a thumbnail more than an inch long, evidence of what is only obvious — that field labor is outside his experience.

Village government has changed little in Java in the last two centuries. Essentially the headman's function is to maintain order and assist in the collection of taxes. In return he is given exclusive rights to a large amount of land instead of a salary for as long as he holds his position.

Other local officials are compensated in the same way; even the man who sweeps the village office is given an acre and a half. By definition then, it is government by the landed.

Sometimes it is alleged that this basically feudalistic system impedes development. But Mr. Sojitno is at pains to be sure that the latest methods and seeds are used on the 35 acres — three times as much as he could legally own outright — that have been set aside for him. Crops on that much land could bring in as much as $8,000 in a year, which is breathtaking by the standards of rural Java.

Mr. Sojitno, not oblivious to the plight of the small holders and the landless, hopes that eventually there will be small-scale industry in the county to employ them. In the meantime he advocates family planning.

Birth-control pills and the intrauterine device, commonly known as the loop, were first introduced in Sawahrejo two years ago. According to records kept by Mrs. Sojitno, 52 women accepted the loop and 45 women started on the pill. But the pill-takers gave up within a few months, complaining of headaches, and no loops have been accepted for a year.

It is not so much resistance to birth control as skepticism over the methods and a certain fatalism about the results. By Asian standards the rate of population increase in Central Java is relatively low — 1.7 per cent a year — and with the high density the advantages of a small family are widely recognized. But high infant mortality undercuts the very notion of family planning.

The question was raised in one of the small colonies of the landless on the banks of the canal. Not a single man or woman there, it was said, had used modern contraceptives. Several times they were asked why. The answer was given by a 15-year-old named Lukimah, who had just had her first child. "It doesn't matter," she said. Asked what she meant she merely repeated herself.

In the final analysis each small holding is an overcrowded lifeboat. A young farmer named Kasmari was asked how many people had to be sustained on the slightly more than an

The New York Times / Joseph Lelyveld

Workers harvesting rice in Sawahrejo, Indonesia.

acre and a half that his father had farmed; he recited 22 names.

Half the holding had been deeded to two elder brothers; seven siblings had equal claims on the rest. This season they contrived to rent an additional two-fifths of an acre by selling their last water buffalo. Next season there will be no buffalo to sell.

WILLIAM ROBBINS | # The United States

Sweet Home, Arkansas: Hunger in the U.S.

The house was a faded gray, squatting in the dust beside a crumbling macadam street.

In one of its two rooms Mrs. Luteller Peters, 84 years old, her eyes fiercely bright in a face deeply seamed like black leather stitched loosely over bone, sat under a sign that said in crude red letters:

"We reserve the right to refuse service to anyone."

The sign, a relic from an old restaurant, is a grim reminder of years of indignities met by Mrs. Peters as a black in the South and yet another indignity that she encounters now. Despite billions spent by the United States Government on food aid, she is living out her days in hunger.

A local volunteer agency, aided by Federal funds, delivers a hot lunch to Mrs. Peters every day. But she says she cannot use food stamps for the rest because she is too feeble to go to the store with the coupons, which she says local merchants insist she must present in person. And to provide morning and evening meals for the whole month, she has only $9 of her own available.

Thus, in one of the most fortunate of nations — one with a wide margin of plenty in a world where more than 400 million people suffer from malnutrition and many live on the edge of famine — hunger persists.

And while it is a much smaller problem on the whole in this country than in many others, it is no less harsh for the individuals who endure it.

Hunger in the United States has many faces. It exists, a trip into two randomly chosen areas shows, among all types of the poor — the young and the old, the urban and the rural.

Many of the hungry are elderly and rural, like Mrs. Peters and like Cornelius Butler, 70, who sits through each long day, weak and underfed, on a rotting porch near Jacksonville, Ark.

But there are also many in the cities who are young, angry, unemployed and confused, like William Parish, 27, who is white and who has only bread and peanut butter to eat in his house in Little Rock, or like a black mother of three in Detroit, who survives on the same fare.

The hunger persists even though great sums of money — $4-billion in 1974 — are spent on food stamps under a Congressional mandate to administrators to give the eligible needy "an opportunity to obtain a nutritionally adequate diet" and to try "to insure the participation of eligible households."

And there is much evidence indicating that the situation is worsening because of inflation. Hunger-related crimes, for example, are reported increasing and food-stamp applications are reported up sharply in many areas.

Yet, 10 years after passage of the first food-stamp legislation no one really knows how big the problem is.

Such evidence as exists is based on limited studies — limited in both scope and depth. But that evidence indicates that millions of Americans are hungry at least part of their lives, that many suffer from malnutrition, and that many children in the United States suffer permanent mental and physical damage as a result.

Recent testimony before the Senate Select Committee on Nutrition and Human Needs alleged that 37 million were poor enough to be eligible to receive food stamps, with only 14.1 million now receiving such assistance.

Other estimates have ranged as high as 50 million people in eligible families.

The 37-million estimate given in the Senate testimony, as it turns out, stemmed from a projection by an economist at the Department of Agriculture, who based his work on census data.

That projection is now disowned by officials of the department, who point out that figures on incomes reported by census-takers are undocumented and that many of those represented by low-income census figures would be ineligible for food stamps because of assets held, because they are served by institutions, or for other reasons.

Acknowledging, however, that there might be "a high degree of correlation" between the census figures and the number of eligible people in low-income families, one official said: "The truth is we really don't know how many there might be."

The officials also say that food-stamp figures themselves are misleading, because the rolls change constantly. As many as 20 million people may be served during a year, they estimate.

One of the best and the broadest studies of the effects of hunger and dietary deficiencies resulting from poverty is a "Ten-State Nutrition Survey," produced by the Department of Health, Education and Welfare. Though it is now dated, reaching only through 1970, it was based on clinical examinations, and thus is revealing.

The survey found evidence, for example, of deficiency in vitamin A in more than 40 per cent of children of the low-income black families studied compared with 10 per cent or less among children of white families.

It also found that more than 8 per cent of the low-income black families studied showed evidence of iron deficiency.

As an assumed result of malnutrition, it found that children from low-income families tended to show retarded development, including smaller head sizes. Other studies have shown that young children suffering from malnutrition are penalized throughout life by retarded brain development.

Thus, specialists say, poverty and the blighting effects of poverty are passed on from one generation to another.

Better evidence may become available when the Department of Health, Education and Welfare begins reporting, as it is expected to do in a few months, on a new and improved

The New York Times / Pat Patterson

Luteller Peters is one of millions of ill-fed Americans.

"health and nutrition examination survey." But as of now the department cannot report even the incidence of such nutrition-related health problems as rickets and goiter.

In this country, few deaths are reported as malnutrition or starvation. But numerous "high nutrition risk" cases result in early deaths from a variety of common diseases, experts say.

Although food-stamp applications are said to be rising, increases in the distribution of food stamps have not offset even the number of people who had been benefiting from surplus commodities under a discontinued program for which food stamps were substituted.

The worst of the food problems persist largely without reason and at least partly because of administrative foot-dragging, many critics say. They note that food-stamp programs are now available in virtually every section of the country and that several other food programs are in operation, though supported with too little funds to respond to all needy applicants.

One provides supplemental feeding for needy lactating mothers and young children. Another called "WIC" (for women, infants and children) is for low-income families considered "at risk" nutritionally, and school lunch and school breakfast programs are widely available.

Critics of the basic program for the hungry, the food-stamp plan, say that the problem lies partly in the legislation itself. It provides for a "nutritionally adequate diet," but regulations drawn up by the Department of Agriculture relate such a diet to its "economy food plan."

That plan is a carefully selected and measured list of foods designed to provide the minimum needs of basic nutrients. It is "technically possible," one Washington official said, for a shopper to get an adequate diet with a food-stamp allowance based on the plan, but it is practically impossible for the poor and often poorly educated families to make the meticulous calculations required in shopping to fill their needs.

In addition, inflation is racing far ahead of adjustments in the food-stamp allowances.

A family of four with income of $6,000 a year or less can qualify for $150 in stamps, but it must pay a large part of the face value in cash. The cost of the stamps rises from zero for such a family with less than $30 a month income to $126 for a family of the same size with $450 a month.

It is difficult for poor families to set aside enough money to pay at once for the stamps after paying such basic costs as rents, utilities, medical expenses and other necessities that cannot be bought with food stamps.

But more serious problems of hunger persist, the critics say, because of failure of both the Department of Agriculture and local officials who are responsible for distribution of food stamps.

They say the department has failed to impose on responsible local officials the legislative requirement of an "Outreach" system to find eligible hungry but nonparticipating families and try to insure their participation.

At the local level, they say, the problem is also administrative, with too few social workers generally to handle the program.

"It's an administrative morass," said Ronald Pollack, director of the Food Research and Action Center, an organization that has filed many lawsuits seeking improvement of the system. There are too few workers and too few offices, he said, and applicants have to travel long distances, sometimes for several days in succession before managing to get through long lines of people waiting for certification. "The working poor just cannot afford all that time," he added.

The critics' charges are disputed by officials here.

"My feeling is that nonparticipation is based more on the fact that they generally have to pay for the stamps and on the attitudes of many people about accepting public assistance," Roger Shipp, director of the Agriculture Department's Food Stamp Division, said in an interview.

"I get the feeling that the states are very serious about making the program work."

But a Federal court ruling in one of Mr. Pollack's lawsuits as well as evidence observed in Detroit and rural areas near Little Rock tended to support the charges.

Judge Miles W. Lord of the Federal District Court in Minneapolis blocked an effort by the department to return to the Treasury $280-million in unspent food stamp funds for the fiscal year 1973. Noting that the department had spent only

$80,242 in the United States that year in the "Outreach" effort, Judge Miles found:

"The [Agriculture] Secretary's response to the Congressional directive, when viewed in its totality, is fairly described as a total failure on his part to do what the Congress clearly intended him to do."

Mr. Shipp and aides questioned whether a greater effort might have produced more participation. Besides, he said, the 1,300 field employes in the program were mainly assigned to monitoring of grocery stores with "relatively few left to keep tabs on what local administrators are doing."

In both Detroit and the Little Rock area, the cases among the poor illustrated complaints heard elsewhere.

Telling of long lines and days of waiting that discouraged applicants for aid, the Rev. William Cunningham, a Roman Catholic priest who is director of a volunteer Detroit agency called Focus: Hope, asserted: "the programs seem programmed to fail."

Mrs. Eleanor Josatis, head of the Mayor's Task Force on Hunger and Malnutrition, provided the results of a study indicating, however, a higher percentage of participation that appears to prevail elsewhere.

Of 236,102 persons said to be eligible for the food stamp program, the number in need but not being served was put at 26,843.

Among those getting assistance was a 70-year-old widow, Mrs. Estella Smith, who explained why she could not take full advantage of the program.

Her rent and utilities absorbed all but $70 of her Social Security and welfare checks, totaling $194 a month, she explained. With medical and other expenses, she had available only $16.50 of the $33 that would be required for a full monthly stamp allowance with a face value of $46.

With the $23 worth of stamps that she can buy, she explained, she survives toward the end of each month on oatmeal and "pots of greens I cook up."

Wistfully, she added: "I can see plenty of people buy so much groceries it's pitiful. I just stand there and look at it."

But far hungrier was a young mother, living with her three children on the top floor of the building pocked with broken windows. She was out of work since being laid off at a restaurant several weeks earlier.

The young woman, whose name cannot be used because she feared retribution, had also been without welfare aid since, she said, she cashed an aid check made out in a name similar to hers but missent to her address. And because she had been unable to buy food stamps as a result of the cut-off, her food-stamp certification had been voided.

She and her children had been living, like the young man in Arkansas, on homemade bread and peanut butter. Focus: Hope came to her assistance with emergency supplies.

The young Little Rock man, Mr. Parrish, was encountered in a welfare office, waiting angrily in his third attempt to see a worker and gain certification for food stamps. The waiting room was crowded with about 50 other applicants, many of whom gave similar accounts, some with repeated long and costly trips.

The office serves an entire, sprawling county.

A far different fact of hunger was that of Aline Johnson, of Jacksonville, Ark. a woman so fat that she could not rise from her chair unaided. Yet she, too, was often hungry, surviving with her children on two meals a day of "greens and beans" for the last few days of each month.

Her very obesity, experts say, is a sign of malnutrition.

With her, sitting on old, cloth-draped furniture, were two grown daughters, one with an infant lying listless despite crawling flies, a sign, nutritionists say, of malnourishment.

Miss Johnson's case is one of a type that has drawn attacks from critics of food and welfare. She is unwed but the mother of 11 children. Of the daughters with her, both also unwed, one has four children and the other six.

Critics charge that public assistance in such cases encourages the spawning of still more children and new burdens on society.

Defenders say that, without food assistance, defenseless children would be condemned to the environment in which they were born and to perpetuate it in later generations.

Mrs. Peters, the 84-year-old widow here in Sweet Home, says she is unable to endure either a trip to the welfare office or the waiting for certification by a worker. And if she did qualify and receive stamps, she is too infirm to exchange them in person for her food as she said local stores require.

As a result, she said, she "gets by" on the $9 a month she has left from her monthly income of $75 a month as the widow of a Spanish-American war veteran, and the hot meal brought to her door once a day by a volunteer agency with funding from the Department of Health, Education, and Welfare.

In the mornings and evenings, she usually eats "a little rice."

"I don't mind. I like rice," she said proudly.

Mr. Shipp said there was no reason why she could not also get a welfare check that would automatically qualify her for food stamps or why, according to regulations, she could not make arrangements to send the stamps to a store for her food.

But, for some reason, no one had explained that solution either to Mrs. Peters or to the local food stores.

| **The World**

Malnutrition, the Global Scourge

In parts of rural Bangladesh, during relatively good times, villagers hope to eat one meal a day. In 1974, during the aftermath of the summer floods, many of them were eating only once every other day, sometimes only once in every three.

An authority on world malnutrition, Dr. Nevin S. Scrimshaw, cited these grim figures recently to put in human terms the impact of hunger in 1974.

The consequence of prolonged hunger is malnutrition. It is widespread in the underdeveloped world. It appears to be getting worse. It hits children hardest, killing many and stunting the growth of many others both mentally and physically so that they are likely to be handicapped for life.

Since early 1974, nutritionists say, there have been sharp increases in serious malnutrition among young children in many regions, notably Barbados, Guatemala, Bangladesh, Thailand and India.

There are no good global figures on malnutrition and never have been, but some experts estimate that a billion or more people suffer from it during at least part of the year. That means that about one quarter of the human race are suffering today from hunger and its consequences.

Malnutrition and its ultimate form — starvation — are the real causes of world concern over the teetering balance between food supplies and population across the globe.

Real progress against malnutrition has been made during the last two decades. But some specialists, including Dr.

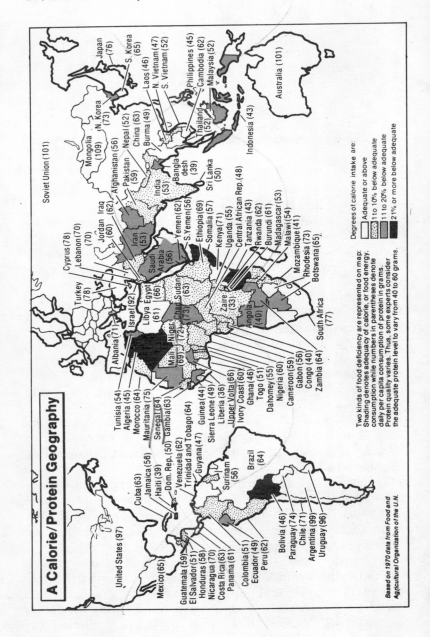

A Calorie/Protein Geography

Two kinds of food deficiency are represented on map:
Shading denotes adequacy of calorie, or food energy,
consumption while numbers in parentheses denote
daily per capita consumption of protein in grams.
Protein quality varies. Thus, some experts consider
the adequate protein level to vary from 40 to 60 grams.

Degrees of calorie intake are:

- Adequate or above
- 1 to 10% below adequate
- 11 to 20% below adequate
- 21% or more below adequate

Based on 1970 data from Food and
Agricultural Organization of the U.N.

United States (97)

Mexico (65)
Guatemala (59)
El Salvador (51)
Honduras (58)
Nicaragua (70)
Costa Rica (63)
Panama (61)

Cuba (63)
Jamaica (56)
Haiti (39)
Dom. Rep. (50)
Venezuela (62)
Trinidad and Tobago (64)
Guyana (47)
Surinam (56)

Colombia (51)
Ecuador (49)
Peru (62)
Bolivia (46)
Paraguay (74)
Chile (71)
Argentina (99)
Uruguay (96)
Brazil (64)

Soviet Union (101)
Mongolia (109)
Japan (76)
S. Korea (65)
N. Korea (73)
Afghanistan (56)
Pakistan (59)
Nepal (52)
China (63)
India (53)
Burma (49)
Bangladesh (39)
Sri Lanka (50)
Laos (46)
N. Vietnam (47)
S. Vietnam (52)
Philippines (45)
Cambodia (62)
Thailand (52)
Malaysia (52)
Indonesia (43)
Australia (101)

Turkey (78)
Cyprus (78)
Lebanon (70)
Jordan (70)
Iraq (60)
Iran (53)
Albania (71)
Israel (92)
Libya (61)
Egypt (66)
Saudi Arabia (56)
Yemen (62)
S. Yemen (56)
Ethiopia (69)
Somalia (57)
Kenya (71)
Uganda (55)
Central African Rep. (48)
Tanzania (43)
Rwanda (62)
Burundi (61)
Madagascar (53)
Malawi (54)
Mozambique (41)
Rhodesia (73)
Botswana (65)
South Africa (77)

Tunisia (54)
Algeria (45)
Morocco (64)
Mauritania (75)
Senegal (64)
Gambia (63)
Guinea (44)
Sierra Leone (49)
Liberia (36)
Upper Volta (66)
Ivory Coast (60)
Ghana (46)
Togo (51)
Dahomey (55)
Nigeria (60)
Cameroon (59)
Gabon (56)
Congo (40)
Zambia (64)
Mali (69)
Niger (72)
Chad (73)
Sudan (63)
Zaire (33)
Angola (40)

Scrimshaw, head of the Department of Nutrition and Food Science at Massachusetts Institute of Technology, say there has been a sharp turn for the worse in recent months.

Among the underlying causes are bad weather, inflation in energy and food costs and the inexorable growth of world population. Rising petroleum prices have sent the costs of fertilizer and transportation up, too, blunting the promise of the "green revolution."

Floods, droughts and other anomalies of weather have hurt crops in some of the world's main food-producing regions and in other places where shortage can be least tolerated.

Nations that appear to be particularly hard-hit include India, Pakistan, Bangladesh, the sub-Saharan countries of Africa, Indonesia and parts of several Latin-American countries.

It has been estimated that roughly 15 million children a year die before the age of 5 of the combined effects of infection and malnutrition. This annual toll represents a quarter of all the deaths in the world.

Some experts believe virtually all of the children born to poor parents in the underdeveloped nations have some degree of malnutrition at one time or another. For millions the malnutrition is severe.

The human tragedy of this is clear to anyone who has ever seen the staring, apathetic eyes, match-stick limbs and swollen belly of a seriously malnourished child. The whole social and economic cost is harder to grasp, but no less tragic.

In adults, malnutrition can ruin health and productivity; in a child it can all but foreclose the future. The world malnutrition covers many possible deficits, sometimes simply too little food of any kind, sometimes the lack of certain crucial nutrients. The results can vary too — anemia and apathy, or deformed bones, or stunting of growth in both mind and body. When prolonged and drastic enough, malnutrition becomes starvation — a word that needs no definition.

In regions where malnutrition is common, Dr. Scrimshaw observed during a recent interview, laborers often have to be given tasks that take only two or three hours a day. Men and women can't work longer on the calories their meager diet provides. This lack of productivity tends to be self-perpetuating. The person who can work only a few hours a day can't earn enough to buy the food that would make a longer work day possible. Even when the malnutrition reflects primarily deprivation of certain specific nutrients rather than overall lack of food, the loss of productivity can be drastic.

A field study in Indonesia last year, sponsored by the World Bank, showed a strong correlation between iron-deficiency anemia and reduced take-home pay among rubber tappers. The study, by scientists at M.I.T., showed a 38 per cent rise in income when the rubber workers were fed extra iron to correct the anemia.

Malnutrition is bad enough by itself, but it almost never occurs alone. The malnourished person suffers more severely than others from infectious diseases. In places such as Africa, where malnutrition is a common childhood experience, measles is a killer.

Furthermore, repeated bouts of infection can intensify and aggravate malnutrition. When a malnourished infant develops diarrhea — often a combined effect of too many germs and too little food — the mother responds by withholding solid food. When the only alternative is a thin gruel of little nutritive value the malnutrition inevitably gets worse.

In many poverty-stricken regions of the world, infant diarrhea and respiratory infections in the young are among the leading over-all causes of death. Many experts agree that this toll is as high as it is primarily because of malnutrition.

While malnutrition can be disastrous at any age, health workers concerned with the problem are most alarmed about the effects on children and pregnant women. The alarm is over those who survive as much as over those who die.

The combined assault of poverty and its social deprivations along with the lack of good nutrition, both before and after birth, can leave a young child permanently handicapped virtually from the start of life. For at least 20 years, evidence has been accumulating that infants thus deprived may grow up with permanent mental as well as physical handicaps.

"The world is producing literally hundreds of thousands of children who will be at risk of poor mental development later on," said Dr. Myron Winick, who has done pioneering studies on the effects of malnutrition on the developing mind and brain.

"These are the very countries that are underdeveloped and can least afford to have many of their 20-year-olds retarded 20 years from now," he said. Dr. Winick is director of the Institute of Human Nutrition of Columbia University's College of Physicians and Surgeons.

The same worry has been expressed recently by many experts, including Dr. Scrimshaw of M.I.T.

"We will see an increasing threat to the population on which the developing countries will depend to bring them into the modern age," he said.

That is a factor of utmost concern to health scientists: Today's malnutrition may already be shackling tomorrow's generation of adults.

Part of the evidence for this lies in the way the human brain develops. There are two relatively distinct key periods in its growth. The first of these is a rapid multiplication of nerve cells coming during the second trimester of pregnancy — months three-through-six.

The second key phase extends through the first two years of a child's life. During this phase, according to Dr. Merrill S. Read, of the National Institute of Child Health and Human Development, comes major growth of the brain's non-nerve cells and of the intricate multiple connections between cells.

This latter phase is particularly important to human mental performance. Dr. Read said in a survey report on the effects of malnutrition on learning.

It had once been thought that the human fetus was almost entirely protected against malnutrition while still in the womb and that the infant could recover satisfactorily from even severe temporary lack of nourishment. Today, both of these views seem overly optimistic. A malnourished mother may not be able to give the fetus the optimum nutrition that it needs. The infant lacking proper food during early critical stages may never recover completely.

There are at least three ways in which early malnutrition can permanently stigmatize its victims, Drs. Read, Winick and others agree. Evidence from humans and animals shows that malnutrition at key times early in growth may affect the development of the brain so as to impair learning ability. The second and third factors appear to be as much social and behavioral as physical. The seriously malnourished baby tends to be apathetic, less demanding of attention from its mother — and therefore getting less. The result is likely to be further malnutrition and withdrawal into a bleak empty world of its own. It's a situation that tends to perpetuate itself among the survivors with later changes in personality and behavior that may interfere with learning and almost everything else.

Experiments with nonhuman primates have shown that severe malnutrition in the young results in emotional problems and difficulty in adapting to change later on.

From long studies of deprived children in Latin America and Cambridge, Mass., Dr. Ernesto Pollitt of M.I.T. has concluded that the victims of early malnutrition inhabit a world virtually separate from the more fortunate, and that food alone would hardly suffice to bridge the gap.

Yet, for millions, enough food seems to be getting more and more out of reach.

In oversimplified summary, this is the picture several specialists have drawn recently:

In poor areas of the world, inflation in both human numbers and the cost of everything is driving rural people off the land and into appalling city slums. Work is scarce and government dole of food offers the only hope of survival. In this natural breeding ground for malnutrition, infants are further compromised because their mothers can't both breast-feed and look for work.

In city after city in countries where hunger is already a problem there seems to be a trend away from breast-feeding. Nutritionists are concerned because they see evidence that it is reflected in serious malnutrition at the age when the baby is most likely to suffer irreparable damage. The reason is that the infants often get their substitute food under unsanitary conditions and the formula food itself is often watered down to save the family money.

"It's too dilute to do any good," one doctor said, "but it still looks white."

Some nutritionists say a major aggravation of the problem is the tendency of some poor mothers to abandon breast-feeding in emulation of more prosperous women — but without the resources or knowledge to provide their babies with adequate substitute nutrition.

The result, all too commonly, is a grave type of malnutrition called marasmus. It results from a prolonged deficit in total food — too few calories, too little protein, too little of everything else that is important in food.

Dr. Winick said marasmus in the very young is particularly dangerous because it hits during a stage of development when the risk of permanent brain damage is probably greatest. Dr. Joe Wray, a pediatrician who has worked in community health projects in many parts of the world as a field staff officer of the Rockefeller Foundation, says he has been appalled by the extent of urban malnutrition.

His most recent assignment was several years in Thailand. There he said, breast-feeding was still the custom in rural families. Malnutrition was neither common nor often severe.

Dr. Wray said that when he left Bangkok earlier this year, the drift away from breast-feeding was so strong that most women were no longer doing it after the first six months. In the urban slums of that city, he said, well over half of the babies were malnourished and as many as 15 per cent suffered from marasmus. He suspects that the same thing would be found in many of the other big cities of Asia.

Dr. F. James Levinson, director of M.I.T.'s International Nutrition Planning program, called the lack of breast feeding among the poor "a dreadful syndrome" that is having effects all over the world.

In the midst of all the evidence of malnutrition in various regions of the world, there are a few notable exceptions.

Dr. Georgio Solimano, head of the nutrition programs under the Allende regime in Chile, said his country had made significant progress against infant malnutrition by intensive programs of giving milk supplements to poor women and children, together with a large-scale public health education program.

Dr. Solimano, who is now at M.I.T., said the program began before the Allende regime but was accentuated during his presidency. Infant and maternal death rates have declined in Chile in recent years, he said, partly under the impact of the long-term policy.

Others familiar with the situation in Chile said the present regime was continuing to follow a strong nutrition policy under the direction of Dr. Fernando Monckenberg, an internationally known scientist.

Several nutritionists and experts in child health have been surprised and much impressed by the lack of visible malnutrition in mainland China. Evidence of severe and widespread malnutrition would not be easy to hide from the visitors' expert eyes. Many who have been to China believe she has indeed managed to provide adequate food for her 800 million people. Visitors to North Vietnam in recent years have reported much the same thing.

Decades ago, China and Indochina had the reputation of being the traditional home of periodic famines. Today, in much of the rest of Southeast Asia, malnutrition is widespread, some experts say.

As Lester R. Brown of the Overseas Development Council notes in his new book, "By Bread Alone," published in 1974 by Praeger, neither malnutrition nor famine is particularly new to the human race. Millions died of famine in the Soviet Union during the early nineteen-thirties; millions died in Ireland during the potato famine of more than a century ago.

In 1943 floods destroyed the rice crop in West Bengal, India, causing a famine in which some two to four million died.

There have been smaller famines since World War II in various parts of the world and one case in which a large-scale threatened famine was avoided in India because of food aid shipments made largely on American initiative.

Mr. Brown, who has devoted much time and energy to warning of world food problems, said India might have experienced one of the worst famines in history in the mid sixties had it not been for the nearly 10 million tons of food aid shipped in during two successive years.

Observers say it appears that India may need several million tons of food aid this year, possibly as much as their annual needs for aid during the episode of the mid sixties. But this

year, one American nutritionist said, we don't have the surpluses to send them.

Some of the great famines of history have devastated whole
countries or regions, threatening almost everyone when food
supplies ran out. In his new book, Mr. Brown worries about
subtly different famines that may confront today's world.
The modern version, influenced by population pressure and
rising prices, could affect primarily the poor, leaving the affluent, even in poor nations, largely untouched.

"The modern version of famine does not usually confront
the world with dramatic photographs such as those of the
morning ritual of collecting bodies in Calcutta during the
Bengal famine of 1943," he said, "but it is no less real in the
human toll it takes. Reports in 1974 of rising rates of nutrition-related deaths in several poor countries underscore the
need for closer attention to this ominous trend." In a recent
conversation, Dr. Wray of the Rockefeller Foundation also
underscored the ominous look of things today, particularly in
the urban slums of major Asian cities.

3 SUPPLY AND DEMAND

The United States and World Needs

KATHLEEN TELTSCH

The new report to a Senate committee that the needy in the United States are hungrier and poorer than they were four years ago has raised doubts that a bountiful American harvest may forestall the threatened world food shortage.

In effect the report by a group of experts to the Senate Select Committee on Nutrition and Human Needs, published yesterday [June 19, 1974], shows that neither increased spending nor rising agricultural output is sufficient answer, domestically or internationally, to an increasingly critical food problem.

Agriculture Department policy-makers had estimated a harvest of 2.1 billion bushels of wheat, which they insisted should be ample for domestic needs, put at 750 million bushels, and for a billion-bushel provision for profitable sales abroad — leaving a carryover of 350 million bushels for emergency foreign assistance.

However, economic analysts outside government and some members of Congress object that such calculations are perilously dependent not only on American harvests as good as forecast but on the absence of major crop failures in other grain-producing regions. World food stocks have fallen to their lowest levels in 20 years, it is emphasized.

And with population growing at 2 per cent a year and with rising pressure for richer diets, demand is increasingly outrunning productive capacity.

The immediate outlook abroad is not reassuring. Poorer countries such as India have had to cut back on fertilizer imports because of quadrupled prices and scarcities. The same is true for diesel fuel for tractors and for irrigation

The Chicago Board of Trade

pumps. Capricious weather has damaged Soviet winter wheat, hit Ukrainian fields with dust storms and slowed spring sowing in Canada.

"The world situation in 1974 remains more difficult and uncertain than at any time since the years following the devastation of the Second World War," the Food and Agriculture Organization concludes in a report for the World Food Conference.

The difficulties and uncertainties cited by the United Nations specialized agency are reflected in a survey by The New York Times, which also suggests that sketchy and frequently contradictory information is being provided by many governments because of pride or politics or simply inadequate data.

According to New Delhi officials, India will be able to meet food requirements without much difficulty; they assert that there is no dearth of fertilizer and no danger of famine. At the same time an Indian supply mission has been sent to Washington to buy as much wheat as possible to offset deficits expected to reach 10 million tons.

The food agency warns that the drought-ravaged countries extending in a wide belt across Africa south of the Sahara are experiencing acute shortages and that drought is spreading east and south and can be expected to reduce harvests in Dahomey, Egypt, Guinea, Kenya, Nigeria, Somalia, Tanzania and Zaire. However, some qualified authorities returning from the area south of the Sahara say original estimates that 10 million people were threatened by famine were grossly inflated.

"Photographs of bleaching animal carcasses in the desert, which are offered around as current evidence, are no longer valid and the situation has improved radically," according to Dr. Pascal J. Imperato, First Deputy Commissioner of the New York City Health Department, who recently revisited the area, where he had spent five years.

He and others acknowledge that foreign assistance will be needed for years. A new United States report said it would take decades after the emergency relief phase to carry out rehabilitation and irrigation projects to halt the desert's advance.

Some relief experts here note that the full dimensions of the famine last year in Ethiopia were suppressed by the Cabinet in Addis Ababa — since ousted — and maintain that United States officials were lax in reporting the disaster because they were unwilling to antagonize the Ethiopian Government.

Concern for the Indian subcontinent and the sub-Sahara area in Africa prompted recent warnings by the director of the United Nations Children's Fund, Henry R. Labouisse, that 400 million to 500 million children were threatened by severe malnutrition. For the first time in many years there are reports of severe malnutrition in Central America.

Theoretically, according to the experts, global grain production of 1.2 billion tons should be enough to meet minimum needs if supplies were spread evenly, which, of course, they are not. To attain bare minimums for the 30 to 40 poorest countries would require radical cuts in consumption in affluent countries, which consume a ton of grain per capita a year, mainly as feed grain to build costly protein in meat, milk and eggs. The prospect of such redistribution is slim.

The first signal that the world was once again veering toward a food crisis came in 1972, when disastrous weather cut production in the Soviet Union, China, India, Australia, Southeast Asia and the sub-Sahara region.

The Soviet Union, which in previous shortages had tightened its belt, chose to go to the world market, largely for feed grains for expanded livestock production. It was principally its purchase of 20 million tons from the United States that pulled down American reserves and pushed prices up.

Any assessment of this year's food outlook is complicated by the Soviet practice of withholding forecasts and China's refusal to disclose output. Recent reports have said winter wheat was hard hit by bad weather in the Soviet Union and spring planting delayed. So far there has been no indication, according to American agricultural experts, that Moscow will again be buying on the world market.

Although 1973 was a good year and the United States put idle cropland back under the plow, reserves have not been rebuilt. The experts, maintaining that the shortages are not the result of temporary conditions such as the poor 1972 weather, point to long-term trends that are not yet fully understood. They suggest that the world food economy, after decades of abundance — albeit maldistributed, so that many were hungry while some had surpluses — is moving into an era of chronically tight supplies.

Scarcities are developing because the global system is overloaded, according to the Overseas Development Council, a private group. As growing populations and improved diets raise demand, it notes, prices soar and competition for scarce energy and fertilizer intensifies.

The United States has had an agreement with the fertilizer industry since October barring new export sales, which is having damaging effects, particularly on developing countries.

While Agriculture Department spokesmen tend to belittle gloomy forecasts on world output, the F.A.O. report supports the gloom to the extent of estimating that by 1985 the poorer countries will face grain shortages they will be unable to meet with imports. Assuming that increases in population and demand will continue, the agency estimates that by then the majority of developing countries will be left with a big cereals gap.

Senator Hubert H. Humphrey recently proposed a food action program that has bipartisan support. Formulated after consultation with Secretary of State Kissinger, it could be a basis for American policy at the Rome conference.

The program, elements of which will stir domestic opposition, urges a substantial increase in assistance to needy countries, which has been scaled down as American surpluses disappeared, calls for helping the poorer countries increase production and provides for participation in a global system of food reserves.

Many proposals are being offered to ease the food shortage, ranging from the advice of the economist Barbara Ward that the more affluent forgo a hamburger a week, to the urgings of Dr. Jean Mayer, the nutritionist, that a worldwide campaign restore breast feeding. Another proposal is that the family pet be fed with scraps from the table instead of commercial food, a $1.5-billion item in the American budget. Senator Humphrey is appealing to Americans to change their rich diet and affluent life-style to save grain and asking that the three million tons of fertilizer spread on lawns and golf courses be sent abroad.

Some of the suggestions evoke from specialists the reaction that they would be merely symbolic. Among farm interests there is fear that the principal effect of big crops and reduced domestic consumption would be a sag in prices. "It's tough to make the bread and gravy come out even," a farm spokesman remarked.

WILLIAM ROBBINS | # The Domestic Picture

We Could Run Short

"There is no excuse for us ever getting into a position where we won't have enough food," Tony T. Dechant, president of the National Farmers Union, told a reporter.

Agricultural experts in and out of Government agree that, barring a national calamity of inconceivable proportions, American farmers will never fail to produce more than Americans can consume. And yet, most of them also agree, the United States could run short of food.

The reasons for this paradox hinge on Government decisions and raise hard questions of policy: Should United States export policy always be an open door? How much does the richest nation owe to the world's poor and hungry? Must the Government accumulate grain reserves if the country is to be a reliable supplier to its customers?

All such questions focus on one generally accepted fact. Under current world conditions, to produce enough food for the United States is not enough, because this country has become the major supplier to food-deficit nations, rich and poor.

In 1973, the world depended on the United States for 44 per cent of all wheat exports and for half of the shipments of livestock-feed grains.

On the other hand, American agriculture, which would otherwise smother in its plenty, depended on foreign markets for three-fourths of all farm sales of wheat, half of the farmers' soybean sales and a third of their corn sales.

"Food is power," Secretary of Agriculture Earl L. Butz said in an interview, noting the diplomatic leverage that world dependence on American grain provides. But he also stressed the role of the farmers' export in preventing unmanageable trade deficits. The United States agricultural trade surplus was $9.3-billion last year.

Despite this country's agricultural resources, the United States very nearly ran out of one basic food commodity, soybeans, in 1973 and perhaps would have run short if the Government had not stepped in to cut off exports. In 1974 the country's bakers warned at one point that the nation might soon find its wheat bins empty.

Even now, with farmers beginning to harvest a record wheat crop — expected to yield two billions bushels — and with the biggest corn crop ever already planted, grain brokers nervously watch each new estimate of prospective yields. For corn, the Agriculture Department predicts that the harvest will be 6.4 billion bushels, about 750,000 more than the record production of 1973.

So sensitive is the question of supplies, and so narrow the current margin between enough and not enough, that each new development starts gyrations on commodity markets.

And because grains are basic to people's diets — they are the basic ingredients in bread, cereals and feeds for meat production — price changes on commodity markets echo in family budgets.

A relatively small sale, by Canada to China, made wheat prices spurt one day on the Chicago Board of Trade. They dropped later in the day on news of good weather for harvests in Kansas and Illinois. On the same day, corn prices soared because of an estimate by growers that the crops might not come up to Government expectations.

That kind of sensitivity to food supplies is likely to continue for the next year or so.

The sensitivity is partly a result of Government food policy, past and present, or what some economists and politicians say is a lack of policy.

"Our food policy is chaos," Senator George McGovern, Democrat of South Dakota, who is chairman of the Senate Select Committee of Nutrition and Human Needs, told a reporter. And a Government economist, Kenneth Tedor, administrator of the Cost of Living Council's office of food, said in an interview:

"We don't have a food policy, we have an agricultural policy. We have a Department of Agriculture, not a Department of Food."

But he added that this in itself was a form of policy — or at least a free-market philosophy.

"We do have a food policy — a policy of plenty," the Agriculture Department's chief economist, Don Paarlberg, said. This view was also stressed by Secretary Butz.

In the past, a free-market policy would have led to overwhelming surpluses and plummeting prices. Now, it increases concern on the part of many economists and consumers about food security.

When harvesting began in 1974, the United States had about a 26-day supply of wheat left in its storage bins, a slender margin against scarcity. In 1975, the Government hopes to have twice as much, but that is still regarded as less than a comfortable stockpile.

"The world food supply-demand equation is precariously balanced," Lester R. Brown, an economist with the Overseas Development Council, a private research organization, said. "A poor harvest in any major producing country would send economic shock waves not only throughout the food sector of the world economy but, as it fueled the fires of inflation, throughout its other sectors as well."

It was a harvest failure, in the Soviet Union in 1972, that

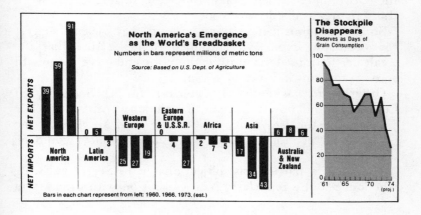

North America's Emergence as the World's Breadbasket
Numbers in bars represent millions of metric tons
Source: Based on U.S. Dept. of Agriculture

Bars in each chart represent from left: 1960. 1966. 1973. (est.)

The Stockpile Disappears
Reserves as Days of Grain Consumption

brought a trade mission to buy up one-fourth of this country's wheat crop. That action has been blamed by many economists for the tight supplies and much of the food inflation of the last two years.

Arthur Okun, former chairman of the Council of Economic Advisers and now an economist with the Brookings Institution, estimates that because of increased exports United States domestic supplies were reduced 5 to 10 per cent below normal levels last year.

"That had a dramatic impact," he told a reporter. "Instead of 5 per cent inflation, we had 9 per cent. A shortage of food translates into a shortage of money, and that raises interest rates and reduces the availability of money for such things as home building."

Such uncertainty has led many consumers and some economists and businessmen to wonder whether the United States can always maintain an open-door policy to foreign buyers and many of them to think about measures to protect American food interests first.

"If the United States consumer has to compete with export demands of an increasingly crowded and hungry world, providing adequate nutrition to millions of lower-income Americans could become an impossible dream," C. W. Cook, chairman of General Foods Corporation, recently told the Senate's Nutrition Committee.

He proposed that the United States make an estimate each year of domestic needs and expected production, and that the Government then make only the difference between those figures available for export.

Some economists have gone beyond that idea to suggest that available exports be rationed to make sure that the wealthier nations don't outbid the poor and leave them with starving millions in times of scarcity.

Others, such as Peter G. Peterson, former Secretary of Commerce and now chairman of Lehman Brothers; D. Gale Johnson of the University of Chicago, and Mr. Fedor, the Government economist, argue that such a policy would be unworkable.

The idea is particularly objectionable to Secretary Butz, who once told a reporter: "You can ration with prices, you know." He hastened to add that the United States would not ignore its humanitarian obligations to nations hit by hardship and unable to feed their people.

There is no question, however, that the needy abroad have been hardest hit by the current squeeze on food supplies. One measure is the amount of food relief shipped by the United States.

As grain prices have risen, shipments under the Food for Peace program have declined. After aid in the form of wheat and wheat products had continued for many years at the level of six to seven million tons, the total dropped last fiscal year to 4.1 million. This year, such aid is expected to be no more than 1.24 million tons.

Recent experience and continuing uncertainty have generated growing support among economists for national and international systems of grain reserves.

Whether Dr. Butz will be able to resist the rising tide of opinion on food reserves is unclear. A majority of economists on several panels that reported to Senator McGovern's committee recently favored Government action.

Support for a national reserve came also from a panel headed by Ray A. Goldberg of Harvard University and from a vice president of Cargill, Inc., one of the major grain companies.

For the near future, however, the whole question remains academic. Until a bumper crop creates a wider margin between supplies and needs than is expected within the next two years, no major power can accumulate a substantial grain reserve without driving world food prices to unacceptable levels.

Thus, in the midst of plenty, American consumers are likely for some time to live in uncertainty about both supplies and food prices.

Diverse Views on Inflation

Representatives of farmers, farm-related industries and consumers gathered in Chicago tonight [Sept. 12, 1974] to seek common ground for an attack on food price inflation, widely regarded as the most serious element in current economic problems but also, perhaps, one that is most susceptible of solution.

The meeting is one of a series before the conference on inflation called by President Ford for Sept. 27 and 28 in Washington.

As the delegates listened to opening remarks and prepared for the serious business that will get under way tomorrow few seemed under any illusion that areas of unanimity would be broad. Yet Secretary of Agriculture Earl L. Butz, chairman of the conference, expressed optimism.

Noting that the gathering included delegates from farm organizations, commodity groups, consumer groups, labor organizations, food businesses, educational institutions and others, he said:

"We expect a lively meeting will come from that mix of interests. We fully expect that this group will come up with some positive suggestions for things that the Government and private industry can do to help control inflation."

"Lively is hardly the word," one delegate remarked. "Some of these people couldn't walk into the same room without striking sparks."

The names of some of the participants offer strong clues to the diversity of opinion that will be offered.

They range from Ford Administration officials, who believe tight money and fiscal austerity provide the only promise for a cure, to others like Willard Mueller, former director of the Federal Trade Commission's Bureau of Economics, who maintains that "the old-time religion won't work."

Clarence G. Adamy, president of the National Association of Food Chains, which would like to cut its labor costs, including those in meat departments, is a delegate. So is Patrick E. Gorman, secretary-treasurer of the Meat Cutters and Butchers Workmen of North America.

The delegates also include William Kuhfuss, president of the American Farm Bureau Federation, which has always maintained that the Government should keep out of agriculture, and Tony Dechant, president of the National Farmers Union, which is at the opposite end of the farm-policy spectrum, urging higher farm-price supports.

All the delegates have provided papers outlining views on the general economy, food inflation and means of dealing with the problem, which will be summarized by speakers at tomorrow's session. Those by Mr. Adamy, Mr. Dechant, Mr. Gorman and Mr. Mueller are expected to span the diversity of opinion, and each will have some following.

Mr. Adamy is expected to support the Administration's stand on fiscal austerity and to call for guidelines that will relate wage increases to improvements in the productivity of labor.

"That might mean less money in the pay envelope for some," he said, "but it would also mean more real income for all of us."

Mr. Adamy discussed steps that the food industry could take to increase productivity, including reductions in the labor force of retail stores. One such move would be a plan for the carving of beef into the ultimate retail cuts on assembly lines at central butchering plants.

This would be opposed by Mr. Gorman.

"It would eliminate millions of people," he said. "Naturally, we're not going to stand for that. We've agreed to plans for boxed beef, but I don't see that it has cut the price of your steaks."

The distribution of beef that has been broken down into the primary sections and boxed for shipment is a growing practice among wholesalers and retailers. Many experts say that more savings could be achieved by reducing the meat at central points into the final cuts for consumers.

The view on fiscal austerity backed by Mr. Adamy will be attacked by Mr. Mueller, a professor of economics at the University of Wisconsin, who once served as executive director of President Lyndon B. Johnson's Cabinet Committee on Price Stability.

Mr. Mueller's position was generated in part by his leading role in widely respected studies of the food industry made by the F.T.C. for the National Commission on Food Marketing in the nineteen-sixties.

"The old-time religion of strict monetary policy hasn't

worked before and it won't work now," Mr. Mueller said in an interview. "It had an uneven effect on the various segments of the economy when it was tried in 1969. In concentrated industries, market power can frustrate the effectiveness of monetary and fiscal policies."

Concentrated industries are those in which a few companies have a major share of the sales volume.

"When they tried tight money in 1968 and 1969, the competitive industries were affected and some did cut prices," Mr. Mueller said. "But in the non-competitive industries, they just cut production. That means fewer jobs, and that can't help the economy. The economic environment is even less favorable for that approach now than it was then."

The Administration's policy of free markets and a reduced Government role in agriculture, which is backed by Mr. Kuhfuss's organization, will be opposed by Mr. Dechant.

His National Farmers Union has called for increases in price supports, with the Government prepared to buy and store commodities until prices rise well above the support level.

Mr. Butz is opposed to Government storage of reserves.

Mr. Dechant's top Washington assistant, Robert Lewis, asked about the farm organization's position, remarked:

"Shortages of foodstuffs are the major problem. To combat that, you've got to encourage more production, and to do that, you've got to give farmers some assurance that they are going to get a fair return for their crops."

Another strong Administration stand, for free international trade in agriculture, will be opposed by others at the conference, led by the American Bakers Association and some consumer groups. They will call for some restrictions on exports as a means of fighting food inflation.

In general, the food industry, the largest segment of the economy and one in which inflation has most seriously troubled consumers, is believed to be the richest ground for ideas for improvement.

In 1972, consumers spent $132-billion for their food, the largest share of which went to the industries that market it rather than to the farmers who produce it. The farmer's share of the dollar is 39 per cent, the processing and marketing industries' 61 per cent.

The food industry, meanwhile, has been marketed by lagging productivity, though that of farmers has been among the highest in the nation. Last year, it used as much labor to market less food than it moved in 1972.

Of the marketers' share of the food dollar, the biggest percentage goes for packaging and the next largest for transportation. Both are considered ripe areas for improved efficiency and productivity.

Waste and Grocery Costs

The inflationary cost of food has disrupted many a family budget, leading Americans to wonder: Does food really have to cost *that* much? Now economic analysts have an answer for harassed consumers: Maybe not.

The food industry, they say, probably has more opportunities than any other major sector of the economy to eliminate waste and inefficiency — invisible items that add up at the supermarket check-out counter.

One promising area is productivity, where the food industry in general lost ground last year. Compared with the year before, it used just as much labor to move less food from farm to consumer. And food retailing in particular, which had a scant productivity gain of 1.5 per cent in the previous three years, apparently slipped last year.

How to overcome such problems was among the challenges tackled by economists and food experts at the food conference on inflation held last week [Sept. 1974] in Chicago. One thing they discussed was a proposal that emerged from the Agriculture Department recently.

While others were cursing the darkness, a group of specialists in the agency's Agricultural Marketing Service ignited one small candle to help light the path out of food inflation. They produced a new grading plan that could lead Americans to eat leaner meat and thus save millions of bushels of costly feed grains. The plan could mean important savings for both the food industry and consumers.

The food industry as a whole took in $132-billion from United States consumers last year, and by year's end it was collecting money for food at an even faster annual pace. Since then, shoppers have noticed that more of their money is going to farmers, but they have failed to realize that an increasing proportion of it is going to the processors and marketers that come between them and the original producer.

When the housewife forks over a dollar bill at the check-out counter, only about 38 cents finds its way to the farmer. Here's what the food industry does with the remaining 62 cents: It pays about 30 cents for labor costs, 7 cents for packaging and 4½ cents for transportation. The next biggest item is corporate profits, roughly 4 cents. Then business taxes get 2½ cents, and interest and repairs combined also get 2½ cents. Advertising, depreciation and rent take 2 cents each. The 5½ cents that remain is spent on a variety of expenses, such as utilities, promotion, fuel and insurance.

Nearly all of these outlays are fertile ground for improving productivity and reducing costs, recent studies have found.

The National Commission on Productivity discovered in 1973 that increases in productivity in the food sector were below the national average. Had it not been for farmers' enormous and steady improvements in productivity, the average would have fallen to a far lower scale. Over recent decades farmers have increased their productivity at an average annual rate of more than 5 per cent. Oddly, it was at the farm level that the first step came last week toward cost-saving.

The new meat-grading plan, by reducing the amount of feeding time to fatten cattle, could save as much as 5 cents a pound for beef at current grain prices, the American National Cattlemen's Association has estimated. Others say that, by stretching out supplies, the plan could reduce grain prices and lead to still further reductions in feeding costs.

As much as farming productivity has increased, however, it offers still further scope for improvement.

The Agriculture Department has noted, for example, that the top 10 per cent of producers get crop yields that are 50 per cent above the national average. Experts believe that, by adopting known practices, many of the average and below-average producers could increase their productivity.

Meanwhile, agricultural researchers are developing new improvements. Among them are increased fertility of beef cattle, which would lower the required size of breeding herds as a proportion of beef produced, and improvements in plant architecture, which would increase the exposure of leaves to sunlight and thus increase their efficiency.

But the biggest opportunities for better food efficiency are in the farm-to-consumer sector, the so-called marketing margin.

Packaging, which next to labor accounts for the largest percentage of the consumer's dollar, offers perhaps the greatest chance for savings. Food-packaging costs totaled $10-billion last year. Aside from "convenience" foods (which many consumer studies have found offer little convenience and add substantially to labor costs), packaging is often quite wasteful, contributing to further waste in other operations.

American processed foods are packaged in more than 2,500 different sizes and shapes, according to several estimates, in addition to 1,400 different packages for fresh produce.

This multiplicity of packages aggravates the expenses involved in processing, storing and handling food. And it raises obstacles to automated warehouse systems that could be introduced with present technology.

"There has to be a better idea," said Grant C. Gentry, executive vice president of the Jewel Companies, Inc., summing up packaging inefficiencies in a presentation at the last annual meeting of the National Association of Food Chains.

The diversity of packages also contributes to waste in transportation, which already has inefficiencies of its own. Because of the wide variety of packages, it is nearly impossible to stack goods without wasting space. Often, movement of unevenly stacked pallets, with boxes bulging over edges, leads to damaging of goods.

"Almost half of the trucks engaged in food transportation are empty at any one time," Mr. Gentry noted. Part of this waste results from Interstate Commerce Commission rules that many trucks must make backhauls (return trips) without a paying load.

Still less efficiency is found in the use of railroad cars. The

National Commission on Productivity found in 1973 that, although rail rates had increased 33 per cent since 1967, railroad cars were still moving food across the country at a slower pace than they did 20 years ago. The cars were moving only 12 per cent of the time and moving with a load only 7 per cent of the time.

"Enormous productivity gains could flow from an improved transportation system, not only from faster service but from the more efficient packaging and handling that it would make possible," the commission said.

Among the business interests that take a share of the food marketing dollar, the largest goes to the processing industry, which got $28-billion in 1973. Retail food stores received the second largest share, nearly $24-billion. Restaurants and similar institutions took the third largest portion, $18.9-billion.

Some segments of the family's budget cut across all these areas. Meats, which account for more than $3 out of every $10 spent at the grocery store, offer many opportunities for cost savings, according to a recent study by a special task force of the Agriculture Department.

One saving could be achieved by increasing shipments of boxed beef after carcasses are broken down into primary sections, allowing efficiencies through manpower savings with assembly-line cutting and use of trimmed bone and fat for by-products, plus additional savings in transportation.

More savings could be gained by the further reduction of beef at central cutting points to the final retail cuts, the task force said, and still more savings through marketing of frozen beef, which could eliminate much of the spoilage now paid for ultimately by consumers.

"Of the meat we transport, 27 per cent is bone and waste — that is, garbage," Mr. Gentry of the Jewel Companies had said in his presentation.

Other studies have shown that producer savings could be achieved by marketing bulls instead of steers because bulls grow faster and make more efficient use of feeds. Young bulls are only slightly less palatable than steers, food experts say.

Meanwhile, processor savings have been made possible through studies resulting in greater control over the arrival of animals at slaughtering plants, allowing better planning and use of labor and facilities.

But perhaps some of the greatest savings, at least in the labor segment of the food marketing dollar, are available in the stores, retail analysts say. One reason is that each individual item a shopper buys must be handled at least twice — once when it is marketed and stacked on the shelves and again at the check-out counter.

A development of some promise is experimenting now under way in the automatic coding of retail goods for electronic, hands-off check-outs before the shopper pays for the groceries.

Perhaps a long-range dividend of the current inflation will come from the increased urgency brought now to the examination of these and other means of increasing productivity and elimination of waste.

The United States Sets Grain Export Controls

On Oct. 7, 1974 the Ford Administration announced a limited system of controls over large scales of grain for export.

It said it wanted to prevent sudden, excessive drains on diminished supplies and to avert a recurrence of the "very embarrassing" cancellation over the weekend of two large deals with the Soviet Union.

The plan, calling for advance approval of sales above 50,000 tons of wheat, corn, sorghum, soybeans or soybean meal, was described by Secretary of Agriculture Earl L. Butz to a gathering of grain executives.

While the system calls for voluntary cooperation on the part of the grain companies, Dr. Butz acknowledged that it was "at least a partial" form of export controls.

In response to a question, he said that the alternative, if the newly announced system failed, would be imposition of mandatory controls.

The secretary made it clear that the system was also a limited form of rationing designed to insure an equitable distribution of limited supplies.

H. J. MAIDENBERG

The Controls and What They Mean

The traditional flow of basic foodstuffs from American farms to the world market has been radically altered by President Ford's moves in October, 1974 to monitor exports of grains and soybeans.

With worldwide shortages of food raising for millions abroad the prospect of starvation, physical and mental disorders and economic decline, American grain traders view the President's moves as the first steps toward apportioning food exports.

And some traders even foresee some forms of controls on food consumption in this country — at the extreme, perhaps, a breadless or meatless day each week — if world hunger becomes widespread and the United States acts to alleviate it.

A report issued this month [Oct. 1974] by Cargill, Inc., a leading grain exporter, said that limitations on the supply of food "absolutely preclude" consumption levels anywhere close to what they were in the last 12 months. "Rationing must occur in both domestic and export consumption," the report added.

There was a temporary embargo on exports of soybeans and other oil seeds in mid-1973. But basically, until recently, American food sales — large or small — to friendly nations were handled by private companies under free-market conditions.

The concern of traders was underscored in the Ford Administration's current announcement of a $400,000 grain sale to the Soviet Union. The United States agreed to sell 2.2 million tons, but it was a million tons less than in a sale scheduled earlier this month but blocked by President Ford.

Under the Administration's food-export controls, commodity traders must get Federal approval before shipping more than 50,000 tons of wheat, corn, sorghum, soybeans and soybean oil meal to a customer, or 100,000 tons or more to a country in a single week.

Moreover, exporters are required to keep the Government informed of major deals and, perhaps more important, any changes in destination of cargoes previously reported to the Department of Agriculture under the new rules.

The American controls on grain exports place the Government at the center of the complex, interlocking domestic and international forces that are of basic importance in the world food situation.

When a large-scale foreign buyer of American grain, for example, places an order, it affects not only the price of the commodity but also the price of the meat that comes from livestock feeding on the grain.

As Dr. John H. Knowles, head of the Rockefeller Foundation, noted in a recent speech, there is now a potential imbalance between world supply and demand. Increasingly, large parts of the world have become heavily dependent on three grain-surplus countries — the United States, Canada and Australia.

In 1973, the United States exported 73.5 million metric tons of grain; Canada, 14.5 million, and Australia, 7 million tons. The major importing regions were Asia, 39 million tons; Eastern Europe and the Soviet Union, 27 million; Western Europe, 21 million, and Africa and Latin America, each 4 million.

Dr. Knowles observed that before World War II, all these importing areas, except Western Europe, were net exporters of grain.

Because the largest exporter, the United States, has been unable to increase its surpluses substantially, most leading commodity traders have become resigned to what the grain trade terms "the rationalization of supplies around the world."

The once burdensome American surpluses were wiped out by the sale of 19 million tons of grain and soybeans to the

Soviet Union in 1972, the re-entry of China into the American grain market, and steadily increasing purchases by others since then.

Since 1972, the world market in basic foodstuffs has been governed by "price rationing." This means, in the words of one Chicago grain exporter:

"If foreign buyers have the funds, they get the stuff. If they don't, they go hungry. Obviously, this situation can't go on forever."

As the commodity traders view the situation, President Ford's action in imposing controls of exports of basic foodstuffs are intended to achieve the following:

● Persuade American farmers to sell the record amount of grain they have held off the market in 1974 in expectation of still higher prices, with the hope of deferring much of their taxes into 1975.

● Discourage foreign commodity speculators from buying up large quantities of scarce foodstuffs, thus exacerbating shortages and spurring inflationary pressures.

● Get domestic exporters to provide more information — foreign orders, shipping schedules and names of customers — in order to keep track of the flow of available food.

● Get wealthier foreign food importing nations to reveal their needs so as to prevent them from suddenly and secretly buying up huge amounts of foodstuffs, as the Soviet Union did in 1972.

● Assure the poorer nations, hard-pressed to pay for either energy or food today, that available American surpluses would be shared more equitably.

Ordinarily, any one of these goals would be a difficult undertaking. But given today's critical worldwide food situation and the interrelated nature of the domestic and international factors, commodity experts point out that all the goals must be met at once.

As they see the situation today, a major element limiting the present flow of American food to the world market is the American farmer's "retentions" of grain.

In 1974, for example, the nation's wheat growers will have harvested a record 1.8 billion bushels, or 4 per cent above the mark set in the preceding season.

But some 60 per cent of the wheat crops were held by growers early this month, according to Roderick Turnbull, an official of the Kansas City Board of Trade and a recognized grain expert.

The "retention" figure is considered a record because two-thirds of the nation's wheat crop — hard and soft winter grades — were harvested by early July as usual. And corn and soybean growers, who are now completing their harvests, are also expected to hold on to much of their crops.

Obviously, the farmers want better prices. Many also want to postpone sales until after Jan. 1, to spread out their heavy tax liabilities caused by record income early this year.

Domestic supply-demand factors will not shake loose the grain. A halt in the price rise will. Farmers are aware that the nation can only consume a third of its wheat, half of its soybeans and four-fifths of its corn output.

Despite adverse crop weather in 1974, the same consumption ratios hold. Consequently, the farmer depends on the export market. So does the Treasury if it hopes to retrieve the dollars being paid for costly fuel imports.

As for grain growers, they have three options: They can store their crops on the farm or in nearby grain elevators for a fee; or they can "pawn" their crops with the Government's Commodity Credit Corporation and get a loan in return of roughly one-third of the market price; or they can sell their crops.

If grain is stored in elevators today, the farmer pays about 1.5 cents a month for each bushel of 60 pounds of wheat and soybeans, and a bit less for a 56-pound bushel of corn. Naturally, farmers count on higher prices to offset such storage costs.

To discourage farmers from "pawning" their crops during this time of critical worldwide food shortages, Washington first raised the interest it charges for storing grain from 5.5 to 7.25 per cent a year last April, and then to 9.375 per cent early this month [Oct. 1974].

The Commodity Credit Corporation system, known as the "loan program," permits farmers immediate cash for their crops. Nowadays, the loan levels are termed "target prices." Born of the Depression and later sustained by post-World War

II surpluses, the system was meant to provide the farmers some income to tide them over until prices improved.

More often than not during those years, farmers found it profitable to let their loans expire rather than redeem their crops. That was how the Government acquired the once burdensome surpluses, which it either had to store at taxpayer expense or give away to friendly foreign countries under various aid programs.

Given today's prices, farmers could be expected to redeem whatever grain they have pledged for Government loans.

Once the farmer decides to sell grain, he usually calls his local grain elevator operator. (Many of these concerns are cooperatives owned by farmers.)

The elevator operators, in turn, sell their grain to either food manufacturers or exporters and make shipping arrangements accordingly.

If the buyer is, say, a baking or flour milling company, the transaction is relatively simple. But if an exporter is involved, the elevator operator becomes the first party to the highly secret world of international commodity dealings.

The larger exporters have storage facilities at major marine shipping terminals, which are often used to obfuscate their operations. Once the grain moves from the country elevators to their facilities, it becomes part of the secret trade pattern, or at least that was the case before President Ford imposed limited controls on exporters.

To mask their operations, exporters may order ship captains to change course in midocean. Grain sent to one foreign port may be reshipped to another. Large orders may be split into seemingly unimportant cargoes.

Foreign importers are frequently speculators who have neither the storage facilities nor the desire to accept delivery of grain and use similar tactics to hide their operations. These speculators must be nimble and find buyers and sellers before their cargoes depart or arrive.

Because of the large amount of such trade, which the Department of Agriculture classifies as "unspecified destinations" in making their calculations on export business, the Government's figures have often been proven wrong.

Many commodity traders contend that a close watch on the

movement of shipping is often a better indicator of who is buying and selling in the international market.

Not too long ago, for example, the Soviet Union bought large amounts of wheat and corn in Argentina, apparently for its own use. But sharp-eyed Chicago grain men quickly noticed the booking of cargo space between Buenos Aires and Havana in the British shipping market.

Moscow was buying grain in behalf of Cuba, which has no problem getting its own grain from Canada and elsewhere. It was part of the international commodity shell game.

Long before President Nixon reopened trade with China two years ago, American grain often found its way there indirectly. As more than one Chicago grain dealer explained the practice:

Perhaps an Italian importer bought a cargo of wheat in Buenos Aires for a client in Rotterdam; a similar amount of American grain for shipment from Galveston, Tex., to the same destination, and then reshipped one of the two cargoes from the Netherlands to Shanghai on a Dutch ship.

"Grain doesn't carry a brand name," a dealer noted, "the stuff moves like the tides around the world."

Moving grain is easy. What exporters pay heavily for is information on weather patterns, crop development, changes in currency values and officials in key posts in foreign lands who handle import orders and the like.

Suppliers of reliable information on such matters on both sides of the Iron Curtain often become wealthy quickly. The value of this information was highlighted by the 1972 Soviet grain deal, which involved 19-million tons of American wheat and feed grains, including a quarter of the nation's wheat crop that year.

Grain traders in the Midwest are still debating whether Washington intelligence sources knew the extent of Moscow's crop failure at that time, and if so, how much weight the information carried in subsequent trade negotiations between the two nations.

In any event, the Soviet Union used the traditional secrecy that covers international grain dealings to buy up 19-million tons of grain here and 11-million tons elsewhere.

Not one of the many exporters involved knew the over-all

total of grain and soybeans involved in that deal, according to sworn testimony before Congress as well as private comments of usually reliable sources in the commodity trade.

Adding the much smaller exports of grain to China and Japan that year, which were also well wrapped in secrecy, surplus stocks of key foodstuffs were wiped out around the world.

Moreover, the resulting shortages served to deepen the secrecy that enveloped the trade at a time when inflation was prompting many holders of doubtful paper money to exchange their currency for commodities.

Today, large amounts of foodstuffs are held by speculators and other hoarders, public and private.

At the time the Soviet buyers were seeking grain in 1972, each of the several export houses involved were approached individually in secrecy. And each obtained the grain and made shipping arrangements in secrecy. Each house thought it was a large but routine bit of business it had snared.

Their surprise came, according to reliable sources, when the Government totaled the statistics and revealed them. Others were also unaware, particularly foreign officials and newsmen in Moscow.

All during the summer of 1972, news dispatches told of the uncommon heat in Russia and the peat fires it caused on the outskirts of the Soviet capital.

But Washington officials say that they were unaware that the heat was also burning up that part of Russia's grain crop that the extremely cold preceding winter had spared.

As far as the grain dealers are concerned, all would have paid a fortune at the time to know the condition of the Soviet crops then — and even now — in order to buy up supplies in anticipation of purchase orders from Moscow.

In Washington, meanwhile, the Soviet crop failure in 1972 proved a boon. The once burdensome surpluses vanished, and the nation's export earnings soared.

Until the summer of 1974, Washington officials said, the sharp rise in domestic food prices sparked by the soaring exports were expected to be temporary.

After all, they noted, the increased prices stimulated growers to utilize every available acre. Domestic needs were considered ample even without the expanded acreage, and the increased harvests were supposed to soak up some of the billions of dollars being spent on costly foreign fuel.

But the Administration had to change its game plan recently for several reasons. First, inflation worsened beyond expectations and added to the cost of moving food from farm to the supermarket.

Domestically, grain moves through a complex system before it reaches the final consumer in the grocery store. The average foreigner consumes 600 pounds of grain a year; Americans use 2,000 pounds, but only 200 pounds in the form of bread and other baked goods. The rest goes into meat products, eggs, beer, liquor and many other things.

It takes, for instance, a pound of grain to make a pound of bread; two to produce a pound of poultry; four to make a pound of pork and eight to produce a pound of beef.

Regardless of how grain is consumed, today's inflation makes each of the many steps from the field to the table a bit more costly.

Equally important, grain growers experienced an uncommon time of adverse weather; heavy rains in the spring, followed by drought and, most recently, early frost. Each factor cut into the expected total supply and erased the gains from the expanded acreage.

Of late, Department of Agriculture officials appeared confused by the margin of wheat, corn, sorghum and soybeans that would be safely available for export.

And many Midwest grain dealers were set to wondering whether the nation wasn't exporting just surplus foodstuffs, but also the supplies needed for domestic consumption until the 1975 harvests.

Finally, the commodity experts noted, the plight of the poorer lands unable to pay for soaring food imports, prompted the President to take the initial steps toward rationing supplies around the world.

The poorer lands have more than humanitarian claims to American foodstuffs surpluses, which have sustained many of their people for years.

Often in the past, these nations were discouraged from developing their agricultural potential by the easy availability of our surpluses, and spent their limited financial resources on industrial projects instead.

Usually, the governments of the poorer countries acted as the importer. Depending on the political form of government, the importing nation either distributed the foodstuff itself for cash or as a welfare grant, or turned it over to private companies for a fee.

According to United States aid officials, only in a relatively few cases of so-called American food giveaways of the past did the ordinary hungry consumer in the poorer lands actually receive supplies without charge.

However, the availability of these supplies tended to keep food prices low. Too low, some aid officials said, to spur farmers to switch from cash crops to foodstuffs.

In Latin America, for example, the flow of American surpluses was often such that farmers were forced to grow coffee, sugar, cotton, cocoa and other exportable cash crops, rather than food.

Looking ahead, most commodity experts see a different pattern emerging. Although all the motives behind the President's moves to monitor foodstuff exports have yet to be revealed, they expect a greater emphasis on aid to foreign agriculture.

By being able, in effect, to channel American food surpluses overseas openly, all exporters and importers of basic human energy should be able to judge available supplies and markets.

Thus, food would be prevented from becoming more of an economic and political weapon. By guaranteeing basic needs, the food gluts of past decades in this country could be avoided.

Conrad Leslie, the respected commodity statistician and partner to the Chicago brokerage house of Mayer-Gelbort-Leslie, Inc., said the other day:

"All the farmers in the major exporting nations — the United States, Canada, Australia, Argentina and those in Western Europe — are presently geared to produce everything they can.

"If the weather, worldwide, returns to normal next year, we will see a tremendous amount of food available. But the problem of distributing it fairly will still remain."

H. J. MAIDENBERG

Cutbacks in United States Aid

When World War II ended, Washington embarked on an unusual and far-reaching program to feed millions of hungry people overseas, most of whom paid little or nothing for the basic foodstuffs they received.

Now, with even greater numbers in desperate need of food, Washington is quietly winding down its so-called "Food for Peace" programs.

One such program has already ended. There were no shipments of powdered milk, upon which millions of children depended, during the fiscal year that ended June 30, 1974.

Lester R. Brown, a food expert at the Overseas Development Council, observed in Washington recently that in 1972 some 90 million of the world's poorest people depended on food received from these programs. He added:

"An estimated 20 million nutritionally vulnerable people have been cut off from these programs in the past year."

In addition, many more millions are now confronted with costly food bills they cannot afford. Shamsher Singh, chief of the commodity division of the World Bank, declared the other day:

"The poor countries have had their energy bill raised by $10-billion the past year. Their minimum imported food bill equals that unobtainable sum. Obviously, their situation is untenable even in the short term."

It was also obvious to the many commodity specialists interviewed recently [Oct. 1974] that producers of basic foodstuffs are attempting to use their surpluses to pay for their vastly increased energy bills. That is one reason, the experts pointed out, that prices of such key foodstuffs as grain, soybeans and sugar have recently risen almost as much as petroleum.

Another reason is that the current tonnages of surplus foods, while they equal those in the years immediately after World War II, must now feed far greater numbers of people born in the last generation.

The tradition of American food aid for stricken foreign countries dates back at least to 1891 when a famine in Russia moved voluntary relief organizations to send shiploads of corn there. The Secretary of Agriculture advised on the methods of processing and shipping and sent a corn specialist to teach the Russians how to prepare dishes from the unfamiliar grain.

During World War I the Government formally took up food aid by asking Americans to observe wheatless Mondays and Wednesdays, beefless Tuesdays and porkless Thursdays and Saturdays to conserve food for shipment to American allies. After the war, President Wilson established the American Relief Administration to help the hungry of war-torn Europe.

Food aid by the United States to allied countries also played a role in World War II, with the Lend-Lease Act of 1941 permitting them to buy food on concessional terms. It became even more widespread after the end of the war, which left Europe ravaged and in the midst of a "cold war" between Communist and non-Communist blocs.

Once the war ended, the task of war relief was assigned to the United Nations Relief and Rehabilitation Administration (UNRRA), to which the United States was the leading contributor. Then, in 1947, as the UNRRA period came to a close, the United States continued its aid through a series of other organizations.

In 1947 President Truman appeared before a joint session of Congress to announce the Marshall Plan, named for the then Secretary of State, Gen. George C. Marshall. The Marshall Plan concentrated on industrial reconstruction, but it also embraced a sizeable American commitment to send food and technical assistance to rebuild European agriculture.

The aid was made conditional upon European initiation of "self-help" programs.

Domestic as well as foreign considerations were involved in

the evolution of American policy on food aid. American agriculture had been geared for massive production during World War II and food shipments abroad provided vital support for the agricultural economy. Further, the aid programs were stimulated by scientific advances that stunningly raised corn yield per acre, for example, from 30 bushels to more than 90 bushels in the postwar years.

So great was the productive power of the United States farmer that, by the end of the Korean war in 1953, it faced a flood of surplus food each year. So did Argentina, Canada, Australia, New Zealand, South Africa and other countries that had geared up to help feed the world during World War II.

Thus, Washington strengthened its tariff barriers to imported food and, in 1954, consolidated its food aid with the passage of Public Law 480, the Agricultural Trade Development and Assistance Act. This became known as the "Food for Peace" program.

Under Title I of the program, foodstuffs were shipped to America's political allies under extremely attractive terms. The recipient country usually paid in local currency or over a period of up to 40 years at very low interest rates.

Washington aid officials point out that the large sums amassed by their food loans were often used in the recipient countries for improving health, communications and education systems, all of which also eventually increased the demand for food.

American surplus food was also given away outright under Title II of P.L. 480, which accounted for roughly half the $1-billion to $1.5-billion a year involved in the over-all plan.

But the cost was often canceled by Washington's ability to unload tremendous tonnages of surplus foodstuffs, which it had to carry at taxpayer cost. These surpluses accumulated because farmers often didn't redeem their crops after they had pawned them under the various subsidy programs offered by the Government since the Depression.

The American merchant marine benefited, too, by carrying the bulk of the food surpluses at a time when foreign-flag carriers were driving the nation's shipping companies out of business with lower freight charges.

Washington also earned the friendship of millions of hungry

people abroad who received the precious food either at no cost or at subsidized low prices.

Until the Soviet Union's massive grain purchases in the United States and elsewhere in 1972-73 and the surge in petroleum prices late in 1973, the private traders and exporters of basic foodstuffs depended largely on a crop failure somewhere, a minor war or some natural disaster to bring them business.

The bulk of this nation's surpluses were finally erased by Moscow's purchase of 10 million metric tons of grain and soybeans here and 11 million tons elsewhere in 1972 because of a poor Soviet crop.

Equally important, President Nixon opened the American food market to China for the first time in 24 years at a time when Japan and other developed nations were becoming increasingly dependent on North America for their key agricultural products.

For the millions of poor who depended on American food giveaways, the events of 1972-73 mean more than an economic disaster — their very lives are at stake. Indeed, their exposure to starvation today is far greater than it was in the post-World War II period, when the aid programs began.

First, there are about 900 million more people on this planet now than in the late nineteen-forties. Science has not been able to duplicate its earlier crop miracles because of shortages of pure water, cheap fertilizers and other chemicals made from crude oil as well as the normal vicissitudes of weather.

The last quarter century also has seen vast movements of people from rural areas, where they could provide their own basic food, to urban centers. It was the availability of relatively cheap food that permitted this mass migration.

The decades of surpluses also permitted the wealthier countries to indulge in their taste for animal protein. For example, meat consumption in the United States and the Soviet Union doubled between 1960 and 1972.

In this country beef consumption exceeded pork consumption for the first time in 1954; the average American ate 56 pounds of beef that year. Now with the United States population much bigger and beef prices much higher, the per capita consumption of beef is 109 pounds a year.

Commodity experts point out that most of the grain and soybeans grown in the United States are consumed by animals, and so is an ever-increasing amount elsewhere in the world.

Another factor that the experts stress is that there will be 72 million more humans for the world to feed one year from today. They will require 30 million tons of grain. That is 40 per cent of America's present grain exports — or the combined sales of Canada, Australia, Argentina and South Africa last year.

Meantime, the poorer nations that require food aid now face another problem. During the years of American aid, many of these countries either neglected their own agricultural potential or used it to produce cash crops for export.

One obvious need, the experts insist, is some worldwide control on population growth. Another need is to invest heavily in unused land in the less developed countries to make them productive.

Much of this land is now owned either by the state or by private persons who are unwilling or economically unable to develop it for crops or as pasture for animals.

As the commodity experts see it, piecemeal land reform measures are not the answer because small holdings preclude efficient production. In this country, where only 2 per cent of the farm and ranch acreage is owned by large corporations, 25 per cent of the units produce 80 per cent of the nation's agricultural output.

The pressures on the poorer countries have placed a heavy burden on global aid agencies such as the International Bank for Reconstruction and Development (better known as the World Bank) and the younger regional lenders, the Inter-American Development Bank and the Asian Development Bank.

The World Bank, by far the largest of the three major lenders, will make loans totaling a record $4.5-billion this year, of which $800-million is expected to involve agricultural projects. The rest of the loans are earmarked for industrially related or socially oriented programs.

Another needed measure in the poorer countries, commodity specialists insist, is incentives for rural people to stay on the farm.

Several Chicago grain exporters observed recently that China has apparently taken the lead in this sector. They commented recently that only 11 per cent of China's land mass is arable but that 80 per cent of that country's population works there, often double-cropping arable acreage.

THEODORE M. SHABAD

Why the Soviet Union Buys Grain

Moscow

In October, 1974, with memories of the huge Soviet grain deal of 1972 still fresh in Americans' minds, the Russians moved quickly into the United States market to order wheat and corn worth half a billion dollars. In an unusual move, President Ford abruptly held up the purchase and introduced a system of export controls. He was evidently keenly aware of the adverse political impact of the 1972 sales, which resulted in higher prices for the American consumer.

However, a smaller sale to the Russians, amounting to $380-million, was authorized.

The continuing Soviet purchases of grain abroad have in the past been explained by the fact that the Russians are both importers and exporters of grain, that they need increasing amounts of animal feed for a livestock expansion program and that their farm output, because of climate and inefficiency, has been subject to considerable fluctuations from year to year.

What was puzzling about the 1974 grain order was that it followed the record Soviet grain harvest of 1973 and a crop this year that has been officially described by the Russians as the second highest in their history.

Moreover, the Soviet Union, a nation with one of the greatest economic potentials, apparently found it necessary to buy food from the United States at a time when the world is intent on alleviating the threat of starvation in third-world countries that have geniune needs.

American specialists on Soviet agricultural policy and

grain-trade practices have sought to analyze the reasons why the Soviet Union has been buying increasing amounts of grain abroad in recent years, particularly from the United States, Canada and Australia.

In the absence of official Soviet explanations of current grain policies, the analysts account for large Russian imports in years of bumper crops in the following terms:

The Soviet Union has standing grain export commitments of at least five million metric tons a year, mostly in wheat shipments, to its allies such as Cuba. It often finds it economical to purchase wheat in Canada or in the United States for direct delivery to Cuba instead of shipping the wheat all the way from the Soviet Union. (A metric ton equals 2,204 pounds.)

In response to increasing demand for a rising standard of living, the Kremlin has embarked on an ambitious livestock expansion program to augment with more meat the starchy bread-and-potato diet of Russians. Soviet agriculture has traditionally stressed food grains and potatoes and is now hard-pressed to provide enough feed for livestock.

These developments are taking place against the background of an inefficient Soviet farm system of low productivity. It is highly dependent on vagaries of the weather and has not been able to provide a relatively stable output from year to year.

The poor performance of Soviet agriculture, when compared with Western farming systems, also reflects the low priority traditionally given to agriculture under the Communist system while most investment went into heavy industry and defense. Only in the last decade or so has the Kremlin allocated more money to farming to right the imbalance.

There is a great amount of controversy as to whether the huge labor-intensive operations of the Soviet Union's 48,000 collective and state farms are inherently more or less economical than the highly mechanized 2.8 million farms of the United States, most of them family-owned and worked by one or two persons.

Studies are now under way among Western experts on Soviet and East European agriculture to determine how farm performance compares, under a similar set of conditions, be-

Workers at a collective farm near Krasnodar, in the Soviet Union, turning over a huge pile of wheat to dry it.

tween small private family farms and the large Soviet farms with an average of 500 workers each.

Some Western scholars have attributed at least part of the low productivity of Soviet farming to a lack of incentive among farm workers and excessive central planning that often fails to take account of changes in local conditions. However, climatic factors also enter into any comparison between the Soviet Union and the United States.

The Kremlin's decision, made in the late nineteen-sixties, to expand meat production appears to have pointed up some of the weaknesses of the Soviet farm system.

Historically the Soviet Union has stressed the production of food grains such as wheat and rye. It appears to have difficulties in reorienting its crop structure in the direction of greater emphasis on livestock feed.

The Russians harvest about twice as much wheat as the United States and produce normally far more wheat than they need for human consumption and for export. In fact, over the years, one-third of the wheat crop has been fed to livestock. In some cases even bread has been used as fodder despite official criticism of such a wasteful practice.

Corn and soybeans, which are the basis of the United States' livestock industry, do not do well in the Soviet climate.

The current expansion of livestock herds and the increased feed rations per animal have raised Soviet feed requirements substantially. The problem has been compounded by continued inefficiency of converting feed into liveweight.

D. Gale Johnson, an agricultural economist of the University of Chicago, noted recently that it takes the Russians one year — twice as long as the Americans — to produce a hog of 190 pounds, the optimal slaughter weight. He added that with an animal inventory roughly equal to that in the United States, the Russians obtain only three-fourths the size of the American yield in animal products.

Writing in the fall, 1974, issue of the Association for Comparative Economic Studies Bulletin, Mr. Johnson said:

"There appears to be little possibility that Soviet livestock output growth can keep pace with growth in demand during the present decade unless the Soviet Union is willing to embark upon a massive import program for feeding materials."

An analysis of trade statistics shows that since 1967 the Soviet Union has become a net importer of corn. Previously the Russians had exported corn. Although they are short of high-protein feed, they have not, for the time being, undertaken an import program for soybean oil meal, a highly effective feeding material.

The Soviet Union continues to be a net wheat exporter except after poor harvests like the ones of 1963, 1965 and 1972. In the wake of the 1972 crop failure it bought 40 million tons of grain abroad, including one-fourth of the United States' wheat crop.

The Russians keep their grain-stock figures secret, but the massive purchases of 1972 and 1973 have suggested to analysts abroad that the stocks might have been drawn down to critical levels, perhaps because of the added feed requirements of the new livestock program.

Under normal conditions, a large portion of Soviet grain purchases abroad are actually intended for third countries that have regular grain-supply commitments from the Soviet Union. They are mainly Poland, Czechoslovakia, Cuba and North Korea.

These third-party deliveries were analyzed earlier this year by Valentine Zabijaka of the United States Commerce Department's Bureau of East-West Trade.

Writing in the spring, 1974, issue of the Association of Comparative Economic Studies Bulletin, Mr. Zabijaka noted that Soviet wheat contracts with Canada contained a provision permitting shipments to other countries on Soviet account.

Published figures suggest that Canadian wheat purchased by the Soviet Union has been shipped regularly to Cuba as well as to some East European countries and the Soviet Union itself. Similarly, some wheat bought by the Russians from Australia has moved to North Korea and possibly, in the form of Soviet aid, to North Vietnam.

The Soviet Union evidently also finds it far less expensive to supply its Far Eastern regions by low-cost shipments across the Pacific Ocean from Canada instead of hauling domestically produced wheat by rail across Siberia.

In its effort to raise the living standard of its own people, the Soviet Union now finds itself in direct competition for the world's tight grain supplies with millions of people in the third world near starvation.

Ironically the Kremlin has embarked on its meat-expansion program at the very time when pressure is being put on the Western industrial countries to reduce their meat consumption as a way of enhancing the grain supply available for the countries where millions are still thinking about their daily portion of gruel, let alone meat.

BOYCE RENSBERGER

The Visitors are Impressed with China

China appears to have raised agricultural production and evened the distribution of food so successfully that she seems well protected against the food shortages now afflicting the underdeveloped world, according to 10 leading American farm researchers who recently visited China.

"We were tremendously impressed everywhere we went with the high quality of Chinese farming," said Dr. Sterling Wortman, the group's leader, in an interview.

"I came away feeling I'm going to worry less about whether China is able to feed her people or not," said Dr. Wortman, a plant breeder who oversees agricultural research grants for the Rockefeller Foundation.

With nearly one-quarter of the world's people and a history of widespread poverty, malnutrition and episodic famines, China has long been a major concern of those working to improve the world food supply. Until recently the country's isolation had restricted available information about Chinese agriculture.

The 10 scientists, experts in nearly all major crops and other aspects of farming, found on a four-week tour that although China's isolation had kept her from achieving some of the scientific advances that have helped improve yields elsewhere, major strides have been made by combining traditional farming methods and domestic scientific advances.

For example, to supply growing quantities of fertilizer needed to increase yields, the Chinese have augmented the traditional use of compost, manure and human excrement with inorganic fertilizer produced by some 800 "backyard factories" that turn coal and water into nitrogen fertilizer.

Each such factory produces a few thousand tons of fertilizer a year. Together, they supplied half of China's consumption of inorganic fertilizer in 1973. The balance was derived from fertilizers produced domestically on an industrial scale or imported. In addition, China has planned or is constructing eight fertilizer factories capable of producing a thousand tons a day.

The American scientists said the backyard fertilizer plants, which produce ammonium bicarbonate, a chemical not generally used as a fertilizer outside China, appeared to be using a simple technology that might well be adapted to other areas of the world.

Dr. Norman E. Borlaug, a world authority on wheat and a member of the group, visited one of the small fertilizer plants.

Dr. Wortman said he and his colleagues, who toured most of the major farming regions, by train and private vehicle, found a wide variety of other innovations and techniques that might also be adapted for use in poorer countries.

The group, organized by the American-based Committee on Scholarly Communication with the People's Republic of China, stopped in Peking, Shanghai, Nanking, Sian, and Canton and visited farms and research centers in the surrounding provinces and in Kirin Province, north of Korea.

Although the group had high praise for the quality of the crops, they noted they had not visited drier western and northern regions, where agriculture might still be poor.

One of the biggest surprises to Dr. Nyle C. Brady, director of the International Rice Research Institute in the Philippines and a member of the group, was that the rice being grown was almost entirely of a new, high-yielding dwarf variety similar to the "miracle rice" developed at Dr. Brady's institute. The Chinese varieties, it turned out, had been developed before the Philippine center was established.

Members of the group also noted that special cropping systems — such as growing several crops simultaneously or in close succession on a piece of land — were widely used.

Farmers would, for example plant rows of wheat, wait for it to sprout and then plant two rows of corn between the wheat rows. Before the corn was high enough to shade the wheat, the grain would be ripe and harvested. Two months later the corn would be ready.

Chinese farmers told the scientists that this particular system yielded 40 per cent more food than would the same acreage if the two crops were planted separately.

This sytem is obviously impossible with American-style mechanization. But China, lacking the machinery, does have the labor for hand harvesting.

One of the American group's major conclusions was that innovations such as intercropping and backyard fertilizer production are found throughout China. One of the major problems of upgrading farming in many poor countries has been the difficulty in persuading farmers to adopt new methods.

"They have been tremendously successful in getting all available knowledge into use at the farm level," Dr. Wortman said. He added that agriculture seemed to be organized in a way that facilitated the spread of new techniques.

The basic farming unit in China is the "production team," a group of 30 to 40 households that till large individual plots of land. Each family also has its own smaller plot, mostly for its own vegetables.

From 20 to 40 production teams are organized as a "production brigade." Ten to 20 such brigades constitute a commune. A commune may include 25,000 to 30,000 people.

Management decisions are made at commune level, though brigade and team leaders share in responsibility. Each commune specializes in one crop, which is sold to the government. But communes also devote a portion of land to a variety of other crops in an attempt to be as self-sufficient as possible.

A family's income is determined by the success of the crop raised by its production team. The scientists said they felt that this maximized the incentive for hard work. The method contrasts with that of other collectivized-farming countries where the farmer's income depends less on the result of his work.

In China, the government buys the team's major crop at stable prices, the scientists were told. Accountants for each production team then subtract costs from income, take out a

A group of Chinese fruit researchers at a conference to help improve the quality of apples.

further 6 to 7 per cent in tax for the government, and apportion the remaining money equitably among the member households.

Whether this system makes China truly self-sufficient in food has been a matter of some disagreement. Figures published by the United States Department of Agriculture show that last year China imported about six million metric tons of wheat and corn but exported 1.3 million metric tons of rice. A metric ton is 2,200 pounds.

Ton for ton, rice costs more than wheat and China has for several years sold rice and used the money to buy larger quantities of wheat. Considering that the per-capita grain consumption in China is about 400 pounds a year, the country can be said to have exported enough rice to feed about seven million people and imported enough wheat to feed 33 million.

Whether this means that 26 million people — the net difference — would have gone hungry without imports is unclear. The purchases may represent an attempt to provide more than the bare minimum of food.

The American scientists found it difficult to get exact figures on Chinese crop tonnages or per-capita production. "Whenever we asked," Dr. Wortman recalled, "they would say production is up 'twofold' or 'threefold.' "

In any event, without highly detailed information, it could be misleading to infer the adequacy of nutrition in China from crop-production statistics.

For one thing, the scientists found, each family is urged to be as self-reliant as it can. Each farm family raises most of its own vegetables and usually keeps a few chickens and pigs for eggs and meat.

The pigs live mostly on vegetable material that is not used in many other countries — leaves and stalks of vegetables, corn stalks, table scraps and cottonseed hulls. In turn, the pig provides manure that is spread on the fields.

"They recycle everything in China," Dr. Wortman said.

He told of one commune that specialized in carp and silk. Dirt dug out to make ponds for the fish was heaped for the planting of mulberry trees on which silkworms live. The carp, considered an underwater pig, is fed much the same way. Droppings from the silkworm, rich in digested mulberry leaf, are also fed to the carp.

Periodically the rich bottom sediments from the ponds are scraped out and spread under the mulberry trees as fertilizer. The ponds are set among the trees to share the moisture.

One of the chief goals of the visiting scientists was to begin an exchange of seeds so that plant breeders outside China might be able to cross Chinese varieties with their own to improve plants. Chinese scientists might have new seed types to work with in the same way. A wide variety of seeds were exchanged and plans were made for further exchanges.

One of the more significant exchanges involved soybeans, a crop rich in protein that has so far defied plant breeders' efforts to develop a higher yielding type. Because China is the home of the soybean and many wild varieties grow there, Dr. Richard L. Bernard, a soybean expert with the United States Department of Agriculture, rambled along hillsides and fences collecting wild soybeans. He brought back the only new soybean varieties that American breeders have had in many years.

The group found China still needed more fertilizer. Dr. Wortman said that while no obviously deficient fields were seen, he and his colleagues did believe that yields could be improved with more fertilizer.

They said a more serious problem for the long run, however, was the disarray of agricultural research and training programs.

China's efforts to sharply modify the nature of some educational and research institutions for political reasons have meant few new scientists have been trained in recent years, the group found. Dr. Wortman said the highly trained scientists and scholars were nearly all over the age of 60.

Unless schools and research centers could enjoy some stability, Dr. Wortman said, his group feared that further agricultural progress over the next few decades could be seriously retarded.

Dr. Wortman said that a detailed report on the group's observations in China has been written and is being prepared for publication.

Other scientists in the group were Dr. Glenn W. Burton of the University of Georgia, an expert on forage grasses and millet; Dr. John L. Creech, director of the United States National Arboretum and formerly head of the United States Plant Introduction Service; Dr. Jack R. Harlan of the University of Illinois, an authority on the origins of agriculture and cultivated plants; Dr. Arthur Kelman of the University of Wisconsin, an expert on the diseases of small grains; Dr. Henry M. Munger of Cornell, a specialist in vegetables, and Dr. George F. Sprague of the University of Illinois, an authority on corn and sorghum.

JONATHAN KANDELL

Latin America's Narrowing Surpluses

Lima

Under the crush of a rapidly increasing urban population and a strong government bias in favor of industrial growth, Latin America is theatened with losing its status as a net exporter of food in coming years.

The region has always suffered from widespread problems of malnutrition. According to studies by the Food and Agriculture Organization of the United Nations, as many as half of the 280 million Latin Americans live on moderately to seriously deficient diets.

But the area has traditionally maintained a favorable trade balance in agriculture on the basis of strong exports from key countries — beef and grains from Argentina, fish products from Peru and Chile, sugar from Cuba.

The concern of food experts is that Latin America — with its vast, but unrealized potential for strong agricultural surpluses — will become instead an increasingly heavy buyer of costlier and scarcer food supplies on the world market.

"It is no longer possible to consider the food crisis in regional terms," said an official of the Food and Agriculture Organization. "Even if Latin America manages to maintain its deficient food standards in the coming decades, it may be doing so by placing even more afflicted Asian and African countries in deeper crisis."

With one of the highest birth rates in the world, the region almost tripled its population from 1930 to 1970.

Even more dramatic was the migration to the cities. Urban population accounted for less than 40 per cent of the area's inhabitants in 1950. The proportion rose to 56 per cent in 1970. By 1990, two out of every three Latin Americans will be living in urban areas.

Along with this shift to urban living, there has been a deterioration in the strength of the agricultural sector in the regional economy. In general the prices farmers pay for goods and services have increased far more rapidly than the prices of farm products.

Faced with volatile and more politically demanding urban constituencies, governments have tended to depress agricultural prices artificially in inflationary times.

Often such measures backfire, leaving governments with even more difficult options. In Bolivia, for example, strict food-price controls led to a booming contraband trade that sent thousands of tons of agricultural products into neighboring countries.

To counter the growing food shortages, Bolivia's President, Hugo Banzer Suárez, increased the prices of basic necessities by almost 100 per cent in January, 1974. Ensuing protest strikes by miners and professional employes, and a peasant revolt in the Cochabamba Valley almost toppled the regime.

In Argentina — the most important agricultural exporter in Latin America — farmers have long complained that they are subsidizing both the urban population and the country's efforts to industrialize.

Food prices in Argentina — even for beef — remain among the lowest in the world, and heavy taxes on farmers have prevented them from benefiting fully from rising food prices on the world market.

There are no significant food shortages in Argentina, but there is a heavy contraband trade across the country's borders that the Finance Ministry estimated earlier this year to be running at more than $500-million annually. More important, the inadequate farm income has discouraged farmers from investing more heavily to increase production.

As a result of such factors, Argentina — which some experts assert could double or triple her agrarian production — has failed to increase food exports notably for decades. The country achieved its highest wheat exports in 1929.

At times, government attempts to ameliorate the plight of

agriculture have caused serious disruptions in farm production.

In Chile, for example, a badly managed agrarian-reform program under the Government of President Salvador Allende Gossens resulted in the formation of overcrowded, inefficient agrarian cooperatives and numerous illegal land takeovers that created widespread insecurity among private farmers. Agrarian production fell 30 per cent from 1970 to 1973, and food imports cost more than $600-million — four times the previous annual record.

The right-wing military junta now in power in Chile sought to stimulate agrarian production by allowing food production to rise according to demand. But the resulting inflationary spiral has created the threat of widespread malnutrition among the poor urban majority.

In Mexico, increased government credit to food producers has not increased agricultural output. Food production continues to fall further behind the demand for food, which is rising at about 5 per cent a year compared with a 3.6 per cent increase in the population growth rate.

A long drought through the last two winters followed by rare frosts and serious flooding brought by two hurricanes this summer are largely responsible for reduced agricultural production. But peasant unrest and insecure land tenure have also discouraged many farmers from investing.

As a result, Mexico is importing large quantities of basic grains. Beans, another staple food, were hit badly by recent frosts and about 10 per cent of the 1-million-ton consumption will be met by imports. There have been sharp increases in food prices, in the case of beans and cooking oils, over 75 per cent during 1974.

The Central American republics have also suffered the effects of droughts and hurricanes. Honduras will be forced to import large quantities of corn, wheat and oil seeds.

Crops in Guatemala, El Salvador and Nicaragua were also damaged by heavy rains, and the eruption of three volcanoes in Northwest Guatemala has covered farmland with sulphurous ash.

Even with normal harvests, malnutrition affects the rural populations of Central America. With a food shortage and the consequent increase in prices, intensified malnutrition is inevitable.

The Latin American agricultural picture has been further clouded by adverse developments abroad, including world inflation, the energy crisis, shortages of fertilizer, and increasing protectionism.

Although Venezuela is in good shape because of her oil revenues, other nations have felt pressures. Argentina has seen her beef exports to the Common Market countries drop from 270,000 tons in 1973 to 65,000 tons this year after European Governments met their farmers' demands.

The situation has been far more critical in Uruguay, which imports all her oil. In an attempt to increase export income, the government banned domestic beef consumption, only to see its efforts thwarted when the Common Market restricted meat imports.

Haiti offers the classic example of a population permanently undernourished.

Although the Haitian economy has begun to improve, 85 per cent of the rural population are worse off because inflation has placed many foods out of their reach.

4 ANATOMY OF THE FOOD PROBLEM

The New York Times/Thomas A. Johnson

WALTER SULLIVAN

Food is a Complex System

Few, if any, problems confronting modern man are more complex than that of assuring an adequate food supply to the peoples of the world in the decades to come.

With near-famine conditions in some parts of the world pushing the problem to the forefront, specialists in the analysis of interacting global issues have begun to apply their expertise and their computers in search of possible solutions.

Success, they emphasize, will depend on identifying those key factors that will control the outcome and, not unexpectedly, they have found that curbing population growth is by far the most vital element.

One projection, in fact, suggests that, if this is not done soon and with special vigor where food supplies are already short, mass starvation by the end of this century is inevitable.

This has emerged from an international effort at computer analysis of all factors believed to bear on food production and population growth over the next half century. The analysis indicates that, unless births in South Asia are brought down to the death rate level within a few decades, half a billion children will die between 1980 and 2025.

The analytical method consists of developing a computer "model" that can project trends by simulating the interactions of all factors believed to determine the direction of such trends.

Those persons responsible for the model that projects mass starvation, unless population is drastically curbed, emphasize that their motive is to identify measures most likely to avoid such a catastrophe, rather than to make "doomsday" predictions.

They are mindful that in the past such projections have been criticized on a variety of grounds — notably that the models did not take into account the "common sense" reactions of humanity to situations that obviously call for changes.

Other long-term projections indicate that total world food production will remain adequate, at least for a decade or two, assuming that the problem of getting food from surplus-producing countries, like the United States, to hungry lands can be solved. On this score, however, there is not much optimism.

It is expected that the countries most in need of food to avert famine will be the least able to pay for it. Some projections set the needs so high that they could be met only if the industrialized countries slaughter much of their livestock to release feed grain for human consumption, assume a considerably greater tax burden and voluntarily lower their living standards.

One proposal for averting famine is setting aside bumper crops to cover the needs of lean years.

It is likely, however, that such granaries would be in surplus-producing countries, leaving unresolved the question of who would pay for the relief shipments.

Some projections envision such widespread famine that a form of "national triage" will be necessary. Triage is a term of French origin (rhyming with camouflage) that refers to a procedure for sorting battle casualties.

Normally, the purpose of triage is to minimize deaths by focusing medical attention on those who can only be saved by immediate attention. It denies such attention to those fated to die, regardless of efforts to save them.

"National triage" would direct limited available relief resources to those countries best able to use them effectively.

The possible need for such measures was predicted as early as 1967 by William and Paul Paddock in their book (widely discounted at the time) entitled, "Famine-1975!" One of the Paddock brothers is an Iowa agronomist and the other a retired Foreign Service officer.

National triage is treated at length in a study nearing completion at the Massachusettes Institute of Technology. It deals with "The Ethics of Humanitarian Food Relief" and is being drafted by Dale Runge of the System Dynamics Group led by Prof. Jay W. Forrester.

Its conclusion, in essence, is that food relief — if it promotes further population growth in the relieved area and denies food to those elsewhere committed to population control — can be "unethical."

As the world food situation has approached a crisis state, there has been a proliferation of efforts to look at it from a "systems" point of view — that is, to look at it in terms of all the interacting factors. It is argued by some experts that so many factors interact to determine the food supply in any one region that only a computer "model" of those factors can make even remotely reliable projections.

Thus, in an interview last week [Aug. 1974], Dr. Howard Raiffa, head of the International Institute of Applied Systems

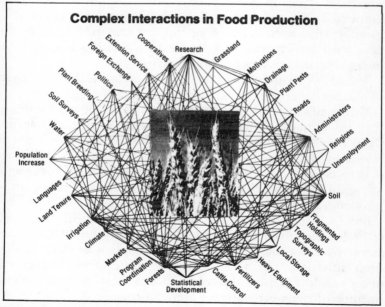

Complex Interactions in Food Production

This diagram shows less than half of the key interrelationships found by many scientists to be major factors in solving food shortages.

Analysis near Vienna, said that, if abundant energy were available, there would be no major food problems.

Energy can be used to produce fertilizer. It drives tractors, harvesters and other farm equipment. It turns the pumps used for irrigation in many hungry lands — notably South Asia. It moves food from surplus to needy regions. And it can be used to desalinate water and make the deserts bloom.

But the world's energy supply is limited by a complex of factors including fossil fuel reserves, economic and environmental considerations, and constraints on the development of nuclear power or more exotic energy sources.

As growing world population has placed an ever heavier burden on food-producing lands, adequate food production has become increasingly energy dependent. The outlook for future food supplies has therefore become inextricably entwined with the energy picture, which itself is a classic "systems" problem.

The International Institute of Applied Systems Analysis, which set itself up last year in a palace outside Vienna, was founded on joint American-Soviet initiative. Its assignment is to apply the techniques of operations research — originally developed for strategic and big-business decision-making — to such problems as the world's energy supply.

Before taking over as its director, Dr. Raiffa was professor of managerial economics at Harvard University.

The institute decided, initially, to avoid taking on problems that involved the whole "world system," concentrating instead on what seemed more manageable issues, such as water resources and energy. The problem of food supply, linked as it is to delicate problems of population control and economics, seemed too touchy for an institute with equal representation from the Soviet bloc and the West.

But in recent months the increasing severity of the food crisis has dissolved such inhibitions. Plans are under way to assess what can be done in its 1975 program bearing on the food situation. Furthermore the institute recently devoted one week to assessing the world modeling effort that has led to some of the most alarming predictions.

The world effort, known as the Mesarovic-Pestel Model, was devised by Mihajlo Mesarovic, director of the Systems

Research Center at Case Western Reserve University in Cleveland, and Eduard Pestel, director of the Institute of Mechanics at the Technical University of Hanover in West Germany. Maurice Guernier, French specialist in problems of tropical agronomy, collaborated.

They present a summary of their findings, with particular regard to South Asia, in the July-August 1974 issue of the UNESCO Courier, journal of the United Nations Educational, Scientific and Cultural Organization. Their efforts have been carried out under the auspices of the Club of Rome, an international organization of scientists, industrialists and economists formed in Rome in 1968.

The "club" seeks to apply modern techniques of business management and systems analysis to the more threatening global problems. It promoted the study, carried out at M.I.T. by Dennis L. Meadows of Dr. Forrester's group, that resulted in the 1972 report entitled "The Limits to Growth."

The latter was criticized in some quarters as a simplistic analysis of world trends, based on generalizations with little meaning for the real world.

According to Dr. Meadows, now at Dartmouth College, a detailed explanation of the computer model that led to the report will be published under the title "Dynamics of Growth in a Finite World."

The Mesarovic-Pestel Model is an attempt to meet some of the criticisms leveled at the Limits to Growth study. The data relating to food, fertilizer, energy, population and other factors on which it is based are stored in computers in Cleveland, Hanover and Grenoble in France. These can be interrogated by telephone from anywhere in the world.

Two years of work by a large team of specialists went into the study, according to the Courier account. Financial support was provided by the Volkswagen Foundation, which has long aided Club of Rome efforts.

Because issues affecting the "world problem complex" tend to be regional, the analysis has been done in terms of 10 large regions. In each of them, 87 age groups are considered. The local diet is defined in terms of 26 varieties of food, and the model also takes into account effects on the population of protein deficiencies arising from various shortages.

The model makes it possible to test the effects of various attempts to avert mass starvation. One such "scenario" envisions a population policy in South Asia that 50 years after its initiation in 1975, would reduce the birth rate to match the death rate.

Because older people would survive while the younger ones were reproducing, population would continue to grow for several more decades. The only way to feed the resulting population of South Asia, according to the analysis, would be to import more grain than the most optimistic predictions for the entire production of all northern countries.

Since this is unlikely, according to the report, "the catastrophe would start some time in the early nineteen-eighties and would reach its peak around the year 2000, when deaths related to food deficit would more than double."

After that, the report says, the population would be so cut back that deaths from starvation would begin to decline. However, the cumulative total, by 2025, would come to some 500 million. The report continues:

"Starvation would not be limited to isolated small areas from which people could escape, but would extend its stranglehold over vast regions inhabited by hundreds of millions. The population would be trapped and there would be no fertile areas to go to as the recent events in semi-arid Africa have so tragically shown.

"There is no historical precedent for this kind of slow, inexorable destruction of the population of entire regions which at their peak were inhabited by several billion people."

In a more optimistic scenario, by the same group, a reduction of births to a one-for-one level is envisioned in 25 to 30 years, rather than in 50. The excess population would then be considerably less, and wide starvation might be averted through reasonable imports.

However, for South Asia to be capable of such imports, the region must develop export industries. To that end, Dr. Mesarovic said in a recent interview, the industrialized nations, between now and 2020, will have to make capital investments in the area totaling about $300-billion.

It is significant that South Asia was chosen for this prognosis, rather than Africa, where population density is not so severe and where some residents suspect demands from the north for population control are racially inspired. The same issue of the UNESCO Courier carries an article entitled "False Prophets of Doom," attacking the "numbers game" carried out by men and machines in more advanced countries.

Its author is Maaza Bekele, an Ethiopian educator, who points out that whereas Africa, in 1650, was home for 20 per cent of the world population, today it accounts for 9 or 10 per cent occupying a little more than 20 per cent of the world's land.

Africans, he writes, must achieve their "true potential" before putting severe brakes on population growth. Indeed it is widely believed that no form of voluntary control can be achieved until a society has become sufficiently stable and affluent to offer security to its citizens in old age. Until that comes, producing capable offspring is the only hope of such people for security.

One problem, however, as noted by the Paddocks, is that the United States and Canada account for 22.7 per cent of all cultivated land in the world. Yet, for example, South America, with a comparable population, has only 6.5 per cent. Other analysts point out that, while more South American land could be brought under the plow, earlier hopes for cultivation of the Amazon Basin no longer seem very promising in that much of the land is unsuitable for cultivation.

There are a variety of dissenters from the school that believes in elaborate computer modeling and analysis of world problems. There is the "garbage in — garbage out" school that believes most of the data put into the analysis are so unreliable that the results have little meaning.

Some would prefer a much simpler computer analysis, using only what seem determining factors. Others avoid computers entirely, relying on intuition (based on long experience) or blackboard calculations.

Thus, in 1969 the United States Department of Agriculture developed a relatively simple computer program to predict American harvests as well as demands by the less-developed countries for American grain.

Its long-term predictions were thrown off by such unforseen developments as the huge Soviet and Chinese grain purchases of recent years, fertilizer shortages resulting from fuel limitations, and droughts like that which has struck Africa.

According to Dr. Quentin M. West, director of the Agriculture Department's, Economic Research Service, 25 million acres of unused American crop land were put back into production in 1973 and by 1985 27 million more acres should have been added to this figure. As a result, in the next 15 years corn crops could grow 25 per cent and soybean yields, 20 per cent.

"Our projections," he told a meeting last April, "suggest that the United States could meet nearly all the world's increased import demand for coarse grains," through 1985. However, he said, poorer nations may continue to depend on food donations that will not always be forthcoming.

"In this connection, we see no easy solution to the agonizing problem of localized famine in this otherwise increasingly prosperous world."

Lester R. Brown of the Overseas Development Council, who has long specialized in such prognoses, makes far less optimistic predictions. In a book entitled, "By Bread Alone," published by Praeger in 1974, he and his colleague Erik P. Eckholm predict that starvation may strike "millions, perhaps tens of millions."

A fundamental change in the world situation, they say, calls for a reordering of American priorities. With countries like the Soviet Union periodically dependent on the efficiency of American farmers, as well as on imports of American technology, they write, such nations are unlikely to attack the United States.

"It is becoming more and more difficult," they say, "to justify the current scale of U.S. global military expenditures." Profligate consumption of energy by the industrialized countries, they add, "may be a greater threat to future global security than many commonly recognized dangers."

Their study was done, essentially, without recourse to computers. Next door to the Washington headquarters of their Overseas Development Council the Brookings Institution has also began studies of world food prospects for the remainder of this century. A computer model with limited inputs is being used.

Early results of these studies have led to no predictions of severe global food shortages before the year 2000, although local crises may occur like that associated with the drought and southward march of the Sahara.

It is in the year 2000, on the other hand, that according to the Mesarovic-Pestel Model, population loss by famine would hit its peak in South Asia if population growth is not checked relatively soon.

Among other efforts to project future food needs is a computer program of the Food and Agricultural Organization of the United Nations in Rome. It was initiated in the nineteen-sixties as an "Indicative World Plan," directed primarily at crop yields and movements of foodstuffs between nations.

According to specialists here its published findings have run into difficulties when they clashed with national findings that sought to paper over unfavorable statistics.

GLADWIN HILL

Mouths to Feed: More and Still More

A world fragmented by differences in race, religion and social and economic conditions is at last taking cognizance of one of its most fundamental common problems: population.

The worsening world food situation, long regarded mainly as a problem of production, has become one also of consumption: How many mouths have to be fed?

Recent shortages of oil and other commodities likewise have elevated to uncomfortable urgency the long-avoided issue of how long the inhabitants of a finite planet — only 8,000 miles in diameter — can keep on multiplying.

The earth's surface, experts say, has the potential of producing adequate nutrition for far more people than there are now. But realization of that potential seems farther away than are additional billions of hungry people.

In recent months other shortages, imminent or incipient, have been highlighted — energy, fertilizers, chemicals and minerals.

In the last generation, social and economic pressures have impelled many nations, from China and India to Mexico, to institute fertility-reduction programs, usually under the title of "family planning."

But any worldwide effort to slow humanity's proliferation was so controversial that government leaders sedulously ignored the problem until recent years.

By 1972, concern had crystallized sufficiently for the U.N.'s General Assembly to designate 1974 as World Population Year, a period for concerted international attention to the problem, and to convoke the first global population conference at the governmental level at Bucharest in 1974.

India began a family planning campaign in 1952, including the distribution of the poster shown here, suggesting that two or three children are enough. The birth rate is still 37 per 1,000 population, against 41 in 1968, but the program has been curtailed in order to save money.

There was no expectation that the conference would produce any miraculous global plan for quickly defusing the "population bomb." What was hoped for was a consensus on the problems of unbridled population growth, recognition of the manifold options for mitigating those threats, and agreement, at least in principle, on remedial efforts.

When there were only a few hundred thousand humans on earth, their rate of multiplication was insignificant in relation to the space and resources available.

Indeed, proliferation was the prime objective — to offset the attrition of disease and other calamities, to furnish more hands for a civilization depending upon manual labor for its physical accomplishments.

By A.D. 1000 — after a million years of unwritten human history — there were not many more people on earth than there are in the United States today, about 275 million.

By 1800 there were still less than one billion. By 1900 there were only 1.6 billion.

Then modern medicine began making inroads against the maladies that had kept population down. People began living longer and producing more children, who survived to become adults and produce more children.

Between 1900 and 1970, the world's population more than doubled, according to United Nations demographers, from 1.6 billion to 3.6 billion.

Today the total is approaching four billion. It is compounding at a rate of 2 per cent a year — a deceptively small number that actually means two more persons each second, 200,000 more a day, over six million more a month and about 74 million a year. Each additional person pushes all of those numbers a little higher.

Unless that rate is reduced, in less than 35 years — within the lifetime of many of today's adults — there will be twice as many people on earth as there are now.

And unless the supportive elements of the meager standards of living now endured by much of humanity are augmented as population increases, living standards inevitably will decline, aggravating deprivation, discontent and disorder.

The Government of India, for instance, has observed that adequately serving its annual population increase of 12 million calls for 2.5-million more homes, 400,000 teachers and four million jobs — four new homes a minute, 1,000 new teachers a day, 11,000 new jobs a day. India makes no contention that the quotas are achieved.

Brazil would have to double its food production in the next 18 years to keep up with its population.

A classic case of the losing race is that of the Aswan Dam in Egypt. In the decade that it was under construction, population growth more than offset the additional agriculture and energy it provided.

The same situation exists, in various degrees, in many countries.

Globally, the prospects are dim that supportive elements can keep pace with population growth. Limitations on world resources, or on man's ingenuity in distributing them, have become all too obvious.

World population long since outstripped food supplies. The estimates are that as many as half the world's people are chronically undernourished, and that weekly, more than 10,000 people die of starvation.

The global population growth rate of 2 per cent annually derives from national growth rate ranging from slightly less than zero in the case of East Germany to 3.4 per cent in Colombia, Ecuador, Venezuela and Paraguay. The figures are from the authoritative Population Reference Bureau, a research organization in Washington. A 3.5 per cent growth rate would double the population in 20 years.

The world's population growth comes principally from the "developing" or underdeveloped countries of Asia, the Middle East, Africa and Latin America.

The underdeveloped countries have about two-thirds of the world's population and the highest birth rates. For every birth in the developed countries, there are five in the underdeveloped countries.

Of the earth's 71 million new inhabitants in 1972, according to the United States Agency for International Development, more than 13.3 million were produced by the 800 million people of Communist China (although its growth rate is a relatively modest 1.7 per cent); and 12.8 million by the 600 million people of India, which has a growth rate of 2.5 per cent.

The third largest source was Indonesia, with an annual increase of about 3.5 million people.

The fourth largest contributor was Brazil, whose 2.8 million additional people exceeded the Soviet Union's 2.2 million.

Mexico added more people to the world (1.8 million) than Japan (1.4 million), a contribution met by Nigeria and slightly exceeding that of the United States (1.3 million).

Although numerically, the responsibility for population growth rests chiefly with the developing countries, demographers and economists point out that population in itself is virtually an abstraction. Its meaning lies chiefly in its relation to resources and the consumption of them.

From this standpoint, the responsibility is that of the advanced nations.

A person in a developing country may be lucky to get a pound of grain, or its equivalent, a day. In the advanced nations, per capita consumption is five times that. While the developed countries have only about a third of the world's population, they consume about 60 per cent of world energy production. The distribution of other basic commodities is similarly disproportionate.

Accordingly, in terms of world resources — the crux of the population question — rich and poor nations face the same thicket of issues together.

A notion has long been widespread that population control was largely a matter of teaching "backward" peoples about birth control, particularly in countries where the Roman Catholic Church was dominant.

Recent studies and experience have convinced leading demographers that that is an oversimplification.

Birth rates are as high in many non-Catholic countries as in Catholic ones. While papal dogma forbids "artificial" contraception and abortion, the church has been a strong advocate of "family planning" — through such means as the rhythm method of contraception — and has participated prominently in worldwide efforts to curb excessive reproduction.

There is mounting evidence that birth rates around the world are linked to other factors than religion. The annual birth rates in two Catholic countries, Italy and France, are respectively 16.8 and 16.9 per 1,000 population — close to the United State's 15.6 and less than the Soviet Union's 17.8.

The first nation to institute family planning services was the Soviet Union, in 1920 — although not with any avowed aim of lessening population growth.

The first "developing" nation to implement a growth-reduction policy, with an extensive family planning campaign, was India, in 1952.

Today, according to the Population Council, a research organization in New York, of 120 developing nations, about 30 have official policies aimed at reducing their population growth rates.

About 30 others, including most of the Latin American countries, have "family planning" programs aimed at public welfare rather than population limitation.

These two categories cover 87 per cent of the population of the "under-developed" world.

Some 60 developing nations are classified as indifferent or opposed to the idea of reducing population growth.

While national birth-control efforts — including the large-scale distribution of contraceptives and voluntary steril-izations — have had observable results, they have largely been disappointing.

India hoped to reduce its 1968 birth rate of 41 per 1,000 population to 25 by 1976. It has come down only to 37; the target date has been deferred to 1980; and India cut back on its birth control program last fall to save money, as "non-essential."

"The only populous less-developed country which appears largely to have overcome the logistical and economic obstacles through providing family planning services is the People's Republic of China," according to Lester Robert Brown, a demographer associated with the Overseas Development Council.

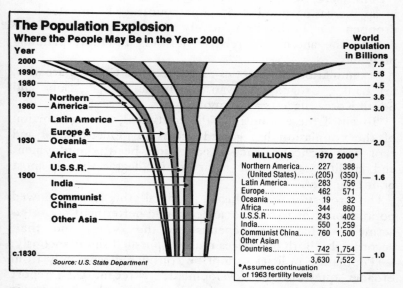

The Population Explosion
Where the People May Be in the Year 2000

MILLIONS	1970	2000*
Northern America	227	388
(United States)	(205)	(350)
Latin America	283	756
Europe	462	571
Oceania	19	32
Africa	344	860
U.S.S.R.	243	402
India	550	1,259
Communist China	760	1,500
Other Asian Countries	742	1,754
	3,630	7,522

*Assumes continuation of 1963 fertility levels

Source: U.S. State Department

This chart shows that population is growing, and will continue to grow, at a faster rate in Africa, India, Asia and Latin America than in other countries.

Studying the paradox of why high birth rates are associated with underdeveloped countries, where people can least afford to have children, demographers have concluded that a prime reason is people's instinct for security: Children are the main protection against the buffets of life.

"Even where a policy discouraging large families is followed, and birth control means are offered," said a recent United Nations study, "the effects are minimal if couples are not motivated to limit the number of children. Motivation for limiting family size oftens seems to be related to economic and social improvements in the society at large."

"Where security is provided, in terms of governmental stability, health care, education and economic improvement, birth rates tend to drop spontaneously, as they have in the advanced nations of the West."

"Birth rates do not usually decline voluntarily," said Mr. Brown, [without] an assured food supply, literacy and at least rudimentary health services."

Conversely, he added, "There is now striking evidence that in an increasing number of poor countries, birth rates have dropped sharply despite relatively low per-capita income and despite the absence or relative newness of family planning programs.

"Examination of societies as different as China, Barbados, Sri Lanka, Uruguay, Taiwan, the Indian Punjab, Cuba and South Korea suggests a common factor.

"In all of these countries," he continued, "a large portion of the population has gained access to modern social and economic services — such as education, health, employment and credit systems — to a far greater degree than in most poor countries."

The professional conclusion from all this is that slowed population growth and socio-economic betterment are interacting — that one depends on the other, and that, accordingly, both objectives must be pursued simultaneously.

"Population policies cannot be considered separately from broader questions of development," a recent U.N. report said. "A high level of social and economic development is generally accompanied by a reduction in fertility.

"Without reduction in the rate of population growth, however, economic development may be severely jeopardized. At the same time, without economic development and without radical transformation in the structures of society, reduction in the rate of population growth will be hard to achieve. Moreover, reducing the growth rate will not be enough to solve the problems of poverty," the report said.

The science — or art — of effectively coupling international population-reduction efforts with economic development assistance is still in its infancy, and was one of the main subjects explored at the Bucharest conference.

The principal governmental effort aimed at stemming the world's population increase is the United Nations Fund for Population Activities, established in 1967. With the task of providing financial and informational assistance for population management programs, its current budget is only about $50-million.

A major nongovernmental effort is the International Planned Parenthood Federation, which is helping family planning organizations in 80 countries, on a far smaller budget.

Mr. Brown, of the Overseas Development Council, estimates that throughout the world, about $3-billion a year is being spent on population control — contrasted with $200-billion in military appropriations.

"There is probably no expenditure of funds which can approach the effectiveness of family planning services in breaking the self-reinforcing cycle of poverty and high fertility," he said.

But, he added that reaching the approximately two billion people who need such services, exclusive of Communist China, at a nominal annual cost of $1 per person, calls for the additional expenditure of $2-billion a year. At least half of that would have to come from the international community.

Given present growth trends and the scope of current population reproduction efforts, many experts do not foresee that human proliferation will even start to taper off significantly before the year 2000, when the world's population has approached eight billion and there has already been an inestimable amount of human misery.

Speaking for a more hopeful school of social scientists, Mr. Brown, in his book, "In the Human Interest," written as a sort of handbook for the World Population Year, outlines ways in which, by massive national and international efforts, world population growth might be slowed down and stabilized at less than six billion "early in the 21st century."

A prognostication on which experts of all stripes find themselves in agreement was voiced by the president of the World Bank, Robert McNamara:

"The population problem will be solved one way or another. Our only option is whether it is to be solved rationally and humanely or irrationally and inhumanely."

VICTOR K. MCELHENY | # The Fertilizer Crisis

A worldwide shortage of fertilizer, gripping rich and poor nations alike, is intensifying a danger that millions may die of starvation in poor countries in 1975.

With inventories of food and the fertilizer needed to grow it at the lowest levels since World War II, many experts are concerned with what they see as a global maldistribution of scarce fertilizer.

They have begun searching for potential emergency supplies to reverse sharp declines in food crops caused by shortages in the three main fertilizers — nitrogen, phosphate and potash — in nations like India and Bangladesh.

One possible source is the fertilizer used on American lawns, flower gardens, golf greens and cemeteries. This comes to nearly three million tons a year and would be easier to tap, politically as well as economically, than fertilizer used by American farmers.

A Senate resolution calling on President Ford to ask Americans to reduce such ornamental uses of fertilizer, freeing it for crops in nations where food is shortest, has gained the backing of 38 Senators. It is an idea that is supported by many food experts as part of a broad program to encourage food self-sufficiency in poor nations.

In this view, scarce fertilizer should be directed to the countries where it will grow the most food. Fertilizer will produce yields at least twice as large on the nutrient-starved soils of Asia, Africa and Latin America as on the already generously fertilized cropland of the United States.

Yet, with food shortages pushing farm prices and farm income to record levels, farmers in developed nations are scrambling for every extra pound of fertilizer they can get to plant more acres and grow more food — some of it for sale to poor nations. The United States and Japan have imposed "quasi-embargoes" on fertilizer exports.

Prices of fertilizer and such fertilizer raw materials as petroleum have doubled and tripled in the last two years. There have been two main reasons — the energy crisis and an exhaustion of reserves because demand outran construction of new fertilizer-manufacturing capacity.

Just a few years ago, spurred by the adoption of the high-yield grain types in the widely heralded "green revolution" in many poor countries, the fertilizer industry built so much capacity that it was threatened with bankruptcy. Construction halted. Then scarcity came again much sooner than expected.

Now, mines and factories are being built and opened all over the world — including eight nitrogen fertilizer "complexes" in China — but not enough of them are expected to go into operation in time to alleviate the present emergency.

For lack of sufficient fertilizer, the green revolution is stalled all over the developing world. With nearly all of the world's land suitable for agriculture already exploited, with a world population of nearly four billion growing at better than 2 per cent a year, experts estimate that generous supplies of fertilizer are essential to avert chronic famines.

They estimate that one billion people, one fourth of the world's population, already depend for their food on the extra food yields from fertilizer. Virtually all the more than two billion extra mouths to feed in the next quarter century will depend on fertilizer.

In the current emergency, close observers are disturbed when a nation like India, for lack of a pound of fertilizer costing 15 cents, fails to grow 10 pounds of wheat that she must try to buy on the world market for at least $1. Such demand from food-short nations is one of the pressures driving American food prices up.

Food experts are convinced that generous supplies of fertilizer are a key to growing the food needed for the world's nearly four billion people, and for the population of more than six billion expected in the year 2000.

Their concern about unequal distribution and worldwide shortages of fertilizer focuses on India, which has been hit with about half of the estimated 2 million-ton "shortfall" of fertilizer in food-short developing nations around the world.

The nearly three million tons of nitrogen, phosphate and potash that Americans use on lawns and rose gardens and for other ornamental purposes each year roughly equals the entire amount that Indian farmers applied — until the sudden shortage of the last year — to a cropland area only slightly smaller than the 360 million acres of United States farmland. American farmers use at least seven times as much fertilizer per acre as Indian farmers do.

In the last year, because the Indian supply of the main plant nutrients fell from three million tons to two, food grain yields have been cut, despite relatively favorable weather, by some 10 million tons. This amount, which is a year's supply for 50 million people, would cost $2-billion to buy on the world market.

According to such observers as James Grant and Lester Brown of the Overseas Development Council, the best place to use scarce fertilizer supplies is the developing countries, where levels of nitrogen, phosphate and potash in the soil are so low that the extra yield from a pound of fertilizer would be at least 10 pounds of grain. Only two to five pounds could be expected from already richly fertilized American or European fields.

Prof. Raymond Ewell of the State University of New York at Buffalo has estimated that an increase in the world grain yield of 100 million tons — above the present world total of 1.2-billion tons — would require 24 million tons of fertilizer if grown on the fields of rich nations like the United States. The same increase would require only 10 million tons of fertilizer if placed on the fields of the developing nations, such as Bangladesh, where food shortages are greatest.

The problems of fertilizer allocation now affect all parts of what many observers see as a single global food community. In testimony before the House Foreign Affairs Committee in

July, Mr. Grant said: "It is no longer possible to insulate U.S. food prices from the outside world. Food prices in the United States are now determined by world price levels."

Mr. Grant said that a $1-billion increase in food and fertilizer aid by the United States would still "be less than half of the more than $2-billion we will receive in 1974 from the developing countries as a result of our higher food prices."

Concern about maldistribution and shortages of fertilizer has triggered these official actions:

• A proposal from the Government of Sri Lanka for establishing a world fertilizer "pool" through which rich nations would share fertilizer supplies with poor ones.

• Creation by the United Nations Food and Agriculture Organization of a special fertilizer commission, which held its first meeting in July 1974.

• Introduction of House Resolution 1155 and Senate Resolution 329 in the Congress, with sponsorship by more than 100 members, urging enlarged food and fertilizer aid by the United States and reduction of "non-critical, non-food-producing uses of fertilizer."

• Pledges by Secretary of State Kissinger, in a speech to the United Nations in 1974, of American technical assistance to help improve the operation of fertilizer factories, to help make more effective use of fertilizers, and help build new fertilizer plants in areas like the Persian Gulf where raw materials for nitrogen fertilizers are plentiful.

Such moves are arousing anger among American farmers, who oppose fertilizer exports that would cut into their own supplies. Their complaints led last fall to action by the Cost of Living Council, now defunct, in which decontrol of United States fertilizer prices was allowed in return for a promise by the fertilizer industry to reserve an extra 1.5 million tons of fertilizer for domestic sale.

This action was termed a "quasi-embargo" by Mr. Grant in testimony before the House Foreign Affairs Committee in July, 1974. Now [Sept. 1974], farmers fear that fertilizer manufacturers might step up exports, since world fertilizer prices are 50 per cent above American levels. A Senate staff aide called the issue "politically red hot."

Ripples from the fertilizer problem have spread all over the developing world, where leaders suddenly realized last fall — when oil exporting nations set their prices sky high — that both industrial and agricultural development prospects were in pawn to the oil-exporting nations.

Developing nations stepped up their plans for self-sufficiency in fertilizer raw materials and products. The most significant moves came in Southeast Asia, where Indonesia, rich in natural gas and petroleum, dedicated one large fertilizer plant at Palembang on Sumatra and promptly signed a contract for one twice as big.

To save up to a year in its drive for self-sufficiency, Indonesia ordered a ship-borne fertilizer plant from Europe. It will be sailed to a point offshore from Samarinda in Kalimantan, as the Indonesians call Borneo.

Some of the ammonia to be produced at this plant will be shipped to the Philippines, where it will be made into ammonium phosphate or ammonium sulphate fertilizer. The sulphuric acid byproduct from the Philippine copper industry can be used to make the ammonium sulphate, or to process imported phosphate rock to put into the ammonium phosphate.

Similar arrangements could make Southeast Asia self-sufficient in fertilizer manufacture within a few years, according to experts from the National Fertilizer Development Center in Muscle Shoals, Ala., who have visited the area.

Discovery of important natural gas reserves 100 miles north of Dacca, the capital of Bangladesh, has led to plans for several nitrogen fertilizer plants, according to observers interviewed at the Muscle Shoals center, which is operated by the Tennessee Valley Authority. The fertilizer plants would not only supply the needs of Bangladesh but also a portion of those of neighboring India.

The fertilizer shortage in India, which has little of its own petroleum or natural gas, has led to the signing of World Bank-sponsored contracts for two nitrogen fertilizer plants meant to tap India's large deposits of lignite, or brown coal.

Such efforts point toward more generous supplies of fertilizer a few years from now — so generous, indeed, that the

World Fertilizer Situation

Consumption Forecast

(In millions of tons)

Developed Nations' Share — Underdeveloped Nations' Share

NITROGEN
1980: 46
1974: 32
11
7

PHOSPHATE
1980: 25.6
1974: 20.4
5.4
3.2

POTASH
1980: 22.3
1974: 17.6
3.3
1.8

Unequal Distribution of Resources

Canada K

United States K P

Venezuela

SOUTH AMERICA

Morocco P

EUROPE

AFRICA

Nigeria

Soviet Union P

ASIA

Iran
Saudi Arabia

Indonesia

AUSTRALIA

Natural gas now flared off could be used to manufacture nitrogen fertilizer

P Major phosphate deposits

K Major potash deposits

An Example of Unequal Fertilizer Use

(Both countries have approximately same cropland area)

UNITED STATES

Nitrogen 8.3
Phosphate 5.0
Potash 4.4

INDIA

Nitrogen 2.0
Phosphate 0.6
Potash 0.3

Source: Tennessee Valley Authority

world might seek to "stockpile" surplus fertilizer factories as part of a world fertilizer "bank" and thus avoid the boom-and-bust sequence being experienced now.

This suggestion was made in the June 1974 issue of War on Hunger magazine, published by the Agency for International Development, by Dr. Donald McCune, head of the international group at the T.V.A. fertilizer development center.

"It appears that adequate capacity is being built to meet long-range needs," Dr. McCune wrote. "In fact, caution may be needed to prevent the pendulum from swinging so far that production may greatly exceed demand."

Fertilizer experts stress that the food needs of a world population growing at 2 per cent a year have long since outrun natural supplies of fertilizer.

Among these are inert nitrogen gas in the atmosphere converted into nitrates by the heat of lightning bolts, at the estimated rate of eight pounds per acre per year. This falls in rain and helps replenish a little of the nitrogen taken from the soil by food plants.

Another natural source is nitrogen extracted from the air by micro-organisms living in nodules in the roots of such plants as soybeans and alfalfa, or in the soil, or in the water of rice paddies.

Also outrun by man's voracious need for extra food are such recycled materials as bones for phosphate, wood ash for potash, manure and slaughterhouse waste for nitrogen — or mined nitrate. The functions of these fertilizers were first understood scientifically in the eighteen-forties.

Although the raw materials of nitrogen, phosphate and potash fertilizers are plentiful in nature, each requires elaborate, massive technology to convert it to substances that plants can use.

Huge centrifugal compressors convert nitrogen from its "aloof" form in the atmosphere, as the fertilizer expert Dr. A. V. Slack calls it, into ammonia, where the nitrogen is combined with hydrogen "donated" by natural gas, an oil byproduct called naphtha, or coal. The plants then use nitrogen compounds as part of every one of the amino acid building blocks of all their proteins, including the enzyme catalysts that carry out thousands of different operations in the cell.

Phosphate rock is mined in Morocco, or scraped from the earth by electric-powered draglines in Florida, separated from other substances and finally treated with sulphuric acid. In the plants, phosphorus atoms linked together in so-called adenosine molecules provide most of the energy for the operations of living cells.

Sulphur, because of its use in sulphuric acid, is a key to phosphate fertilizer supply. As it happens, sulphur itself forms "bridges" within many proteins, holding them to the exact shape that is essential to the proteins' functions.

Almost all the potash, originally named from the source farmers once used, comes today from potassium chloride mined in ancient, dried out, salty lake beds. The potassium, according to Dr. Slack in his book, "Defense Against Famine," helps promote the assembly of proteins from amino acids, and the forming of carbohydrates.

The scale of the nitrogen fertilizer industry, which now accounts for half the fertilizer of the world, jumped dramatically in the nineteen-sixties with the invention of the centrifugal-compressor ammonia plant by the M. W. Kellogg Company, a division of Pullman, Inc., in Houston, Tex. Today's typical ammonia plant, producing 1,000 tons a day, is three times larger than the typical older plant.

The invention meant that if underdeveloped countries wanted to manufacture their own low-cost fertilizer to raise the productivity of their most primeval industry, agriculture, they would have to leap into an enormously complex technology, operating at a vast scale with the help of huge supplies of energy.

If the plants operated below capacity because of bad management or a shortage of spare parts or interrupted electricity supplies, their economies suffered. With the exception of a factory or two in Indonesia, fertilizer plants in developing nations typically operate at 60 per cent of capacity.

Rich resources of natural gas for nitrogen fertilizer are being lost every year in oil-producing nations because markets have not been developed for them. In Venezuela, Nigeria, North Africa and the Persian Gulf region, a total of 4.5 trillion cubic feet of natural gas is burnt, "flared off" into the atmosphere and lost forever each year.

The amount is 10 times what is used in the United States annually to make nitrogen fertilizer. It is enough to make twice the present annual consumption of nitrogen fertilizer.

The existence of such resources, including thousands of years' supply of potash for the entire world in the mines of Saskatchewan, and new discoveries of phosphate rock in Australia and even India, increase confidence that a balance between demand and supply can be established by the end of the decade.

Recent reviews of the world fertilizer outlook by the Economic Research Service of the Department of Agriculture and by the National Fertilizer Development Center indicate that world consumption of plant nutrients, which was 78 million tons in 1973, would rise at least 30 per cent, to 113 million tons in 1980.

While fertilizer experts study how to meet future demands, agricultural researchers are giving new attention to how hundreds of millions of small farmers in developing nations could economize on fertilizer and still achieve larger food yields than they and their families are accustomed to do now.

Laboratories such as the International Rice Research Institute are studying simple ways to apply fertilizers at just the times plants need them.

The National Fertilizer Development Center at Muscle Shoals is pushing development of a sulphur-coated form of the urea fertilizers, which are fast becoming the most-applied type in Asia, as a kind of "timed-release" nitrogen fertilizer for rice paddies that are alternately flooded and dried.

By releasing the nitrogen more slowly to the rice plants, the sulphur-coated urea, which can be applied in one dose at the start of the growing season on intermittently flooded paddies, yields have been increased in trials from Peru to the Philippines.

Nutritious soybeans, whose rich protein now is fed largely to animals, are receiving new emphasis. Soybean plants supply much of their own nitrogen needs, thanks to the work of bacteria living in nodules in their roots.

At the Asian Vegetable Research and Development Center in Taiwan, genetic work has begun to extend the range of the soybean plant from the temperate zones in the United States and China, where it grows best now. This would cut fertilizer needs and aid multiple-cropping plans to enrich diets in rice-growing areas.

At North Carolina State University, plant breeders have been reporting some success in developing hybrid soybean plants, which would allow farmers to increase soybean yields per acre. Up to now, the only way to grow more soybeans has been to plant more acres of soybeans.

One hope, which many scientists had reserved for the distant future, has acquired new sharpness in the last year. This is the idea of genetically "tailoring" bacteria living in the soil or plant roots to do a better job of "fixing" nitrogen from the air.

Scientists in California discovered a new technique of using bacterial "plasmids," small rings of genetic material alongside the main rings of genes, to transfer properties from one strain of bacteria to another.

It is thought that this technique might be used to transfer the genes for the nitrogen-fixing protein called nitrogenase into many soil microorganisms now lacking it. The result might be a significant new way to meet the desperate need of the world's farmers for new supplies of nitrogen for their food crops.

Changing Climates Threaten Food Supplies

HAROLD M.
SCHMECK, JR.

Bad weather this summer [1974] and the threat of more of it to come hang ominously over every estimate of the world food situation.

It is a threat the world may have to face more often in the years ahead. Many weather scientists expect greater variability in the earth's weather and, consequently, greater risk of local disasters in places where conditions of recent years have become accepted as the norm.

Some experts believe that mankind is on the threshold of a new pattern of adverse global climate for which it is ill-prepared.

A recent meeting of climate experts in Bonn, West Germany, produced the unanimous conclusion that the change in global weather patterns poses a severe threat to agriculture that could lead to major crop failures and mass starvation.

Others disagree, but are still concerned over the impact of weather on man's ability to feed the ever-increasing number of human beings.

Whether or not the 1974 events are harbingers of a major global trend, some of those events are, of themselves, causing concern.

The monsoon rains have been late and scant over agriculturally important regions of India, while Bangladesh has been having floods.

Parts of Europe and the Soviet Union have had problems at both ends of the weather spectrum. It has been too hot and dry at some times and places, too wet and cold at others.

There have been similar problems in North America. An American weather expert recently received reports that ice was lingering abnormally on the coasts of Newfoundland and that new evidence showed that the Gulf Stream was fluctuating toward a more southerly course.

In the United States, the world's most important food producer, a severe drought that began in 1973 in the Southwest has spread northward and eastward, and may have potentially serious effects in the Corn Belt. There have also been reports that spring wheat in the United States has been badly hurt by hot, dry weather.

Earlier this year, there had been hopes of bumper crops in North America and elsewhere. But the weather's adverse impact has trimmed back some of these hopes.

The situation is not all bad, by any means. Canada's prospects are said to be reasonably good, depending on what happens during the next few weeks. Aside from some floods, Australia has had no serious problems, according to experts in the United States. The Soviet Union has predicted a high grain yield, largely on the basis of a good winter wheat crop. But spring wheat, accounting for about 35 per cent of that nation's total wheat crop, may be suffering from persistent high temperatures and strong winds.

All of the signs, both good and bad, are being watched closely by specialists in weather and its effects on agriculture.

In the whole complex equation of food, resources and population, the element that is least controllable and probably least predictable is weather. Yet, weather can spell the difference between abundance and disaster almost anywhere.

In 1974, experts in weather, climate and agriculture have given much thought to the prospects for the coming years and decades.

The Rockefeller Foundation sponsored a conference on essentially this subject. A unit of the National Academy of Sciences is preparing a major report on climate change. The Environmental Data Service of the National Oceanic and Atmospheric Administration is organizing a special group of experts to keep close watch on global weather as it relates to food production. And a workshop sponsored by the International Federation of Institutes for Advanced Study pre-

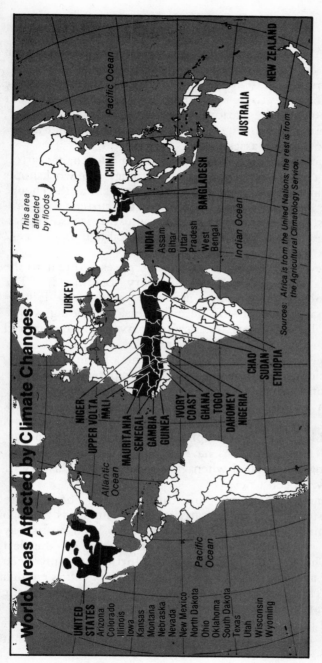

World Areas Affected by Climate Changes

UNITED STATES
Arizona
Colorado
Illinois
Iowa
Kansas
Montana
Nebraska
Nevada
New Mexico
North Dakota
Ohio
Oklahoma
South Dakota
Texas
Utah
Wisconsin
Wyoming

Pacific Ocean

Atlantic Ocean

TURKEY

NIGER
UPPER VOLTA
MALI
MAURITANIA
SENEGAL
GAMBIA
GUINEA
IVORY COAST
GHANA
TOGO
DAHOMEY
NIGERIA
CHAD
SUDAN
ETHIOPIA

Pacific Ocean

CHINA

This area affected by floods

INDIA
Assam
Bihar
Uttar Pradesh
West Bengal

BANGLADESH

Indian Ocean

AUSTRALIA

NEW ZEALAND

Sources: Africa is from the United Nations; the rest is from the Agricultural Climatology Service.

Severe weather changes, ranging from floods to drought, struck many of the world's major agricultural areas in 1974. Climate experts predict even greater variability of weather in the future.

pared a detailed report on the impact of climate change on the quality and character of human life.

The summary statement of that report is one of the grimmest forecasts to be made in recent years. Dr. Walter Orr Roberts, one of the nation's foremost experts on climate, believe there is a growing consensus in his field that agrees with the workshop's assessment.

"The studies of many scholars of climatic change attest that a new climatic pattern is now emerging," the workshop's summary said. "There is a growing consensus that the change will persist for several decades and that the current food-production systems of man cannot easily adjust. It is also expected that the climate will become more variable than in recent decades."

"We believe that this climatic change poses a threat to the people of the world," the summary continued. "The direction of climate change indicates major crop failures almost certainly within the decade. This, coinciding with a period of almost nonexistent grain reserves, can be ignored only at the risk of great suffering and mass starvation."

Dr. Roberts, who is program chairman of the federation, said that scientists of several nations participated in the workshop. Its conclusions were unanimous.

Although not all scientists put the matter in such stark terms and many doubt that a clear change in climate is demonstrable, there is widespread agreement on one point: The weather patterns that have prevailed in recent decades are anything but normal when viewed against the history of the past several centuries.

The mean temperature of the northern hemisphere increased steadily from the early nineteen-hundreds through the early nineteen-forties. Since then, it has been on its way downward toward the colder circumstances of the last century. The drop since the nineteen-forties has only been about half a degree, but some scientists believe this is enough to trigger changes that could have important effects on the world's weather and agriculture.

In recent publications, Dr. Reid Bryson of the University of Wisconsin, one of the chief proponents of the view that climate change is overtaking mankind, has cited India as an example of the possible hazards.

Early in this century, severe droughts seemed to hit northern and northwestern India roughly once every three or four years. In more recent decades, the monsoon rains moved northward and the frequency of droughts declined to about once or twice in 20 years. Dr. Bryson and other scientists now believe that the trend is back toward the less favorable conditions of the early nineteen-hundreds.

Meanwhile, the Indian population has greatly increased and demands on the nation's agriculture have risen accordingly.

Apart from that kind of long-range consideration, the situation in India this year [1974] is being watched with particular attention because, in the view of several experts, it is potentially serious.

The heavy monsoon rains vital to India's agriculture seem to be at least a month late, according to the latest world summary of the weekly weather and crop bulletin, published by the Departments of Commerce and Agriculture.

Dr. Richard Felch, one of the weather experts involved in producing the bulletin, said the latest data available to them showed that three-fourths of the total grain-producing area of India was below normal in rainfall this year. Rainfall was normal at this time last year throughout most of the sub-continent.

The sub-Saharan region of Africa, another area of the world ultimately dependent on monsoon rains, is now in its seventh year of drought.

The region is currently experiencing a brief reprieve as the result of a somewhat wetter rainy season than has been the pattern in recent years. Some observers say the rains may even allow modest crops of sorghum and millet to be harvested.

Even so, most experts view the current rains as only a temporary fluctuation. Dr. Bryson and others believe that the sub-Sahara will continue to suffer the effects of a change in weather patterns that is likely to persist. This, like most other aspects of current climate, is subject to considerable debate among specialists.

One important reason that all of the world's weather signs are being watched closely this year is that the world does not have the margin of safety in food grains that it had a few decades ago.

One specialist said that the world's total grain reserves were equal to the approximate difference between a good crop year and a bad one. Thus, it would take only one bad crop year to draw the safety margin in world food down close to the vanishing point.

That is why experts are keeping a close watch on such diverse phenomena as the tardy monsoon rains over India, hot weather in the Soviet Union east of the Urals, and the moisture in the soil of sun-baked Iowa. Now, perhaps more than ever before in man's history, they all tie together.

Indeed, some scientists believe efforts to build up world food reserves ought to be a major international concern.

Although there is no prospect of a food shortage in North America, specialists are keeping a watchful eye on the Southwest, the Plains States and the Corn Belt because the United States is so important to the world's total food supply.

Lyle M. Denny, who helps Dr. Felch to produce the weekly weather and crop bulletin, said a drought began last fall in West Texas and adjoining areas of the Southwest and has since spread northward and eastward. He said ranchers have had to haul water to their cattle in New Mexico, Arizona and Utah.

Dr. Louis M. Thompson, associate dean of agriculture at Iowa State University in Ames, said hot, dry weather had reduced Iowa's potential corn and soybean crops by at least 10 per cent. A sophisticated statistical study of temperature, soil moisture and their effects on crops has led Dr. Thompson to a rough rule of thumb relating temperature to crop yield.

According to this rule of thumb, he said in a recent interview, the corn crop will be reduced one bushel an acre for every cumulative 10 degrees that the temperature rises above 90. For example, if the temperature rises to 95 on a given day, he would record that as a five. If it rises to 100 the next day, he would add 10.

By the end of the third week in July, Dr. Thompson said, the cumulative total reached 114 degrees above 90. For both corn and soybeans, this would mean a reduction in yield of about 10 per cent, according to his calculations. But Dr. Thompson sees more potential significance to the number than the effect on this year's crop.

The record of 114 has not been approached since the drought year of 1954, when the total through July 21 was 96. The record has not been surpassed since the "dust bowl" drought year of 1936, when the cumulative degrees above 90 in Iowa totaled 236 through the first 21 days of July.

Dr. Thompson said records to 1800 show that the agriculturally important region in which he lives has been hit by a severe drought in a cycle that occurs roughly every two decades. The most recent cycles came in the mid-nineteen-thirties and the mid-fifties, according to his figures. And he notes with little complacency that the next drought would be "due" in the mid-seventies.

Dr. Thompson and those scientists who agree with him think the timing of the current harsh weather in the West may be more than coincidence.

But there is sharp disagreement among experts on this point. Some see no evidence of any cyclical 20-year pattern, and no logical or scientific basis for it.

Specialists in the Department of Agriculture, for example, are among those who disagree with Dr. Thompson. They believe that weather is a random variable, obeying no regular cyclic pattern over the years except, of course, the seasons.

Richard C. McArdle, an economist and climatologist in the Department of Agriculture, doubts the reality of a 20-year cycle and does not think that there will be a global run of bad weather this year or in the near future. The more likely pattern for any year, he believes, is one in which some areas of the world have good weather for crops while other areas do not. This year's pattern is like that, he says.

He and others in the department also argue that modern agricultural technology and irrigation are capable of mitigating the effects of drought in the United States. This, too, is an area of disagreement among experts. Some doubt that American agriculture, proficient as it is, can be "drought resistant" in any major sense.

Regardless of their views on the existence of a 20-year

cycle and the drought resistance of modern agriculture, many scientists are agreed on one important point: The United States has had a run of remarkably good weather during the last 15 years. And many think it foolhardy to expect that good fortune to continue indefinitely.

Dr. J. Murray Mitchell of the National Oceanic and Atmospheric Administration's Environmental Data Service is among the experts who believe that the world should be alert to the probability of change in weather patterns.

Dr. Mitchell, who is one of the nation's leading experts on climate change, says scientists have learned a great deal in the last five years about the fluctuations that have disturbed the earth's climate in the past. He also says there is no doubt that the earth is now at the peak of a very warm period. Change is to be expected.

The point made by many experts is this: World population has soared in the last few decades. World agriculture, adapting to the present norm, has only barely managed to stay ahead. The pressures of population and food need are so great now that the system has lost much of its flexibility. In such a situation, any change from the present "normal" weather could bring serious trouble.

"The normal period is normal only by definition," Dr. Bryson said in a recent article. "There appears to be nothing like it in the past 1,000 years."

JANE E. BRODY | # Man Against Pest

Each year an estimated half of the world's critically short food supply is consumed or destroyed by insects, molds, rodents, birds and other pests that attack foodstuffs in fields, during shipment and in storage.

Experts believe that control of even part of these losses may be the fastest and least costly way of substantially increasing the food availabe to the world's millions of hungry and malnourished people, who survive primarily on grains.

If the field pests and pathogens that attack the world's principal cereal grains — wheat, rice, corn, sorghums and millets — were more adequately controlled, these sources estimate that an additional 200 million tons of grain would be available to feed one billion people each year.

More effective control of storage pests in large and small granaries throughout the world could mean an immediate 25 per cent increase in edible grains without any change in agricultural productivity.

In some cases, solutions to pest problems, such as keeping rodents out of grain stores, are already in hand and need only to be applied, particularly in those poor countries where most of the world's grain eaters live. But other pest defenses require considerable research to develop simple, economical and ecologically sound control measures with worldwide applicability.

The problem of food losses to pests is by no means limited to the developing countries where traditional agricultural practices, haphazard shipping and primitive storage methods often prevail. In the United States, according to the best estimates of the Department of Agriculture, a third of the nation's potential harvest is sacrificed to insects, disease and weeds despite control measures.

Dr. Elvin C. Stakman, plant pathologist at the University of Minnesota, has calculated that American farmers plant "the equivalent of 75 million acres of crop land to feed weeds, insects and plant pathogens instead of human beings."

Up to 10 per cent of crops may be left in the field after harvest and another 5 to 10 per cent are consumed or destroyed by insects, molds and rodents during storage. An estimated total, then, of between 40 and 60 per cent of the potential American crop is unavailable for human consumption.

In the less developed countries, the problem is similar but often of much greater magnitude. In India, for example, losses of 70 per cent of foods placed in storage are reported to be not uncommon.

A half dozen rats consume the amount of grain that could sustain a man, not to mention what the animals may stash away as "reserves." A consultant for the Food and Agriculture Organization in Pakistan dug out a rodent burrow in a rice field and uncovered a 10-pound grain reserve. The consultant, E. W. Bentley, said that local farmers commonly allow poor people to raid these burrows after the rice is harvested, with perhaps 20 per cent of what the rats store being reclaimed for human food.

Insects and micro-organisms that feed on stored grain not only reduce the amount of grain available but also reduce its nutritional quality, since these pests preferentially attack the protein-containing portions of the grain.

On a worldwide percentage basis, losses in the fields of developing countries are not much greater than those in the United States. But sporadic raids by rodents and other animals, epidemics of diseases and invasions of insects can, and frequently do, devastate an area's food supply.

An epidemic of a rice blight disease in India led to the starvation of a million people in the 1940's. During the last major locust plague in Africa, in one month of 1959 in Ethiopia alone the insects devoured a year's supply of grain for one million people, the F.A.O. reports.

An annual African pest almost as voracious as a horde of

locusts is the quelea bird, a small weaver that has virtually no natural enemies and "holds the power of life and death over innumerable small farmers," the F.A.O. says in a report on food losses. The killing of hundreds of millions of these sparrow-sized birds made hardly a dent in their destruction of food grains.

All told, the organization estimated that "55 million Africans could be fed for a year from the [native] grain finding its way to the wrong consumers — rats, locusts, quelea birds, beetles, moths and weevils and countless micro-organisms."

In some areas, pest problems have totally prevented the production of important food sources. Peanuts, for example, could be a valuable dietary item and export crop for many islands in the South Pacific, but plots have been so badly damaged by rats that attempts to grow the highly nutritious peanut have been all but abandoned.

In Africa, 4.25 million square miles of good grazing land is unavailable for cattle production because it is dominated by the tsetse fly, which spreads epidemics of sleeping sickness among domestic animals.

Other sources of "waste" that deprive people of potential foodstuffs include poor use of and lack of erosion control, shipping delays and mishaps and losses during milling and processing.

The quickest gains in reducing food losses can be made by controlling storage wastes, according to various experts.

"Once the grain is produced, we ought to be able to keep it," remarked Dr. David Pimentel, entomologist at the New York State College of Agriculture and Life Sciences at Cornell University.

Noting that "conservatively $2-billion worth of grain is lost each year in storage and transit," scientists from 27 nations who attend a meeting on stored products entomology in Savannah, Ga., in October 1974 sent a resolution to the United Nations pleading for "the patronage and assistance of national and international leaders to accelerate the utilization of available methods and skills" in controlling storage pests. The scientists expressed their belief that "comprehensive adoption of our technology could make a major contribution to mitigation of worldwide food shortages."

In many countries, only a small percentage of the grain is

scientifically stored in large warehouses by government or other agencies. Most is kept by individual farmers or small villages under less than ideal conditions. In India, for example, agricultural experts estimate that 90 per cent of the country's food grains is stored in substandard facilities.

For small farmers in poor countries who store their families' grain supply in burlap sacks or simply heaped in a corner, such simple methods as keeping it in sealed clay pots, burying it in the ground or hanging it in trees can go a long way to reduce storage losses, according to Dr. Robert Davis, a storage pests expert with the Department of Agriculture in Savannah.

A Freedom From Hunger program in Africa promoted the use of corn cribs elevated from the ground with shields on the legs so that rats would be unable to climb up.

Other methods aimed at preventing storage losses that were discussed at the Savannah meeting include the following:

• Hermetic storage of grains in Africa in large, airtight rubber bins. The stored grain and insects already present in it respire, and when all the oxygen is used up, the insects die.

• Pumping cool, dry air into storage bins at night and during the cooler months. This chills the grain, depresses the activity of insects, which are cold-blooded, and prevents the build-up of infestations.

• Storage in plastic bags underwater or in mines to keep grain at a relatively constant low temperature. This method is being used in some Pacific countries, including Japan.

• Partly replacing the air in storage bins with inert gases so that less oxygen is available to support insect life.

More effective drying of grain before storage and sealing leaks in the roofs of storage bins can help to suppress mold growth, which can render grain poisonous as well as distasteful.

Chemical fumigants and insecticide sprays as pretreatments to prevent insect infestation of grain stores are already widely used in developed countries, but their cost and the technology involved in their application is prohibitive in many areas of the world. Therefore, Dr. Burkholder and others are trying to develop simple, low-cost techniques to control the world's most serious storage pests.

His approach includes the use of traps baited with a chemical that attracts the insect, such as a sex attractant. Once in the trap, the insect may be killed by an insecticide or exposed to a disease that it would then spread to its co-invaders.

In India, where treatment of stored grain with DDT is widespread (although illegal), the amount of DDT regularly found in the bodies of the people is the highest in the world. Prof. O. S. Bindra of Punjab Agricultural University has been promoting the use of malathion instead, since this chemical is not stored in the body, is readily broken down in the environment and is relatively nontoxic to mammals.

Since weeds compete with food crops for soil nutrients, sunshine and water, the control of unwanted plant growth, either by hand weeding where labor is cheap or by use of herbicides, can substantially increase yields. Experiments in five Asian countries showed that hand weeding of rice paddies increased yields by an average of 45 per cent.

Partly controlling the rice stem borer in the Philippines by spraying with insecticide produced minimum yield increases of about half a ton an acre, doubling the average yield in Asia, according to a study by the International Rice Research Institute in the Philippines.

But because of their high cost, relative scarcity and difficulty of application, herbicides and insecticides are considered at best only partial solutions to the problem of field pests in developing countries. With the growing problem of pest resistance to chemicals and the environmental damage these chemicals can cause, alternative methods of control are essential in developed as well as in developing countries, according to Dr. Robert L. Metcalf, entomologist at the University of Illinois.

In a large study of control of the alfalfa weevil in Illinois, Dr. Metcalf and his coworkers have shown that instead of spraying the crop eight times a season with heptachlor, a persistent pesticide that contaminates milk and can become a cancer-causing agent, a single chemical application in early spring will protect the crop until the emergence from their cocoons of tiny parasitic wasps that kill the weevils.

"The research to develop such plans is difficult, but the

plans that ultimately evolve won't be difficult to carry out," Dr. Metcalf said, adding that the adoption of such pest management techniques "is the only way modern agriculture can survive in the developing countries."

Much research is being devoted to the development of crop varieties that are resistant to attack by various insects and diseases, obviating the need for any pesticides. The rice institute in the Philippines has released rice varieties that are resistant to five major pests. Such breeding work is a continual process, since sooner or later the pest organism evolves a way of overcoming the plant's resistance, but the use of resistant varieties makes pest control simple and economical for the farmer.

Another approach advocated by Dr. Norman Borlaug, "father of the Green Revolution," is the use in the same planting of combinations of seeds with resistance to different pests. This inhibits the spread of individual pests and lessens the chance that a farmer's crop may be totally wiped out.

Along the tsetse fly belt in Africa, the Agency for International Development is conducting a major study to reduce the population of these live-stock-attacking insects by releasing large numbers of sterilized male flies. Since the female mates only once, mating with a sterile male will prevent her from reproducing.

Control of rodents and birds that attack crops in developing countries is also a major challenge. In Africa, spraying of roosts of quelea birds with parathion kills a lot of birds, but the chemical is getting into waterways and also killing lions and other animals.

A variety of modern-day "scarecrow" techniques, such as alarms, explosive devices and chemical repellents that cause the birds to emit distress calls and frighten their companions, are being used in some areas of the United States. Just as effective, however, is a boy who shakes a string full of tin cans every time the birds land, as is done in India and the Philippines.

Field rodents are trickier to deal with, partly because their invasions are hard to detect — they frequently attack at night and from underground. Poisoned bait, traps, anticoagulant rodenticides, gassing the animals' homesites and running electrified fences through moats around the field have all been used with varying success.

Experts say that long-lasting solutions to the problem of food losses to pests will require intensive study of the natural behavior of each pest and the development of effective methods of intervention.

Then, as with most other approaches to increasing the world's food supply, the problem remains of "getting the new pest control methods out into the countryside," as Ambassador Edwin Martin of the U.S. State Department put it.

"It's not an overnight task," he added, "but it could make a substantial impact on the amount of food available in the next five to ten years."

HAROLD M. SCHMECK, JR.

Little Hope From the Sea

New England haddock has been a staple of American fish markets since Colonial days. Today the fish are so scarce that stocks are endangered and commercial fishermen are forbidden to seek them anywhere off the East Coast.

There used to be a large-scale sardine fishery off California. Today California sardines are commercially extinct. There are a few left, but so few that it is not worth putting to sea after them.

Herring have virtually disappeared from the North Sea and the Atlantic coast of Europe. Fishermen learned all their migration points and systematically fished them out.

Such is the reality behind the popular conception of the teeming seas as a source of limitless food for the world's hungry humans.

In various ways mankind is already putting unprecedented strain on the resources of the seas and showing these resources to be finite. The impetus has come from expanding population, the world's increasing need for food and, in the case of some nations, from affluence.

The lure of large-scale supplies of food from the sea has led to the development of big ocean-going fishing fleets capable of going anywhere on the high seas and virtually fishing out any stock of fish at any depth. The Soviet Union and Japan have been notable for the development of such fleets. Only in its tuna fleet does the United States compare with them, some experts say.

The sharp decline of haddock off New England and the Atlantic coast of Canada is widely attributed to intensive fishing by a Soviet fleet in the late nineteen-sixties. It is expected to take years for the stocks to regenerate. Meanwhile, by international agreement, commercial fishermen are forbidden to take haddock except for small numbers caught incidentally in the quest for other species.

The California sardines seem to have been depleted because of intense American commercial fishing efforts from the mid-nineteen-thirties through the early nineteen-sixties and some bad climate years during that time. There has been no sign yet of any subsequent return. The herring off Europe disappeared more gradually after the assault of fishing fleets of several nations over a span of more than a century.

These are only examples of what over-fishing can do — coupled probably with unknown and unpredictable natural assaults on fish populations.

Specialists say most of the best-known food species of fish and shellfish are already being harvested close to the practical maximum. Some have been pushed beyond that, according to experts on the world's fisheries.

If there are to be substantial increases in the next several years, this apparently must come from wider use of squid, skate, croaker, hake and some other species seldom featured on American menus.

Fisheries experts have singled out some striking examples of fisheries that should be made more productive by taking species that are either ignored at present or even thrown back.

One such case, according to Donald R. Whitaker, of the National Marine Fisheries Service here, is the so-called "by-catch" of shrimp fishing in the Gulf of Mexico. The by-catch means the fish taken incidentally in nets set for something else.

For every pound of shrimp taken in the gulf, Mr. Whitaker said, a shrimp boat is likely to haul in five to 10 pounds of other kinds of fish, primarily croaker, a source of edible, even tasty, food. Thus, he said, in a catch of 200 million pounds of shrimp as much as two billion pounds of fish may be thrown away.

In fact, shrimp-fishing boats aren't equipped to handle the by-catch and would probably have no American market for it if it could.

Nevertheless, some specialists believe it could be developed into a valuable source of food if the necessary effort were made.

The fisheries service has, itself, been criticized for not doing more to popularize some under-used fish species that are plentiful in American waters and for not doing more to help American fishermen make the most of their opportunities.

For example, Mike Weiner, president of a cooperative called the Florida Fishermen's Marketing Association, says the king mackerel is plentiful, but little used in waters off our southeast coast mainly because no effort has been made to promote it.

He also charges that the fish marketing system in this country is antiquated and corrupt and, for years, has exploited American fishermen and fisheating consumers alike.

Yet another example of seafood wastage is that of the tanner crab, plentiful in the seas off Alaska.

A fisheries expert of the National Oceanic and Atmospheric Administration said the Japanese catch more than 100 million of these edible crabs each year in the course of fishing for pollack but have to throw many of them back because the permissible catch is limited by international agreement.

Several specialists say there appears to be large quantities of squid available for the catching if more people could be persuaded to eat them.

There are other exploitable seas, but the total foreseeable gains from using them are modest. Mankind takes some 70 million metric tons of fish and shellfish from the sea each year.

Many experts say this might be boosted, with current technology, as high as 100 million. Some put the possibilities a little higher, but there is widespread agreement that the seas offer no easy answer to world hunger and that seafood is by no means inexhaustible.

One recent estimate was that no more than about 12 per cent of the annual protein eaten by humans comes from the sea. Some experts put the total at about half that.

"We have a finite resource which we have only recently discovered is finite," said David H. Wallace, associate administrator of N.O.A.A. during a recent interview. "It's kind of frightening."

Five years ago, a national commission on marine resources estimated that the total harvest of food from the sea might be raised as high as 500 million metric tons or higher.

In 1969, when the report was completed, the huge anchovy fishery off the coast of Peru was growing dramatically year by year. Its potential seemed all but inexhaustible — and was treated that way.

Not until the mid-nineteen-fifties did commercial fishermen in Peru begin serious efforts to exploit the Peruvian anchovy. By 1958 the anchovy harvest had growth to more than one million metric tons a year and, by 1962 to over seven million — making Peru the world's foremost fishing nation. Most of the catch was used for fish meal.

"Large financial investments were made in the harvesting of this seemingly endless resource until 1970 when the landings were 12.3 million tons," said an analysis published a few months ago by the National Marine Fisheries Service. The catch of that one species off one stretch of the South Ame-

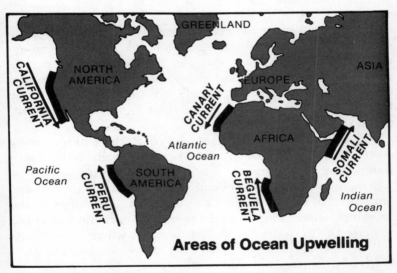

Areas of Ocean Upwelling

Along current paths shown above, prevailing winds and the earth's rotation cause surface water to move away from the coast and be replaced by nutrient-rich water rising from the ocean depths. The upwellings make these waters especially fertile areas for concentrations of fish, but not so fertile that they cannot be depleted.

rican coast yielded more than a fifth of the world's total harvest of fish from the sea.

But in 1971 it became tragically clear that this resource was not endless. A combination of over-fishing and a shift in the Peru current, also known as the Humboldt, cut the anchovy population drastically.

By April of 1973, the Peruvian fishery was in deep trouble. At mid-year anchovy fishing was prohibited to preserve the species. By then only 1.8 million tons had been caught despite all the efforts of a huge fishing fleet. Much of the industry was near bankruptcy.

Some anchovy fishing was permitted again this year, but only on a tightly restrictive quota basis.

Fisheries experts in the United States aren't unanimously agreed on the main cause of this debacle. Some say it was primarily over-fishing. Some change in ocean conditions. Most agree it was a combination of these two factors.

In either case there is a lesson in the experience for a world growing desperate for increased sources of food: Even the vast abundance of the sea can be pushed too far.

The Pacific waters off Peru are usually an almost ideal incubator for anchovies because of something called ocean upwelling. This is caused by complex interaction between prevailing winds, currents and the effects of earth's rotation. Under this influence warm surface waters are blown away from a coast and replaced by an upwelling of cold nutrient-rich waters from the bottom.

The ocean's one-celled plants called phytoplankton thrive on these nutrients when they become available in sunlit waters near the surface.

Upwelling nourishes a complex and abundant food chain, but one that can be subject to perturbation. Changes in the prevailing winds can displace the coastal currents and either disperse the upwelling or shift it to places where its nutrients will be wasted. The offshore crop of phytoplankton fails. Much of the local food chain withers.

In terms of mankind's needs this can be important because there are only a few places on earth where major ocean upwelling occurs dependably. A publication of the National Science Foundation this year estimated that coastal upwelling, occurring in only about one-tenth of 1 per cent of the area of our planet's oceans, yields a good deal more than half of the world's total fish catch.

The principal regions thus favored are waters off the coast of California, off Peru, northwestern and southwestern Africa, along the path of current from East Africa past the southern tip of Arabia. There are also important areas of upwelling in the Antarctic and at midocean spots along the equator, according to the National Science Foundation.

Most of the upwelling areas are already being thoroughly fished today. One that still seems to have great untapped potential is the fertile region of ocean around the Antarctic continent. For more than a century, ships have gone to these icy and dangerous waters for whales — and in recent years have brought most species of these huge sea mammals into danger of extinction.

While some whales are the biggest animals that ever lived, the new interest in the Antarctic waters focuses on animals that are among the smallest. These are little shrimp-like creatures called krill. Dr. William F. Royce, associate director for resource research of the National Marine Fisheries Service estimates it might be possible to harvest 50 to 100 million tons of krill a year from the Antarctic — if anyone knew how to use them effectively.

The Soviet Union has been trying to develop a home market for krill, according to other experts at the fisheries service, offering pure frozen krill for salads, making a paste from it for use with butter and cheese. It is still too early to tell how popular these products will be.

In any case, krill are widely believed to be the ocean's main untapped food resource.

Most of man's effort to gather food from the sea is essentially hunting — whether this be gathering clams by hand or capturing whole schools of ocean fish with huge power-driven purse seines.

In recent years there has also been increasing interest in sea food production of a kind more akin to agriculture on land. The general name for it is aquaculture. It has been practiced in various times and places for thousands of years. These efforts to produce fish and shellfish under controlled conditions give the world some four-to-five million tons of sea-food a year, and the U.N.'s Food and Agriculture Organization has estimated that the total might be increased several fold.

Oysters are produced in large quantity under these semi-domesticated conditions in Japan, the United States and elsewhere. Milkfish are raised for food in brackish ponds and enclosures in many parts of Southeast Asia. Large quantities of mussels are raised in Spain and Portugal. The United States is the world's biggest producer of hatchery-bred trout.

Culture of many other species is under study for early commercial developments here and elsewhere — including shrimp, salmon, scallops and abalone.

For the United States particularly shrimp cultivation could be a major asset, according to Dr. Albert K. Sparks, a National Marine Fisheries Service expert in this field. He noted that the United States catches more shrimp than any other nation — but also eats more and, in fact, has been importing shrimp for more than a decade.

Nevertheless, shrimp growing and most of the other newly developed forms of aquaculture still have a substantial way to go in research and development before they can make much impact on total food supply. In this country particularly such efforts seem more likely to develop further supplies of essentially high cost foods than low cost, mass-produced items that might make a difference to the most drastically food-poor regions of the world.

In fisheries in general, the position of the United States is a tangle of paradoxes. While many American fisheries remain static or are actually in decline, the United States is the world's largest importer of food from the sea. Americans eat only a modest amount of sea food directly — about 12½ pounds for each person every year, but agriculture uses huge quantity of fish products for animal feed and for many industrial uses.

A draft outline of a national fisheries plan now being circulated among Government and other specialists, notes that American total consumption of food-fish products increased from about three billion to seven billion pounds a year between 1948 and 1973. The total per year is expected to rise by three billion pounds more during the next decade.

Roland Finch, a National Marine Fisheries officer who has played a major role in developing the draft plan, said most of the increase during the last quarter of a century has been provided by imports.

It seems clear that the nations of the world are becoming more and more interested in the seas as a major source of food and other needs. As the pressure increases on those resources, food from the sea may increasingly become a source of dispute as well as nourishment for mankind.

Philip M. Roedel of N.O.A.A. said there is recent evidence that nations with extensive coastlines, but no present capacity for commercial fishing, may be interested in leasing off-shore fishing rights to one or another of the major fishing nations.

This potential trend together with recent tragic experiences in the over-fishing of some important food sources, suggests a new era. In this, food from the sea may be more diligently sought than ever before — but also more carefully exploited so that these major resources are kept alive and forever renewable.

5 SEARCHING FOR SOLUTIONS

Wide World Photos

Dr. Norman E. Borlaug

OYCE RENSBERGER | # Down-to-Earth Science

El Batán, Mexico

High on the central Mexican plateau, not far from the village of Chapingo where Norman Borlaug's experimental breeding of high-yielding wheat varieties inaugurated the Green Revolution 30 years ago, stands one of the most crucial research programs in the world.

In a complex of modern buildings surrounded by 160 acres of experimental fields, three dozen agricultural scientists and scores of technicians, most from poor countries, are engaged in a major campaign to feed adequately the nearly two billion people who depend on wheat, corn and related crops for life.

By crossing different varieties of a plant species to combine desirable traits, such as disease resistance and richer protein content, scientists at the International Maize [corn] and Wheat Improvement Center here have produced several new varieties that, if widely adopted, could fill present gaps between food production and demand around the world.

The scientists also estimate that through further plant breeding to build into crops inherited resistance to diseases, insects and drought, it should be possible in coming years to double the global yields of food. They believe it is possible to increase food production in step with the population explosion for perhaps another 30 years.

Such new varieties would also reduce the need for expensive pesticides, irrigation and good land that has largely prevented the benefits of the Green Revolution from filtering down to the poorest farmers.

197

The present drive to increase food production is being pursued with at least as much urgency as motivated the effort 30 years ago when Mexico faced the prospect of famine. In 1943, at the request of the Mexican Government, the Rockefeller Foundation began a program to make the country self-sufficient in food.

A year later Dr. Borlaug, who went on to win the 1970 Nobel Peace Prize for his work, was brought in to develop higher yielding varieties of wheat.

By 1956 the program had succeeded. With better seed and fertilizer, wheat fields that a decade earlier were yielding 6 to 10 bushels an acre gave 50 to 60. Mexico grew all the food it needed and the varieties Dr. Borlaug developed had begun to find their way into fields around the world, beginning what came to be called the Green Revolution. Dr. Borlaug's techniques and strategies were subsequently applied to corn and rice with equal success.

In those three decades the researchers, first at Chapingo and now at CIMMYT (the internationally known acronym from the center's name in Spanish: Centro Internacional de Mejoramiento de Maiz y Trigo) in El Batán have played a major role in doubling world food production.

During those same years, however, world population has also virtually doubled, prompting one of the scientists to comment, "We've been running hard for 30 years and we're still at the starting line."

Because of the population increase, the track is now longer than ever. As a result, the research effort that began on a shoestring budget — at first so slim that Dr. Borlaug had to yoke himself into a harness to pull the plow over experimental fields — has now grown into a major international program supported by more than a dozen countries, private foundations and international agencies.

The same donors, organized into an informal "consultative group," sponsor seven other independent but cooperating international agricultural research centers. They are in the Philippines, Nigeria, Colombia, India, Kenya, Peru and Ethiopia. CIMMYT, 30 miles northeast of Mexico City, is the largest.

Still, as major research programs go, CIMMYT is a lean and independent outfit, oriented sharply toward studies with obvious practical usefulness and chary of too much paperwork, bureaucracy or political affiliation.

"If we ever get into the 'publish or perish' game around here," said Dr. Borlaug, whose no-nonsense operating style characterizes much of the center, "we're dead as far as being able to put food into people's bellies is concerned."

At the heart of CIMMYT's program is plant breeding, the fundamental technique that has led to nearly all the increased yields scored by crops everywhere.

In concept, it amounts to man taking control of natural selection and becoming the guiding force that favors the evolution and increase of whatever new varieties of food plants are deemed to be more useful.

In practice it is backbreaking, tedious labor and, under the burning Mexican sun, it is hot work. In the early days Dr. Borlaug and the other top scientists did it themselves, starting by squatting on short stools in the fields to pluck out with tweezers the tiny male anthers from bisexual wheat flowers before they could produce pollen.

A paper envelope, bearing a catalog number, would be placed over each emasculated spike of flowers to prevent stray pollens from fertilizing the remaining female organs.

Then, days later when the spike had matured, the scientists would return with freshly cut, pollen laden spikes from a different variety of wheat chosen to be the male parent of the new variety. The envelope would be cut open and the spike twirled inside it to pollinate the female parent.

The envelope would be folded over and paper-clipped shut to allow the fertilization and development of new seeds combining the heredity of two different parents.

Each step would have to be repeated thousands of times each season, for chance alone governs which genes from one parent might combine with another. Of thousands of crosses perhaps only a dozen or two would result in desirable new combinations of parental traits.

Today this same procedure is repeated tens of thousands of times over each year at CIMMYT's eight experimental fields in various climatic zones around Mexico.

Now the work, still the same hand operation, is not done by senior scientists but by dozens of Mexican technicians and trainees from many developing countries. The trainees come to CIMMYT each year to learn the methods they can take back to their own countries for use in developing crop varieties adapted to their own soils, climates and plant diseases.

The top scientists, such as Dr. Borlaug and Dr. Ernest W. Sprague, who heads the corn research program, devote more of their time these days to CIMMYT's effort to spread the benefits of a continuing Green Revolution around the world.

In consulting with agricultural experiment stations throughout the world and meeting with government officials in the poor countries to urge more support and better policies to develop local agriculture, Dr. Borlaug and Dr. Sprague spend most of their time shuttling about the world.

During May, June and July of 1974, for example, Dr. Sprague spent only 10 days in Mexico, his home. His itinerary for those months began in Mexico City and went on to Kenya, Tanzania, Nigeria, Ghana, the United States, Canada, Guatemala, back to Mexico, on to Egypt, Pakistan, Kenya again, Zaire, Nigeria again, and finally to Yugoslavia.

"This food problem is a world problem," Dr. Borlaug said. "We can't just sit here in Mexico and expect it to go away. These varieties we develop have to grow in farmers' fields before they'll feed anybody. And if the farmer in Bangladesh or in Tanzania or Colombia doesn't know about them or can't get the money to buy the fertilizer, we might as well close up shop here. If that small farmer can't sell his one bag of grain because the local market is set up to buy it by the ton, what good is it to him?"

Thus, Dr. Borlaug said, it has fallen to agricultural scientists like himself and Dr. Sprague to go to developing countries to lend their advice, expertise and what Dr. Borlaug calls "a little blunt talk where it'll do some good."

Because of CIMMYT's political independence — it is chartered by the Mexican Government and financed by private and public money from 10 other countries — the center's scientists usually have little difficulty in approaching governments of any political stripe.

Despite tensions between India and Pakistan, two of the most food-critical countries. Dr. Borlaug shuttles easily between the two capitals, meeting with agriculture ministers

Dr. Carlos De Leon, a plant pathologist at the international center at El Batán, Mexico, injecting disease organisms into corn to test its resistance.

and other officials to encourage policies that spur more food production.

Because of their global travels and the need to tailor new varieties of crops to the different local climates on four continents, CIMMYT scientists have developed a kind of horizontal consciousness about the planet and its food-growing potentials.

It is said, with not too great exaggeration, that Dr. Borlaug has seen every wheat field in the world. Certainly he visits all the major ones outside the Soviet Union and China each year.

"Wheat talks to Norm," one of his colleagues says, "He just walks into a field, feels a few leaves and looks at the heads of grain and he can tell you pretty accurately what the yield is going to be and what the problems are."

Because their job is, in the end, feeding people, CIMMYT scientists have come to know the food preferences and habits of peoples all over the world. They know, for example, that in Ethiopia and almost nowhere else many people eat a grain called teff. They know it is eaten because it is about the only thing that will grow in the poor soil and arid climate of much of Ethiopia. And they know that it is difficult for most teff eaters to get adequate nutrition from it.

While a new high-yielding CIMMYT variety of wheat may be ideal for irrigated fields in the Punjab of India, or a new race of dwarf corn may be best suited to the intense sunlight of mountain plateaus in Ecuador, and while both varieties may, with some local breeding, be adapted to many other places, neither will grow in the teff areas of Ethiopia.

"Can we tell people they're out of luck because they happen to eat a strange thing called teff and not good old wheat or corn," Dr. Donald D. Winkelman, CIMMYT's economist, asked rhetorically. "As it happens, one thing that might just be ideal for teff eaters is triticale."

Triticale is a relatively new kind of cereal grain, developed at CIMMYT by crossing wheat with rye. It combines the high yield of wheat with the drought and disease resistance of rye.

Before Ethiopian farmers can try it, however, that country must establish a program for testing triticale's potential by growing it in Ethiopian experimental fields. Local diseases may affect it, making necessary a few further steps in plant breeding to find individual plants that have genetic resistance.

Such final stages of plant breeding, sometimes called finishing, are generally best done in the region where the crop is to be grown. For that reason, one of CIMMYT's goals is to encourage developing countries to establish their own domestic plant-breeding programs.

Such national programs are not only scientifically useful; they offer many political and cultural advantages to the wide adoption of a new variety. It is CIMMYT's policy not to develop a new crop variety to the stage where it can be released to farmers but to stop short of the final steps.

The unfinished varieties are given to any national breeding programs that are interested in them for finishing and release. In this way, the new varieties are given local names and come to farmers as the product of and with the backing of their own country's research.

One particularly successful variety of wheat, known to CIMMYT as 8156, has been finished in many national programs and released to farmers around the world under more than 30 different local names.

Before a new crop variety is turned over to national programs, it must pass muster in the biochemical and industrial quality laboratories of Dr. Evangelina Villegas. Her responsibility is to determine the protein content and quality of a variety and to test its suitability for making bread, tortillas, chapatis, spaghetti or any other food typical of the region for which the variety is intended.

In addition to standard biochemical laboratories, CIMMYT has miniature flour mills, spaghetti makers, ovens and other equipment. It also has standard testing equipment used in the baking industry to determine such things as mixing times and stickiness of the dough.

Dr. Villegas said that if a new variety of wheat required bakers to modify their equipment or procedures too much to produce an acceptable bread, it was sometimes easier to go back to the plant breeders to change the characteristics of the variety than to get the bakers to alter their methods.

VICTOR K. MCELHENY

Rice and the Green Revolution

Los Baños, Philippines: The Poor Didn't Get Poorer

Studies in half a dozen Asian countries show that the introduction of revolutionary high-yielding rice varieties is not making the rich richer and the poor poorer, as many social scientists had predicted it would.

The predictions had been that high-yield wheat and rice would favor mechanization of farms, drive labor off the land, concentrate land holdings and generally heighten social and economic inequities in the countryside.

However, studies summarized in Sept., 1974 at the International Rice Research Institute here show that the green revolution, which has spread the new varieties through much of Asia since 1966, has exerted little pressure toward enlarging or mechanizing farms.

The survey, conducted in 1971-72 by 30 social scientists from research centers and universities in Pakistan, India, Thailand, Malaysia, Indonesia and the Philippines, covered 2,400 farms in more than 30 villages in those countries.

According to Randolph Barker and Teresa Anden of the institute's department of agricultural economics, the survey found that the size of farms and the form of tenure had "not changed dramatically since the introduction of the modern varieties."

Furthermore, although more machinery, fertilizers and pesticides were used as output and income grew, over half the farms adopting the new technology used more hired labor from within the village, 40 per cent used more family labor and 30 per cent hired extra labor from outside the village.

"The villages where labor-saving technology had been most widely adopted since the introduction of modern varieties also reported the largest number of farmers with increased employment of family and hired labor," the summary asserted. "Thus, any savings in labor appear to have been more than offset by labor requirements due to the new technology."

Recent estimates are that the new varieties of rice are planted on 40 million to 50 million acres in Asian nations outside China — about 20 per cent of the region's rice land. New wheat varieties have spread even further, to an estimated 30 per cent of the region's wheat acreage.

Whether this adoption of the new varieties, in less than a decade, constitutes success is vigorously disputed. The agricultural technologists who developed the new varieties stress that the rapid spread of the new grain types shows that Asian farmers are eager to adopt higher-yielding grains.

Many other observers say that adoption or proper cultivation of the new varieties has been hindered by ancient social inequalities, which are proving difficult to overcome. They say that glowing predictions in the late nineteen-sixties of rapid movement in Asia toward self-sufficiency in food or even oversupply have proven false.

Such developers of the new varieties as Dr. Robert Chandler, the founding director of the International Rice Research Institute, stick to their opinion that the potential exists to double rice yields in Asia.

Clouding the forecasts is a sharp rise in the price of fertilizer, along with severe shortages in Asia. There are some reports of farmers reverting to traditional varieties for lack of fertilizer.

Interviewed at the Asian Vegetable Research and Development Center in Tainan, Taiwan, which he now heads, Dr. Chandler questioned whether the fertilizer shortage would cut rice yields as drastically as some now fear. He noted that rice varieties more resistant to insects and diseases than earlier modern types, now being planted widely, should give good yields even with low levels of fertilizer.

The surveys summarized at Los Baños were performed before the fertilizer shortage and focused on a point separate from the total spread of the new varieties. The social scientists went to villages where the green revolution would be most likely to take hold and where any social damage would be most likely to be visible. The results of their multi-nation survey differed from reports of increased social disparities made earlier in specific locations, such as the wheat-growing region of the Punjab in India.

Dr. Robert Herdt of the agricultural economics department said the survey was being followed by a much more detailed inquiry into the factors that prevent farmers from getting high yields from the improved varieties. The deterrents include deficient irrigation and shortages of fertilizer and pesticides and of agricultural credit.

The new varieties, short-strawed types that perform best

World Rice Acreage
Total: 330,000,000

N. KOREA 1,700,000
CHINA 85,000,000
JAPAN 6,750,000
NEPAL 3,000,000
BURMA 12,500,000
S. KOREA 3,000,000
LAOS 1,750,000
TAIWAN 2,000,000
INDIA 92,500,000
PAKISTAN 3,750,000
N. VIET. 6,000,000
BANGLADESH 24,000,000
S. VIET. 6,250,000
PHILIPPINES 8,000,000
THAILAND 17,000,000
MALAYSIA 1,700,000
SRI LANKA 1,500,000
CAMBODIA 4,500,000
INDONESIA 20,500,000
AUSTRALIA 100,000

Rice Acreages Outside Asia	
U.S.	1,850,000
BRAZIL	13,000,000
REST OF LATIN AMERICA	3,250,000
AFRICA	10,000,000
EUROPE	800,000

Source: International Rice Research Institute

with high levels of fertilizer and generous irrigation, were largely developed from strains bred at the International Rice Research Institute.

The new varieties are said to have added more than 20 million tons annually to the food supply of South and Southeast Asia, which is the yearly rice intake of 100 million people.

Rice yields have been increased from 1,200 pounds an acre to perhaps 2,500 pounds, though this is still less than half of what is regularly achieved at agricultural experiment stations.

Because the study was looking for effects of the green revolution, it focused on villages that were ready for change. They tended to be more prosperous than average and to have become accustomed to fertilizers and pesticides and, in some cases, machinery.

Dr. Herdt said in an interview: "These are not typical of the situation in Asia at all. These are very advanced villages." Because of this, he noted, the villages could be expected to show the effects of the green revolution early and indicate any social hazards.

The survey was performed at a time when many of the farmers were shifting from a first generation of scientifically tailored rice strains toward even more advanced varieties with wide resistance to insects and diseases.

Varieties with even wider ranges of resistance, with even stiffer straw — the straw keeps the plant erect — and built-in adaptation to special conditions, such as the deep water of Bangladesh and Thailand and the cold of Korea, are emerging from the institute.

The farmers surveyed planted the first-generation modern types during the dry season, when insects and disease reduce yields less than during the rainy season. They told interviewers that insect and disease problems were the chief drawbacks of the types then available.

The survey found new rice varieties being planted on farms whose size varied from less than two acres in Indonesia to nearly 20 acres in Thailand and Pakistan. The new types found favor in villages where farm sizes were disparate, where cultivators were diverse and where either machines or animals provided most of the motive power for plowing. The reliability and completeness of the irrigation systems varied greatly, and the new varieties were often planted with little or no fertilizer.

The Miracle Strains

While the one-third of mankind that lives on rice struggles desperately to grow enough food, scientists in Asia remain confident that harvests can increase faster than the needs of a rice-dependent population that is expected to double by the year 2000.

Their confidence is based on a revolution in rice-growing techniques that continues to spread in Asia, offering what the scientists see as the only pathway of escape from an agriculture of mere survival.

Many observers of the rice-growing tropics dispute this optimism. They focus on widespread hunger today, after years of so-called green revolution, and foresee a continuing threat of famine in regions where agriculture is racing against the greatest population explosion in history. They doubt that problems of landholding, credit marketing, and poor farming practices can be overcome quickly enough to win the race.

They say that the revolution in rice-production methods — based on new rice types genetically designed for high yields — has failed to overcome a host of social and physical obstacles and has hardly kept ahead of population growth. On top of all the other problems, in this view, the green revolution is stalled by a fertilizer shortage linked to the energy crisis.

But the scientists who continue to breed new rice types are confident that the door has been opened to a time when rice yields can increase faster than they did in the first 10 years of the green revolution — when the new types of rice and wheat were all that stood between Asia and declines in per capita production.

The scientists say their confidence does not rest on the first generation of "miracle rices" introduced in 1965 and long since supplanted. Many Asians found the stubby, chalky grains less attractive to eat than traditional varieties. The

densely packed fields of short-strawed rice frequently fell
victim to insects and diseases, particularly in the rainy season.

In response to such problems, scientific institutions here in
Hyderabad and across Asia have made improvements by:
• Armoring the new rice types genetically against an ever-
widening range of pests, reducing risks and costs for farmers.
• Finding ways to grow the fertilizer-responsive dwarf rice
varieties with as little as a third of the previously recommended amounts of fertilizer.
• Developing varieties able to grow in cool seasons or to
stand long immersion in deep water.
• Making practical demonstrations on farms of methods for
growing the new rice types outside the irrigated zone to
which many thought they were restricted.

Because of this situation, the rice scientists see little reasons
for the pessimism and expect a real green revolution to continue many years into the future.

Although so far this revolution has disappointed the hopes
of its most ardent exponents, it has begun transforming the
most tradition-bound and labor-intensive agriculture on
earth.

The scientifically redesigned rice plants are short and densely packed into what look like overgrown lawns. From
Pakistan to the Philippines, they have been displacing the tall,
bushy rice stalks that sustained dense populations for many
centuries amid the undependable monsoon rains of Asia.

According to American agricultural scientists who visited
China in Oct., 1974, similar dwarf varieties are being used in
much of that nation.

On the 40 million acres outside Communist countries on
which they are being used, the new rice varieties have increased yields from the world average of 1,300 pounds of
milled rice an acre to between 1,700 and 2,100 pounds.

The increased yield from the shortened rice varieties is estimated to provide the annual rice intake of 40 million to 80
million people in non-Communist Asia and perhaps 17 million to 35 million more in China.

Because Asia's rice area has increased little in the last 10
years, most of the slow overall increases in Asian rice production are attributed to the new varieties.

The scientists who have been breeding the new rice types, at such places as the 10-year-old All-India Coordinated Rice Improvement Project here or the 13-year-old International Rice Research Institute in the Philippines, acknowledge that they are struggling with strong physical and social obstacles.

The obstacles, ranging from fragmentation of landholdings and shortages of credit to floods and droughts, have brought hunger in 1974 to millions of people in Indian states of Bihar, West Bengal and Orissa.

Critics of the green revolution see other obstacles growing worse in the future. For example, they point to deficiencies in phosphorus and zinc showing up in the fields of the Indian Punjab after nearly a decade of heavy fertilization with nitrogen and frequent double-cropping with new varieties of wheat and rice.

Irrigation water is another problem. There is doubt about how rapidly the investment funds can be found to dig millions of wells in Asia, or how oil-short nations such as India will be able to obtain fuel to run the pumps. There is concern about the long-term effects of uncontrolled well-digging on the total supply of ground water.

But scientists such as Dr. Robert Chandler, founder of the rice institute in the Philippines, or Dr. S. V. S. Shastry, director of the All-India project, believe that the average yield of 3,500 pounds an acre achieved by rice farmers on Taiwan, where virtually all rice acreage is planted in new varieties, is a reasonable goal for all Asia.

About 3,000 pounds an acre would be needed in the year 2000 to feed twice as many rice-dependent people as there are today.

Dr. Chandler wrote early in 1974: "Those who take a more gloomy view of the future should consider the relatively short time during which the new technology has been available and the fact that it is still actively being improved."

"Rice yields are so low now that there is much room for improvement," he added. "I believe it is entirely possible to double average rice yields in South and Southeast Asia within the next two decades."

As for India, Dr. Shastry and his colleague, Dr. D. V. Seshu, estimate that by the year 2000 rice production must double, from 1,000 to 2,000 pounds an acre.

Such confidence is unusual in the thousands of years since Asian farmers began cultivating rice.

In their book "Campaigns Against Hunger," Drs. E. C. Stakman, Richard Bradfield and Paul C. Mangelsdorf added: "In no other region has a single crop plant been cultivated so long and continuously on the same land and its yields maintained at such a high level when the farmers' sole reliance was the simple resources available on their own farms."

And yet, the three scientists noted, the rice farmers often obtained, after backbreaking labor, an amount of rice "scarcely enough to keep body and soul together."

The labor included planting rice seeds close together in seedbeds, so that the seedlings could get a protected start in competition with weeds, and then, after three weeks or more, transplanting the seedlings into flooded paddies at about 28 times the spacing of the seedbed. The flooding of the paddies at the time of maximum monsoon rainfall kept down the growth of weeds. For a good crop, later weeds would have to be pulled out by hand.

Harvesting the rice stalks, with sickles or tiny knives attached to a finger, threshing the grain from the stalks, or drying the grain on the ground, were all laborious and lengthy tasks, performed under constant threat of interruptions and spoilage from untimely rain.

According to the International Rice Research Institute, some 1.3 billion people — nearly all in the tropics and nearly all poor — obtain more than 50 per cent of their food energy from rice. Another 400 million are estimated to receive between a quarter and half their food energy from rice.

The continuing struggle for adequate rice supplies might seem remote from the billion inhabitants of rich nations in the world's temperate zones. The people of these nations prefer wheat for themselves and corn for their animals.

Furthermore, rice is a heavy-footed crop compared with wheat. Very little rice is sent more than a few miles from the fields where it is grown. For example, only about 7 million tons, or 3.2 per cent of the world's estimated 1973-74 crop

The Rockefeller Foundation

In the traditional manner, a Filipino farmer uses a water buffalo to prepare a rice paddy for planting.

of 220 million tons of milled rice was traded internationally. Most of the exported rice came from three countries, the United States, Thailand and China.

Of the world wheat crop, estimated by the United States Department of Agriculture at 390 million tons, some 20 per cent, or 78 million tons, was traded between nations.

Yet, because much wheat is eaten in rich countries and most corn is eaten by animals, rice constitutes the biggest single factor in the continuing world crisis in human food supplies.

Because so little rice is available for trade at a distance from the farm, shortages of rice in a wide area are more threatening than wheat shortages.

The world rice situation has been particularly acute since drought struck wide areas of Asia in 1972, erasing such rice reserves as existed and driving the world price to $600 a ton, or 30 cents a pound.

The same drought, leading to huge Soviet purchases of grain, reduced reserves of grain to their lowest levels since World War II and, for the first time in 20 years, drove food prices up faster than other prices. Food became a leader instead of a follower of world inflation. Food shortages in poor countries affected the income of people in rich nations.

Continued food shortages in poor nations could continue to fuel inflation worldwide because rice-eating nations are experiencing their greatest population explosion in history.

Of the increase of more than 60 million each year in the population of underdeveloped nations, compared with only 12 million in rich nations, more than half occurs in the eight largest underdeveloped nations where rice is the staple.

In 1974 new varieties of rice covered about 20 per cent of the rice acreage of Asia, and the acreage has continued to increase at the rate of 20 per cent a year, according to estimates made by Dana G. Dalrymple of the Economic Research Service of the Department of Agriculture. Yet the effect on over-all production has hardly kept rice output much ahead of Asian population growth.

Indications are that Indian rice production, in the seven years ending in 1972, rose somewhat less than 20 per cent, to a total of 46 million tons of milled rice. Production dropped during the 1972 drought and returned to the former level in 1973. This figure has a major effect on the entire Asian picture, since an estimated 55 per cent of the acreage in non-Communist Asia that is devoted to new rice types is in India.

But India has an even larger proportion of the new wheat acreage, 60 per cent. The spread of the dwarf wheat varieties, first developed in Mexico under a program that began in 1944, was so fast that Indian production of wheat rose in the seven years ending in 1972 from 11 million to 26 million tons.

Because of such trends, wheat has become a far more important factor in the food economies of countries traditionally identified with rice than it was a few years ago. In India, wheat surpluses of millions of tons each year, from the northern states of Punjab, Haryana and Uttar Pradesh, have become mainstays of the nation's distribution of grain in ration shops.

Architects of the green revolution such as Dr. Chandler point to a new government support for increased rice production, such as the support by President Ferdinand E. Marcos of a major effort involving a third of the Philippines rice acreage.

Optimists are also encouraged by a related development in the Philippines, where farmers with unirrigated paddies are growing two crops a year instead of one. To do this in two provinces of Central Luzon, farmers have begun using short-season varieties developed at the International Rice Research Institute.

Because a cheap weed-killing chemical is now available, the rice farmers can direct-seed their crop at the start of the rainy season in May, instead of waiting until the traditional peak of the rains in late summer. The farmers can harvest their first crop by September and then immediately transplant their second crop for harvest in December — the time most farmers gathered their traditional single crop.

This success is considered significant, because about 80 per cent of some 300 million acres of rice land in Asia is not irrigated.

Scientists who helped develop the green revolution varieties of rice see further cause for optimism in the development of numerous systems for growing other crops on rice land, both to restore the fertility of the soil and improve the protein content of the farm family's diet.

Soybeans, planted in southern Taiwan right next to the stalks of harvested rice plants, not only add nitrogen fertilizer to the soil but also provide additional sources of protein, and cash.

These scientists note that the highly productive agriculture of Taiwan is carried on with little mechanization. Furthermore, studies of villages across South and Southeast Asia where new rice types were adopted early show that the chief effect of the green revolution so far has been to increase demand for both family and hired labor.

But these facts are regarded as signs that spread of the new varieties to new land, along with bigger yields from each acre, could hold labor in the countryside rather than drive it away, as some had predicted it would.

A center for research on diet-varying vegetable crops such as soybeans and tomatoes has been established on Taiwan, with Dr. Chandler as its first director.

Interviewed at the center, Dr. Chandler foresaw important future opportunities for growing rice in areas where it is not common now and eliminating rice from areas where its cultivation is extremely difficult.

Dr. Chandler said that large areas, particularly in Latin America, could be converted to rice from less nutritious crops, such as the cassava root.

"If you want to look at malnutrition, look at the people trying to live off cassava," he said. "You see pitiful, pitiful cases. They could be eating rice."

Among the marginal rice-growing regions Dr. Chandler has visited is the Sambalpur district of the Indian state of Orissa, which he called "the sorriest country I ever saw."

"It was pitiful to see the poor farmers out in the field," he said. "You could see their knee joints."

Farmers in such country would do better with such dryland crops as mung beans and soybeans, studied at the vegetable center on Taiwan, or the sorghums, millets, pigeon peas and cowpeas, all the subjects of research at a newly established international center for dryland agriculture here in Hyderabad.

Such developments would fit in with the goal that agricultural scientists increasingly are advocating for developing nations: meeting an increasing share of their food needs from domestic sources rather than depending on limited surpluses from rich nations.

JANE E. BRODY | # The Quest for Protein

No Lack of Strategies

Scientists are juggling plant genes, squeezing juice out of leaves and growing microorganisms on manure in a wide-ranging assault on one of the most fundamental problems of the world's food shortage — how to get more protein for more people.

The push for protein is a major part of the worldwide effort to fight the growing specter of hunger aggravated in recent years by unbridled population growth in already food-poor countries, crop failures caused by droughts and floods, fertilizer shortages and the energy crunch.

As a result, malnutrition is now epidemic in many countries. Experts estimate that nearly a third of the world's people are suffering from hunger and its consequences and that the diets of half the world's children lack adequate protein, the nutrient most essential to proper physical and mental development.

While carbohydrates and fats are most important as energy sources, protein is the core substance of the body's vital organs, including the brain. If a child's diet lacks sufficient protein during critical growth periods, body and mind may be permanently stunted. In adults, protein deficits prevent the proper rebuilding of body tissues.

Protein deficiency also increases susceptibility to infections which, combined with the stress of malnutrition, is the main cause of death among young children in developing countries.

Thus, in laboratories and farm fields throughout the world, scientists from government, industry and the universities are seeking to improve the protein quantity and quality of conventional foods as well as to develop novel sources of protein nutrition.

The approaches, besides extracting protein from leaves, using protein-rich wastes and breeding crops with more and better protein, include fortifying traditional foods and developing new foods from under-utilized proteins.

The United States, the world's major breadbasket, is the leading center for this research and the main source of funds for projects abroad. But the effort is worldwide, with considerable work under way in such industrialized countries as Japan, Scandinavia and England and at internationally supported research centers in Mexico, the Philippines, India, Nigeria and other developing areas.

Proteins (from the Greek for first or primary) are constructed out of about 20 different chemical building blocks called amino acids, all of which contain nitrogen. The human body is able to manufacture 12 of these amino acids from various sources of dietary nitrogen — proteins or parts of proteins that the body digests into molecules called amino groups.

But the remaining eight building blocks, called essential amino acids, cannot be made by human beings and must be supplied as such in the diet. In addition, in order for the body to make the proteins it needs, all the essential amino acids must be consumed in balanced amounts at approximately the same time.

The most balanced proteins (that is, those that supply all eight essential amino acids in adequate amounts) come from animals — meat, fish and dairy products — but they provide less than a third of the world's protein.

Plants, which supply about 80 per cent of the protein for people in developing countries, are normally deficient in one or another essential amino acid. In order to obtain usable protein from vegetarian sources then, two different kinds of plant proteins that make up for each other's deficiencies — say, cereals and beans — must be eaten in the same meal.

Most of the current research has centered on plant proteins, which have the potential of adequately nourishing more people at less cost than meat proteins.

For a steer in this country to produce one pound of beef requires the average consumption over its lifetime of four to five pounds of grain. The pound of beef could provide protein for two persons a day, but the grain the animal consumed to produce that meat could theoretically feed four.

Despite all the research, science has not yet had significant impact on the world's protein deficiency. The complexities of the problems are such that new protein foods can take years, even decades, to move from the laboratory bench to the mouths of the hungry. Such factors as tastes, habits, incentives and price as well as the lack of technical and agricultural resources and adequate number of trained personnel all make for delay.

Nonetheless, the scientists are hopeful. Their efforts are founded on the premise that if the earth's resources were optimally used, it should be possible to provide adequate nutrition for the present world population and the more than six billion people who are expected to inhabit the earth in the year 2000.

A survey of scientific results to date has revealed a wide range of promising prospects — some that are now ready for application, others that need minor further development and many that will require years more research.

Plant breeders, who by increasing productivity of crops have thus far kept the world from mass starvation, are now re-engineering some of the most fundamental characteristics of plants to improve their protein yield and quality. Breeding for better protein is one of the key efforts in the current protein thrust and one that is most likely to pay off in the near future.

Plant breeding is the painstaking, prolonged and somewhat unpredictable task of attempting to change the genes of one kind of plant by crossing it with close relatives that contain the desired genetic characteristics.

Perhaps the best known success of plant breeding toward boosting the world's protein supply is the development of the so-called miracle seed of the Green Revolution. These were semidwarf varieties of wheat (an achievement for which Dr. Norman Borlaug received the Nobel Peace Prize in 1970) and rice that, when properly cultivated with adequate fertilizer and water, can double the yield of grain per acre.

But the grain of the green revolution is still deficient in certain essential amino acids, and the emphasis of most of the current breeding work is on improving the amino acid balance of cereal crops.

Twenty-eight years ago, when American grain elevators were bursting at the seams with excess grain, Dr. Edwin T. Mertz of Purdue University received a state grant "to figure out some way to use up all this surplus food in a nonfood manner." Since Dr. Mertz was a protein chemist, he began by studying the protein in corn.

Seventeen years later, this low-key effort led to an unexpected success — the discovery, with the plant geneticist Oliver E. Nelson (now at the University of Wisconsin), that certain varieties of corn contained twice as much of the amino acids lysine and tryptophan as are found in ordinary corn varieties.

Since these are the two deficient, or limiting, amino acids in corn, the discovery held the prospect of greatly improving the nutritive value of this grain, the principal staple in many countries of Latin America and Black Africa. Indeed, when young rats were raised on high-lysine corn, they grew nearly as well as rats raised on milk protein.

Piglets fed the new variety grew three and a half times faster than piglets fed ordinary corn. In fact, in Colombia a high-lysine corn diet was able to cure children of the severe protein deficiency disease, kwashiorkor, which they had developed from living on a diet of ordinary corn.

But the discovery of high-lysine corn was only the beginning. An incredible amount of work lay ahead to breed the high-lysine gene into otherwise successful native varieties without adversely affecting the desirable characteristics of those varieties.

The high-lysine gene changed the corn kernel from hard to soft, which affected milling characteristics. In addition, explained Dr. Loval (Pete) Bauman, who heads the breeding work at Purdue, the softer kernels were more susceptible to ear-rot and, because the kernels weighed less, the yield per acre was lower.

Ten years of "backcrossing" have virtually solved the ear-rot problem and yields are now up to 90 per cent of normal, Dr. Bauman said. In backcrossing, the original high-lysine corn was crossed with standard high-quality varieties. The resulting new high-lysine hybrid was then repeatedly crossed with the original standard variety to breed out unwanted genetic characteristics while preserving the high level of lysine.

In each area where corn is grown, the breeding work must be repeated with local varieties in order to preserve the disease resistance and other agronomic characteristics necessary in those regions. High-lysine corn is now being tested in many countries around the world, and American farmers grew some 200,000 acres of it last year for animal feed.

Purdue scientists have calculated that by eating only high-lysine corn plus a vitamin-mineral supplement, an adult could eat adequately on 10 cents a day.

As Dr. Mertz put it, the discovery of high-lysine corn "upset the apple cart of plant genetics," which had previously assumed that plant protein could not be changed by breeding. This inspired a search for better quality protein in other cereals.

Thus far, the search has paid off for barley, used mainly as animal feed in this country, but an important food grain for about 200 million of the world's disadvantaged people in Eastern and Northern Europe, the Mediterranean and Near East, India and the Andean countries of South America. A high-protein, high-lysine barley strain from Ethiopia was found in screening 1,000 varieties in the World Barley Collection in Beltsville, Md.

Similar success has been achieved for sorghum, the world's fourth most important grain (after wheat, rice and corn) on which some 300 million of the very poorest people in the developing countries of Africa, East Asia and India depend.

Sorghum grows in towering stands, with heavy heads of edible seeds — produced atop tall, thick stalks.

High-lysine sorghum was discovered last year at Purdue by

Drs. John D. Axtell, Dallas L. Oswalt and Rameshwar Singh. In six years of analyzing the protein of some 10,000 varieties of sorghum from all over the world under a grant from the Agency for International Development, the Purdue scientists found two varieties from Ethiopia that contain nearly a third more protein and twice as much lysine as other sorghum strains.

Tenant farmers of Ethiopia like to roast the nutty-flavored seeds of these two strains and eat them like nuts, Dr. Axtell discovered on a recent visit there. But only small amounts of these strains are grown because landlords, who get a share of what the farmer sells but not of what he eats, discourage their cultivation.

The varieties have been maintained largely because the tenant farmers plant them hidden in the middle of stands of other sorghum varieties so that landlords would be less likely to notice them, Dr. Axtell said.

Dr. Axtell, an enthusiastic but realistic scientist, estimates that a decade of work lies ahead to breed the high protein quality into native sorghums. Work is already under way toward this end in India, Lebanon and Mexico.

Once the scientists have completed their work, the task remains to convince farmers to grow the new varieties. "It's

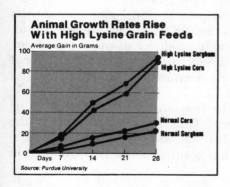

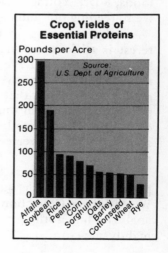

extremely difficult to get farmers to grow something you tell them is nutritionally superior when they've never even heard of nutrition," Dr. Axtell noted. "In Brazil, with high-lysine corn, they're telling farmers to feed it to their hogs. Once the farmers see how well the hogs thrive, it's easy to convince them that the corn is good for their children, too."

A push is also on now to increase the protein content of oats, which have an exceptionally good balance of amino acids and already contain more protein than most cereals, said Dr. Vernon Youngs, a chemist who heads the Agriculture Department's National Oat Quality Laboratory at the University of Wisconsin. Last year, his laboratory analyzed the protein in 28,000 oat samples sent in by breeders throughout the country.

Until now, oat breeding emphasized larger kernels — which gives farmers bigger yields — but larger kernels meant a lower percentage of protein, Dr. Youngs said.

As a result of the new emphasis on protein, two new oat varieties containing about 22 per cent protein have already been released. Their protein content compares to the 17 per cent average of the World Oat Collection and rivals that of meat, which ranges from 20 to 30 per cent.

"Right now, even though oats are such a good food, only 5 to 10 per cent of the U.S. production goes into human foods," Dr. Youngs remarked. "We'd like to change this. We're feeding our animals better than our people."

Another cereal grain that has attracted much research interest is triticale (pronounced trit-i-kaley), a man-made hybrid of wheat and rye that surpasses wheat — the world's main cereal — in both total protein and lysine content. Its main drawback is that its hybrid genes are somewhat unstable, making it an unreliable producer of quality seed, according to Dr. Kenneth Lebsock, an Agriculture Department scientist who is overseeing Government-sponsored work on triticale in India.

Wheat itself appears to be resistant to much change in its protein quantity or quality. Thus far, 15,000 lines in the World Wheat Collection, also housed in Beltsville, have been analyzed but nothing yet has come near the improvement in high-lysine corn.

However, steady progress has been made in developing hybrid wheat, which holds the promise of considerable increases in yield per acre. Scientists at Cargill Wheat Research Farms in Fort Collins, Colo., have just harvested their first crop of hybrid wheat, the seeds of which derived from two high-quality inbred lines.

Theoretically, according to the concept of hybrid vigor, the hybrid seed should produce a crop better than either of its parents. The achievement depends on the development of one line in which the male part of the plant is sterile, preventing self-pollination, and a second line containing fertility-restoring genes so that fertile seeds will result from a cross with the male-sterile plant.

Beans, which Americans look upon as a source of carbohydrate but which much of the world uses for protein, have also begun to attract the interest of plant breeders. Although higher in total protein content than the cereal grains and adequately endowed with lysine, most beans are deficient in other essential amino acids, mainly methionine and cysteine.

At the University of Ife in Nigeria, Dr. Frederick Bliss, a University of Wisconsin plant breeder, helped develop a high-protein (30 per cent) cowpea (also known as black-eyed or southern pea), an important protein source in many tropical and subtropical areas. According to what he calls his "skyscraper" philosophy, he is now trying to improve the productivity of the African pea, in part by changing it from a viney plant that grows along the ground to an upright one.

Dr. M. Wayne Adams at Michigan State University estimates that by changing the architecture of the field bean from a short bushy plant with lots of branches to a taller, nonbranching type that can produce the same number of pods in less space, the protein yield per acre could be increased by a third.

This season, Dr. Adams, who works under a grant from the Rockefeller Foundation, will examine "one by one" some 22,000 plants — the results of crosses he made last year — to select for those that grow tall and narrow.

Cross-pollinating bean plants is in itself an arduous, back-breaking task that requires the dissection and emasculation of flower buds one-sixteenth of an inch wide. Theodore Hymowitz, a plant geneticist at the University of Illinois, has enlisted bees to do the pollination for him. A table of soybean plants in a greenhouse is covered with a screened cage that is home for a hive of bees, whose diet of nectar and pollen from soybean flowers is supplemented with synthetic pollen. The result is thousands of hybrid seeds all year round, Dr. Hymowitz said.

He is seeking, among other things, to breed out some of the plant sugars that humans have difficulty digesting, resulting in the classic "gassiness" of beans. In the search for better soybeans, Dr. Hymowitz had been disturbed that no breeding material was available from the Chinese mainland, where the soybean originated. In Oct., 1974, however, American scientists returned from China with many native soybean seeds, including some wild soybeans, to test in American breeding programs.

Soybeans, with an average of 40 per cent protein (nearly twice that of most meats), contain more and better protein than any other edible plant. But like all beans, its yields are low compared to cereal crops such as corn and wheat, a fact that Richard Cooper, an Agriculture Department researcher in Urbana, Ill., is trying to change by developing a more efficient, semidwarf soybean plant.

As he explained it, when a lot of fertilizer is used to increase the yield of ordinary soybeans, they get so tall that they fall over, or "lodge," which diminishes yield. Using the approach that produced the greatly increased yields of miracle rice and wheat, Mr. Cooper has bred a 22-inch plant that produces as many beans per acre as the 44-inch plant. This year he has planted the short variety closer together to see if yields will increase.

Other scientists at the Regional Soybean Laboratory are trying to create soybeans that will bloom regardless of how long the day or night is, a characteristic that would allow the

The New York Times / Jane E. Brody

To increase the yield of highly nutritious soybeans, Richard Cooper has bred a 22-inch semi-dwarf plant that is more efficient than the traditional 44-inch variety.

soybean to spread into the food-short tropics. One such "day-neutral" variety is now being tested in Puerto Rico.

Rather than wait for desired genetic variants to occur naturally and, following their discovery, breed them into native crops, some scientists are attempting to induce genetic change in existing crops with radiation or chemicals. This approach, which has already succeeded in producing a high-lysine barley and a high-yielding semidwarf rice, can potentially save the plant breeder much time and effort.

Front Runner: The Humble Soybean

One of the greatest hopes in the drive to provide more and better protein for the peoples of the world is the soybean, a bitter-tasting legume that has been used by Asians for centuries as a major protein source.

It has only been in the last two decades that Western food technologists have sought to adapt this most nutritious of vegetable proteins to a wider range of tastes and dietary habits.

Scientists believe that the soybean can do much to resolve the pervasive problem of protein malnutrition, now rampant in developing countries. A protein-deficient diet can increase susceptibility to disease, permanently stunt the brains and bodies of young children and prevent the proper rebuilding of body tissues in adults.

Creating new, protein-rich foods from the old soybean is part of a multi-faceted effort to increase world supplies of this most essential major nutrient. In addition to breeding crops that contain more and better protein, research is also being directed toward fortifying foods with protein supplements, extracting protein from leaves and utilizing protein-rich wastes.

Much of the current popularity of the soybean, which recently surpassed wheat as a cash crop in this country, is due to its oil, a key factor in the fast-growing magarine and vegetable oil industry. Now, however, increasing interest is focusing on the protein-rich residue left in the bean after the oil is extracted.

Americans are already familiar with at least two products

of the worldwide soybean research effort — bacon-flavored bits and hamburger extender (also known as "textured vegetable protein"). Americans also consume breakfast foods, biscuits, breads, sausages and other foods that contain soybean meal.

While such products are currently designed primarily for the American market, the technology involved in their preparation could be readily applied to the creation of highly nutritious foods for protein-starved peoples with vastly different dietary habits and tastes. The price of soybeans is now at a new-record level, but they are still a much less costly protein source than meat.

Scientists anticipate that Americans will be among the hardest to please with novel sources of protein. General Mills, Inc., is currently test-marketing two soy protein meat analogues called "Country Cuts" — frozen, ready-to-eat cubes with the flavor and texture of chicken or ham.

Depsite the ready availability of the "real thing" in this country, General Mills expects the convenience, economy (a savings of 25 to 40 per cent over the meats they imitate) and lack of waste to attract considerable consumer interest.

In producing meat-like fibers from the "defatted" soybean flour with which General Mills starts, first the carbohydrates are removed and the remaining honey-like solution of pure protein is pumped through a "spinnerette" — a showerheadlike device with microscopic holes. As the protein emerges from the holes, it hits an acid bath that precipitates the protein as individual fibrils, which are neutralized and washed.

The resulting tasteless, odorless, off-white fibers are then mixed with flavorings, coloring, fat, water and egg albumin, which acts as a binder. A cooking process coagulates the mass into slabs three-eighths of an inch thick.

The "chewiness" can be varied by increasing or decreasing the stretch on the fibrils as they go through the spinnerette.

At the University of Illinois, food scientists have taken a different approach — using the whole soybean, oil and all. They have come up with a wide range of products, from cereal flakes to "milk" and "yogurt," and nearly all of them have been rated as very acceptable by taste panels. They have developed a simple, inexpensive processing method that skirts the soybean's limitations while taking full advantage of its virtues.

"Since most people who are deficient in protein also need more calories, using the whole bean — oil and all — makes better nutritional sense," said Dr. Marvin Steinberg, who directs the Illinois research.

If calories for energy are in short supply in the diet, the body — which normally uses sugar, starchy foods and fats for energy — burns protein for energy instead, leading to a "wasting" of consumed protein needed for building body tissues.

Previously, processors avoided the whole soybean because the oil imparts a characteristic "beany" or "painty" flavor that is difficult to mask and unacceptable to consumers outside the Orient. Dr. Steinberg found he could get rid of this flavor right at the start by heating the beans to inactivate the enzyme that causes it.

But the heat makes the soy protein insoluble, a limitation that Dr. Steinberg circumvents by "homogenizing" it with a miniature dairy homogenizer. His process also removes most of the gas-causing sugars, and he ends up with a high-protein material that has 90 per cent the nutritional value of milk protein.

As Dr. Steinberg and Drs. Lun-Shin Wei and Alvin Nelson downed a mid-morning snack of soy "milk," a visitor sampled some of their soy products. Soy flakes, mixed one-to-one with flakes of corn, rice or banana, tasted like what they were mixed with and did not get pasty when liquid was added.

A variety of canned goods in which soybeans were substituted for traditional navy beans — three-bean salad, pork and beans, for example — were indistinguishable from their traditional counterparts.

Homogenized soy beverages — 3.6 per cent protein (the same as milk) and 1.8 per cent fat (half that in milk) — were refreshing and good-tasting. The milk-flavored drink had a slight cereal-like flavor, the cream-flavored one tasted like melted soft ice cream and the chocolate drink was indistinguishable from chocolate milk.

The Illinois team has also turned the drinks into flavored yogurt, an ice cream-like dessert and a custard. Other prototype soy products they have developed include a whole soy bean diet margarine, soybean butter and a soy-rice snack.

Soybean beverages are already popular in several countries, where they compete successfully with bottled sodas. As Dr. Steinberg pointed out, the beauty of soy protein products is that their form and flavor can be tailored to the tastes of peoples with vastly different dietary habits.

Other oilseeds besides soybeans also lend themselves to the development of food analogues. Considerable research is now under way on cottonseed protein which, in addition to flour, can also be texturized to make a meat extender or other meat analogues. At Texas A & M University, Drs. Karl F. Mattil and Carl M. Cater are also working on converting peanuts, coconuts, sunflower seeds and sesame seeds into low-cost, high-protein foods.

A variety of areas in soybean research follows:

Fortifying Foods

Rather than improve the quantity and quality of protein in natural foods, some scientists have focused on adding substances that would boost nutritional value.

One approach, already widely used in mills and bakeries around the world and in certain nutritional programs in developing countries, is the use of combinations of flours or cereals, such as corn, soy and wheat, which compensate for each other's amino acid deficiencies. The formula for these composites can be adapted to the dietary customs of the region in which it is to be used. Thus, cassava, coconut, sorghum or other foods can be included.

Several of these fortified cereals have been used successfully to correct protein malnutrition in children.

Another, related approach is simply to add the missing amino acids to the food in question. Thus, artificial rice grains containing the two amino acids in which rice is deficient, lysine and threonine, can be added at the mill to ordinary rice. Lysine produced by the chemical industry can be added to cereal grains, and methionine added to beans to produce a more balanced protein.

The protein content of foods can also be improved by adding a balanced protein concentrate, such as fish flour prepared from species that are not ordinarily used for food. The National Marine Fisheries Service developed a process of producing an odorless, tasteless, off-white flour containing 90 per cent fish protein. This concentrate can be added to processed foods or baked into bread, cookies and crackers.

A Swedish company, Astra, which already produces fish flour for human consumption, is now studying ways to make fish protein concentrate into a form that could be fashioned like soybeans into meat analogues.

Protein from Leaves

Green leaves from grasses, plants and trees are the largest source of protein on earth. Although leaves from such crops as grass, alfalfa and corn supply most of the protein for livestock, they have been used only in very limited amounts in human diets. Anyone who has tasted a leaf, aside from conventional leafy vegetables, can readily tell why they are not popular foods: They lack palatability and they contain large amounts of fibers and other indigestible materials.

But science has found a way around such drawbacks. Rather than use the whole leaf, protein-containing juice is squeezed out and processed into protein concentrates. What remains behind still contains enough protein to make excellent animal foods.

Interest in leaf protein dates back to World War II when Britain, fearing that its food supply would be cut off by the Germans, enlisted N. W. Pirie, a biochemist, to figure out how to get edible protein out of leaves. Although never used to feed the British, the substances he developed led, among other things, to the use of leaf protein to treat malnourished children in India.

Most leaf protein workers have concentrated on alfalfa, although the same process is applicable to any kind of leaf, including pea vines, carrot tops, potato plants and other leaves that are currently just waste. In terms of protein quality and protein yield per acre, alfalfa surpasses all other crops, including the revered soybean.

In experiments at Michigan State University by Dr. J.

Robert Brunner, about 25 per cent of the plant's protein is collected by squeezing the fresh-cut alfalfa. The green juice is spun in a centrifuge to remove the chlorophyll-containing chloroplasts and the resulting amber-colored liquid is treated with acid or heat to precipitate a whitish protein concentrate. The final almost tasteless powder (it has just a hint of hay) can be spun into meat analogues or used as flour or a food fortifier, Dr. Brunner said.

At the University of Wisconsin, a 15-member team has developed pilot equipment for processing leaf protein. Part of their goal is to design a machine with the cost of a hay bailer for use on smaller farms. Among the advantages of extracting alfalfa, they say, is that it reduces losses encountered in drying hay in the field, the juiceless alfalfa makes high-quality silage, and the left-over juice can be used for fertilizer.

George O. Kohler, a scientist with the Agriculture Department, operates a pilot leaf protein processing plant at the Western Regional Research Laboratory in Berkeley, Calif., where farmers harvest seven crops of alfalfa a year. A further advantage of this approach, he said, is that it saves fuel used in plants that dehydrate the crop.

Dr. Kohler said commercial interest in his process is keen. "We receive a steady stream of visitors from food companies, as well as from alfalfa dehydrating firms, but we're not yet ready to hand out large quantities of our white protein for testing by processors."

Protein From Wastes

With the current emphasis on pollution and recycling wastes, it is not surprising to find that the searchers for protein have turned to currently discarded materials as potential sources of food for both man and animals.

Whey, the whitish liquid left after milk is processed into cheese, is one such product that is nutritionally too good to throw away. Yet, less than a third of the 22 billion pounds of liquid whey produced annually in the United States goes into human or animal foods. (Ricotta cheese, for example, is made by coagulating the protein in whey.)

If the whey that is now discarded each year were dried and treated, it would yield at least 170 million pounds of protein, one billion pounds of the milk sugar, lactose, plus water-soluble vitamins.

Whey can be added to fruit drinks (Dr. Steinberg at the University of Illinois mixes it with his soy milk). In addition, coagulated whey protein makes an acceptable ground meat extender and whey protein can be whipped into foam suitable for cake frosting.

At Michigan State, Dr. C. A. Reddy, veterinarian and microbiologist, is fermenting whey and mixing it with ammonia to produce a syrupy, high-quality feed for ruminant animals. The resulting feed, which he calls "bactolac," contains 50 per cent protein (as good as soybean meal in protein quality) "and it is made from stuff that does not compete with the human food chain, as does the soybean," the Indian scientist pointed out.

"It is also a completely recycled process — the cow produces the whey and the whey is fed back to the cow to make more whey-containing milk," Dr. Reddy added.

With his whey feed process about to be used commercially by a new plant in Okemos, Mich., Dr. Reddy is now working on another waste-recycled feed from manure. He said that if only a third of the three to five billion tons of cattle manure produced annually in the United States were used to make feed, it would exceed in protein value all the soybean protein produced in this country each year.

Dr. Reddy is studying a process whereby the microoganisms already in the manure convert it without air into organic acids. When ammonia is added, the acids form ammonia salts that the cattle can use to make protein.

Waste products are also being studied as a substrate on which to grow protein-rich microorganisms — bacteria, and other fungi — that might be used to feed people as well as animals. A Louisiana State University team is harvesting bacteria with 60 per cent high-quality protein that were grown on cellulose wastes, such as paper and plant fibers. Bechtel International of San Francisco is building a $10-million demonstration plant that will use the Louisiana process to make protein supplements for animal feeds.

Much work has already been done demonstrating the feasibility of growing edible microorganisims on petroleum.

As human food, microorganisms (often referred to as "single-cell protein") have a disadvantage of resulting in too much uric acid, which can cause gall stones and kidney stones. But the Louisiana team believes ways will be found to get around this limitation so that someday these organisms may be converted into analogues of steak.

The Japanese, among others, are culturing single-celled algae which, after the protein is separated out and coagulated, can yield a high-protein powder that can be added to flour or other foods or used as an animal feed supplement.

These various approaches represent the major efforts in the current worldwide thrust for protein. Other avenues being explored include breeding crops that can be irrigated with salt water, increasing the drought tolerance of plants so that they can be grown in desert areas and using soil bacteria to fertilize crops that currently require large inputs of chemical fertilizers which are costly and in short supply.

Some of these ideas are currently little more than that — an idea on which a great deal of research must still be done. For others, such as fish protein concentrate and various soy foods, the technology has been nearly completely worked out on a pilot scale and could theoretically be incorporated soon into the diets of protein-starved people.

But the obstacles to such incorporation are substantial. They include such political and economic questions as who should sponsor the effort and is there money in it for private industry. Moreover, needed technology and personnel are usually not available in the developing countries and the new foods often do not suit individual tastes and dietary customs.

General Mills says, for example, that the main stumbling block to introducing soybean "meats" in this country is getting people to try them for the first time. It would be even harder to feed them to undernourished people in developing countries who are unaccustomed to any kind of meat in their daily diet.

Since there can be no one solution for all the protein-malnourished peoples of the world, the search for adequate protein resources continues to go in many different directions at once. In recent years, growing numbers of American scientists, industries and organizations have joined this search, and some of the results of their labors are expected to find a substantial place on the American table before the decade is out.

But the primary goal of this effort is to provide ample quantities of well-balanced protein for the growing numbers of people in developing countries whose diets are protein-deprived. There is little doubt among both scientific and political experts that the achievement of this goal is essential, not only to the well-being of these people, but to the future health of the world as a whole.

BOYCE RENSBERGER

The Wasteful American Diet

As the daily ration of rice becomes steadily smaller in several poor countries, some Americans are beginning to look at their dinner plates of steak and potatoes not with pleasure but with a trace of guilt.

They are among a small but growing number of people who are coming to realize that the dietary habits that are commonplace in the United States are among the most wasteful of the world's agricultural resources.

As a result, a growing number of voices are urging that individual Americans help to stretch the food resources of a hungry world by modifying their traditional diets to favor less wasteful sources of protein.

If there were cutbacks on grain-fed meat, the food experts contend, it would be possible to divert the grain saved to famine-relief efforts. The move would be similar to turning down the thermostat and reducing speed limits to conserve energy for other uses.

Because most Americans eat the way they do, consuming two to four times as much meat as the body can use and excreting the excess protein, agricultural experts say that a sizable share of this country's land, fertilizer and farming skills has been committed to growing food for animals and not directly for man.

Cattle, swine and poultry consume several times as much protein in grain as they yield in meat, dairy products and eggs.

Dr. Lester Brown of the Overseas Development Council estimates that if Americans were to reduce their meat consumption by only 10 per cent for one year, it would free for human consumption at least 12 million tons of grain. This amount, enough to feed 60 million grain-eaters for a year, would be more than enough to prevent the famine now developing in India and Bangladesh.

Humanitarian reasons aside, the American Heart Association is emphasizing personal health in its current recommendation that Americans cut their meat consumption by one-third. Mindful of the contribution of animal fats to deterioration of the arteries, medical doctors say this reduction would go a long way toward preventing heart disease.

Even a few citizens groups, with names like Freedom From Hunger, Bread for the World, and the Hunger Action Coalition, will attempt to persuade Americans to substitute vegetable protein for animal in their diets.

Some authorities say that such campaigns may be unnecessary because rising meat prices have already begun to reduce consumption. The trends are expected to continue.

While most authorities concede that the traditional American reliance on meat, particularly beef, is perhaps the single largest inefficiency in world dietary patterns, it is, of course, not the only one.

In many Asian countries, for example, people prefer a highly polished rice. That the process of polishing removes much of the protein- and vitamin-rich layers of the grain seems to prompt little change in preferences.

In much of South America, where the corn has been yellow for centuries, people spurned a new variety of corn that had protein of as high a quality as milk or meat. The new variety was white and people said it was "sick."

Plant breeders seeking to develop improved varieties of many crops frequently encounter such seemingly arbitrary local preferences for various characteristics in staple foods. In addition to breeding higher yielding or disease-resistant potatoes, for example, plant scientists must remember that if they are to help Venezuela, the potato must have a white skin but that if the neighboring Colombians are to adopt it, the skin must be red.

Traditional taboos also deny available nutrients to some

peoples. Among a few tribes in Tanzania, for instance, women are forbidden to drink milk. In parts of Thailand pregnant and nursing mothers may not eat a variety of fruits and other foods. Some Jews and many Moslems observe proscriptions of pork.

On balance, however, the underdeveloped countries are thought to be making remarkably efficient use of the foods they have, even to consuming plants, animals and organs of animals that many Americans would consider repellant.

Despite the wide variety of unusual sources of food some people draw upon, the vast majority in virtually every country, rich or poor, rely upon a narrow range of foods as staples. They are chiefly wheat, rice and corn.

All of man's food comes initially from plants. The great dietary difference distinguishing affluent societies from those in poverty is the number and kind of "middlemen" between the plant harvest and the dinnertable.

In India the plants are almost entirely consumed directly in a largely vegetarian diet. In the United States only a small fraction of the edible plant products are consumed directly

Growth in Per Capita Meat Consumption in Some Industrial Countries*			
	1960 Meat Consumption	1972 Meat Consumption	Increase
	(Pounds per year)		(Per cent)
United States	208	254	22
Australia	234	235	0
France	168	212	26
Canada	167	211	26
United Kingdom	158	171	8
West Germany	144	192	33
Sweden	109	112	3
Soviet Union	80	104	30
Italy	70	136	94
Yugoslavia	62	75	21
Spain	51	96	88
Japan	14	51	264

*Includes beef, veal, pork, mutton, lamb, goat, horse, poultry, edible offals, other.

Sources: Organization for Economic Cooperation and Development. Soviet Union data from U.S. Department of Agriculture.

by people. A large fraction—mostly corn—is consumed by animals which, in turn, feed man with meat, dairy products and eggs.

Because animals consume so much more food than they return, diets that rely heavily on meat claim a larger share of primary plant nutrients than do diets that are more vegetarian.

Statistics from the Food and Agriculture Organization of the United Nations and the United States Department of Agriculture show that the average Indian consumes about 400 pounds of grain each year, of which about 85 per cent is eaten directly in such things as chapati, an unleavened bread, and gruel.

The average American consumes, directly and indirectly, nearly a ton of grain a year, of which only about 7 per cent is eaten directly in the form of bread, breakfast cereals, baked goods and the like. The other 93 per cent is fed to cattle, swine and poultry for meat, milk and eggs.

Thus the average American consumes about five times as much of the earth's primary food as does the average Indian. In Western Europe, for comparison, per capita grain consumption is about half that of the United States.

Growing awareness of these disproportions is raising questions about the capacity of human societies to work out systems for the equitable distribution of food. The complex food production and distribution systems that operate within and among most countries have largely come into being without plan or control.

Food is generally treated not as a basic human right but as a commodity to be sold to the highest bidder. As a result, the demands of the wealthy can claim disproportionate shares of a finite resource.

"Morally," Willy Brandt told the United Nations General Assembly a year ago, "it makes no difference whether a man is killed in war or is condemned to starve to death by the indifference of others."

In the view of some experts, the demand for food is increasing so rapidly that any growth in production of primary foods, meaning mostly grain and beans, that can reasonably be expected will be too little to meet the need.

"Efforts to insure an adequate diet for all mankind can no longer concentrate almost wholly on expanding the supply of food," Dr. Brown warns in "By Bread Alone," his 1974 book on the food crisis. "Almost equally important is the need to curb the growth in per capita consumption among the more affluent people in the world, those who are already overeating."

As it affects the world food supply, "overeating" means eating meat, particularly beef. Although man is biologically an omnivore and not a carnivore, many Americans believe—contrary to the findings of nutritionists—that a healthy diet must include large quantities of red meat. Beef is regarded as one of the good things that money can buy and one of the most familiar indicators of the affluence a family feels is the frequency with which steak is served. This affinity for beef is of relatively recent origin.

For the first 50 years of this century, figures from the Department of Agriculture show, beef and pork were consumed in approximately equal and unchanging quantities. From the turn of the century until about 1950, for example, consumption of beef in the United States fluctuated little from about 60 pounds per person year after year. But from 1950 to 1972 beef eating soared in popularity, nearly doubling to an annual per capita rate of 116 pounds. In 1973 it declined slightly to 109 pounds, the first decline since the early nineteen-fifties, largely because of rising prices.

Pork consumption has changed little over the same period, hovering at about 65 pounds per person annually. Poultry-eating patterns remained stable at 16 pounds a year per person until about 1940 when it began rising to reach about 50 pounds in the nineteen-seventies. Adding lamb and other minor sources of meat, the average American directly consumes about 250 pounds of meat each year.

It is not fully clear why the sudden boom in beef occurred, but it is generally ascribed to the popular view that large quantities of meat are nutritionally desirable. With the rapid growth of personal income in the United States over the last 25 years, many Americans appear to have chosen more beef as a way of seeming to improve their standard of living.

Few realized that in 1950 most people in the United States

were already consuming as much meat as their bodies could use.

Similar patterns have developed in many other countries where affluence has been spreading. The famous Soviet grain deal of 1972 was a direct result of the Soviet government's desire to sustain increasing levels of meat consumption. Normally, in a bad crop year, cattle would have been slaughtered to conserve grain for human consumption and six or eight years would have to pass before the herds could be built up again. This time the Russians chose to continue feeding the cattle, necessitating massive grain purchases.

Despite the belief that large quantities of meat are nutritionally desirable, meat-heavy diets have not made Americans significantly healthier than, for example, West Germans, who eat about 200 pounds of meat per year, or the British, who consume 170 pounds annually, or the Swedes, who eat about 110 pounds, or the Japanese, who eat about 50 pounds per year.

In the view of many medical authorities the rise in beef consumption may, indeed, be linked with the rise in heart disease. Similar increases in heart disease are being noted in

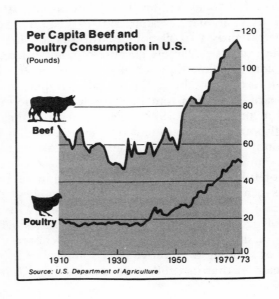

Per Capita Beef and Poultry Consumption in U.S. (Pounds)

Beef

Poultry

Source: U.S. Department of Agriculture

other countries adopting the American beef-heavy diet, and some experts now consider too much meat-eating to be a form of malnutrition.

The beef boom has led to a dramatic increase in the demand for grain. Because Americans want more beef and more "marbled" beef than can be raised on grazing land, livestock producers have increasingly resorted to "feed lots," where young steers that started out on grass are penned together outside slaughterhouses and fattened on grain.

Once a steer is in the feedlot, it consumes about 10 pounds of grain for every pound of meat added to its weight. When it is ready for slaughter, having gained some weight on grass and some on grain, each average pound of meat will have required four to five pounds of grain.

Among the principal meat animals used in the United States, cattle are the least efficient converters of grain into meat. While it takes 10 pounds of grain to add a pound of beef, it takes only four to make a pound of pork. Still more efficient are chickens, which produce a pound of meat on only two pounds of grain.

These differences in grain-to-meat efficiency have prompted some food conservation groups to try to persuade Americans to switch from beef to pork or chicken in their meals.

They note, for example, that if Americans substituted a pound of chicken for a pound of beef (the protein contents are similar), it would reduce the animal consumption of grain by eight pounds. That extra grain could be used to grow an additional four pounds of chicken or it could be used for direct human consumption. In that case, it could feed one adult for a week.

If the American demand for beef were reduced to a level that could be met by grass-fed cattle, it could, hypothetically, release more than enough grain to feed all of India's nearly 600 million people.

The same switch from beef to chicken would also substantially reduce the intake of fat and cholesterol, a fact that the American Heart Association emphasizes in its public education efforts.

Still less wasteful of basic food resources, food experts say, is a largely vegetarian diet that substitutes protein from grains, beans and other plant sources for animal protein.

While there has, in the past, been some controversy among nutritionists over whether a strictly vegetarian diet provides good nutrition, it is now generally agreed that with proper selection of foods, it does. Earlier this year the National Academy of Sciences concluded that "a vegetarian can be well-nourished if he eats a variety of plant foods and gives attention to critical nutrients."

Virtually all nutrition experts condemn as inadequate some vegetarian diets, such as the unvaried "macrobiotic" regimen adopted by some people for religious reasons. Serious, near fatal, cases of malnutrition have been discovered among some followers of macrobiotic diets.

Nutritionists say the most important factor to consider in substituting vegetable protein for animal protein is the balance of amino acids, the building blocks of all protein molecules. In digestion proteins are broken down into their component amino acids. There are 18 principal amino acids, of which eight cannot be manufactured within the adult human body and must be included in the diet. A ninth amino acid is essential in the diet of infants. Once the bloodstream has transported the amino acids to human tissues, each cell constructs new proteins by linking the various amino acids in precise combinations. If one of the requisite amino acids is not available at the time, the others that are present cannot be used and are either excreted or broken down.

Unlike animal proteins in meat, dairy products and eggs, most vegetable proteins are deficient in one or two essential amino acids. Consumption of a single vegetable source alone results in the waste of much of its protein content. But if two or more vegetable sources are properly combined, each can compensate for the deficiencies of the other. The combinations must be made within the meal.

Two groups of protein-rich vegetable foods that nutritionists have found to compensate well for each other's deficiencies are legumes and nuts on the one hand and cereal grains on the other. The first group includes beans, peas, lentils, nuts and peanuts. The second includes wheat, oats, corn, rice and rye in whole-grain products.

Combinations recommended by nutritionists include beans

with corn, beans with rice and peanuts with wheat. The most familiar form of the latter, is of course, a peanut butter sandwich.

Peanut butter is generally regarded as one of the richest sources of vegetable protein. It is also, according to the Agriculture Department's Research Service, the cheapest source of protein in the American grocery store. The quantity necessary to yield 20 grams of protein, the requirement of an adult for each meal, could be bought for 15 cents as of August, 1974.

By comparison, the most expensive source of the same quantity of protein were veal cutlets and porterhouse steak at 74 cents for 20 grams worth in protein. The least expensive meat on a pennies-for-protein basis was whole chicken at 20 cents for the same quantity of protein. Among the most expensive meat sources was bologna at 54 cents.

One of the drawbacks of a strictly vegetarian diet, nutritionists warn, is that it can easily be deficient in vitamin B_{12} vitamin D and calcium, nutrients that are available in significant quantities only in animal products. Nutritionists point out that these deficiencies could be filled by milk, commonly fortified with vitamin D, or by vitamin and mineral supplements in pill form.

Even if the efforts to persuade Americans to cut back on beef and substitute plant protein for animal—sometimes called simplification of diet or "lowering one's self on the food chain"—were successful, there is no guarantee that the grain or fertilizer saved would be diverted to feed starving people or to build a reserve for future famine relief.

While it is obvious that a decline in domestic consumption would initially leave a larger share of grain available for export, the exact amounts could not be determined until the trend had become stable. Increased supplies might, for example, depress prices so much that farmers would grow less. Or the rise in world demand might well be more than enough to absorb the increase.

It is generally held that extending the benefits of an American food conservation program to poor countries would require some form of Government regulation compatible with guidelines on the international food trade.

The Eat-Less-Meat Movement

Some 250,000 Americans fasted yesterday [Nov. 2, 1974] in a demonstration of concern for the famine-stricken population of the world.

College students in large numbers, as well as members of church, civic and business groups, participated throughout the country, reflecting what appears to be a surge of public interest in the issue.

"The tragedy of world hunger has stirred a profound type of concern among students that I have not witnessed in 25 years of college experience," said the Rev. J. Donald Monan, president of Boston College.

The fast was organized by Oxfam-America, in Boston, one of a number of hunger groups that have become active in this country in the last year or so as the dimensions of the food crisis have been increasingly in the headlines.

Another manifestation of the increased concern yesterday was a statement by the American Roman Catholic Bishops meeting in Washington. They called for special parish programs of worship, fasting and abstinence to help alleviate threats of starvation in more than 30 countries.

Oxfam-America, which is the United States branch of the British-based Oxford Committee for Famine Relief, sponsored the 24-hour Fast for a World Harvest along with Project Relief, a Providence, R.I., fund-raising organization.

There are those who question the value of such activities. And, as one church relief official noted, "During the Nigeria-Biafra struggle, all kinds of groups sprang up, but they died away in a year or so. It's part of the American scene."

Among the optimists is the Rev. Arthur Simon, co-founder of a New York-based group called Bread for the World. He has concluded that a surprising number of people would willingly sacrifice and make permanent life style changes if they could find something to do that they felt would really have effect.

The tiny organization, whose president is the Rev. Dr. Eugene Carson Blake, former president of the National Council of Churches, and former general secretary of the World Council of Churches, decided last May to seek a national constituency.

Since then, more than 4,100 people have sent in $10 membership dues, although Bread for the World's appeal appeared only in a few national church magazines. "It's not that we have organizational genius, but that we're filling a vacuum," says Rev. Simon.

Unlike race and other social action issues that have stirred controversy in church groups, hunger relief appeals have always brought immediate responses from liberal and conservative-minded parishioners alike. "It's a motherhood issue; it's not controversial," Rev. Simon observed.

BOYCE RENSBERGER

Cutting Back: Pro's and Con's

As the significance of the world food crisis becomes more apparent to well-fed Americans, the call for people to cut down on consumption of meat, especially grain-fed beef, is increasingly being voiced by citizens' groups, religious and humanitarian organizations and some food and nutrition experts.

Their argument is that if meat consumption were to decline enough, the agricultural resources now devoted to feeding cattle, pigs and chickens could be diverted to rescue famine victims and to build grain reserves against almost inevitable future food shortages.

Several advocates also suggest that such actions would be in the enlightened self interest of the affluent countries because they would help fight inflation. Rising food prices, they note, are now leading the over-all inflation rate. In a world competing for the same food resources, any effort to expand the supply in one place would tend to hold down prices everywhere.

On the other hand there are a number of agricultural economists, meat industry representatives, and experts on the food problems of poor countries whose views range from less than enthusiasm to opposition.

They contend that such a voluntary campaign would be unlikely to overcome a well-developed American preference for grain-fed beef and that, even if it did, the action would not be likely to result in food for starving people, especially in the near future.

The skeptics contend that such an outcome would require the Federal Government to buy the diverted grain specifically for famine relief. Otherwise the grain would simply go to the highest commercial bidder. If the Government must take that step anyway, the argument goes, it might as well enter the grain market now and buy what is needed.

In addition, some economists see that too hasty a retreat from beef would not only wreck one segment of the agricultural economy but also sharply drive up the prices of other foods. For example, the price of milk would be higher if dairy farmers could not sell their calves to the beef producers as a byproduct.

Only a few years ago, when the American cornucopia was still full, such a debate would have seemed unthinkable. Now that the more or less unplanned drift of American tastes and farming priorities have been called into question, experts on all sides are finding they have little hard data from which to predict the results of sudden shifts in consumption and production trends.

While the debate on this issue is sharpest on the question of whether much extra grain could be diverted to humanitarian purposes in the short run, there is somewhat more agreement that a long-term change in American dietary patterns could indeed result in the availability of larger quantities of grain for export.

In fact, some of those who doubt that charitable motives will cut the beef demand significantly note that the high price of beef is already lowering the demand. Per capita beef consumption dropped in 1973, for the first time in nearly 20 years, from a peak in 1972. There are indications the decline continued through 1974.

Because cattlemen now benefit little from the high retail price of beef and must pay high prices for corn, grain feeding is becoming uneconomical and the industry is already shifting toward more use of grass and other forage crops.

Thus there seems to be agreement that whether or not the steak given up today results in more food for people starving now, it could be the beginning of a trend that over the next few years would increase the United States ability to help prevent or relieve future famines.

Many of those urging a cutback in meat eating say that even if it didn't release enough grain to meet the present crisis, there are likely to be similar crises recurring with increasing frequency in the next few years. If a trend in reduced meat eating can be begun now, they contend, American corn farmers will soon shift to growing desirable food grains such as wheat, thus increasing the quantity available for export or for donation to a world food reserve for future emergencies.

Background

Twenty five years ago the average American ate about 60 pounds of beef a year, about equivalent to the rate of pork consumption. Poultry consumption stood at about 25 pounds a year per person. Americans were not, on the average, malnourished then.

These days Americans eat about the same amount of pork, but the annual consumption of poultry has doubled to about 50 pounds per capita and beef eating soared to 116 pounds before declining slightly to 110.

Nutritionists agree that the swollen meat consumption is not necessary or even desirable for health. Many heart specialists believe the increased eating of meat, particularly the more expensive grades with more fat, sometimes called marbling, has contributed to the rise in disability and death due to heart disease.

The extraordinary surge in beef eating is generally attributed to the then rising affluence of the middle class and to the development of a taste for soft, juicy beef. The juiciness comes largely from melted fat.

A large share of the increased beef production demanded by this change in preference has come not from pasture and grazing lands which yield a leaner, often tougher beef but from the use of feedlots where young steers that are started on grass are virtually force-fed on fattening grains.

Because meat production consumes several times as much food in grain as is returned in meat, the growth in meat eating has used up grain at a disproportionately high rate. The American meat-heavy diet uses up five times as much grain each year as does the Indian grain-heavy diet.

In the nineteen-forties only about one-third of the beef cattle slaughtered had received any special feed but by the nineteen-seventies about 82 per cent of the beef cattle were coming from feed-lots. The animals that are still grass fed are largely ground into hamburger, a fact that those urging the sacrifice of "one hamburger a week" have apparently overlooked. Skipping a hamburger will save little or no grain. It is the highest grades of beef that monopolize the grain.

Lately, due to increasing costs of feed grain, the beef industry has been returning to more reliance on grass. The National Livestock and Meat Board, an industry group, estimates that during 1975 as much as 30 per cent of beef will be grass fed, up from about 18 per cent in recent years.

Skeptical Views

While few outside the meat industry itself flatly oppose a reduction in meat consumption, many of the most knowledgeable experts on world agriculture are skeptical that it will do much good, particularly in the short run. They also worry about the impact on American meat producers, already hard hit by costs rising faster than sales.

The first point usually raised by the skeptics is that too few people would cut back far enough to make an identifiable and useful difference.

Even if there were large reductions, the grain that would be diverted would be mostly corn of types that are not widely attractive to human beings. Although corn is a staple in parts of Latin America and Africa, it is not as widely eaten in India and Bangladesh, two of the countries where food shortages are most acute.

It is sometimes argued by skeptics that, if the demand for grain declined within the United States, the price would fall and farmers would be inclined to reduce production or even go out of business.

"In the short run it is not a feasible or consequential idea," said Dr. Kenneth Farrell, deputy administrator of the Department of Agriculture's Economic Research Service. "In the long run, however, the argument is not without merit."

Dr. Farrell said the first result would be a drop in the price of corn, the main feed grain, discouraging corn production.

He said farmers would tend to switch to growing wheat and rice. One requirement for a meat cutback to have effect in famine areas, Dr. Farrell stressed, would be for the Government to announce its intention to buy a specified quantity of grain. Assured of a demand and a good price, he said, farmers would continue to produce.

Dr. Sterling Wortman, vice president of the Rockefeller Foundation, which supports much agricultural research in poor countries, contends that if averting famine soon is the goal, a meat cutback is at best an indirect solution.

He notes that the Federal Government would probably have to buy the diverted grain for famine-stricken countries or at least earmark quantities available for purchase by those countries.

"There are much more direct and forceful ways to get the grain," Dr. Wortman said. "If the American people really want to send food aid, they should urge the Government to buy the grain as the first step."

Another point Dr. Wortman raises is that it is the very lack of ready American food aid in the present crisis that is now motivating poor countries to develop their own food-producing potential.

"For the first time in history we've got people seriously interested in getting food production up in the underdeveloped countries," Dr. Wortman said.

It is generally agreed, even among those who urge meat cutbacks, that the most important solution to the food crisis in the long run is to upgrade farming in the poor countries.

Lowell Hardin, who heads agricultural research programs for the Ford Foundation, notes that whether or not the grain diverted from steers reaches starving people depends on an intricate web of agricultural, economic, and other factors. Not the least of which is the political implication of inflicting further hardship on the already beleaguered meat producers. There are about 150,000 commercial feedlots in the United States, each buying its calves from many sources, including dairies and many thousands of small farmers.

Dr. Hardin suggested that the only way the needed Government action might be politically acceptable would be if it included some measure to ease the economic impact on the beef industry.

Food Conservationists' Views

The most prominent food experts supporting the campaign to reduce meat consumption have been Lester Brown, an economist with the private Overseas Development Council, and Jean Mayer, a professor of nutrition at Harvard Medical School.

Dr. Brown has calculated that if the total American consumption were reduced by only 10 per cent, it would save about 12 million tons of grain, an amount greater than India's food deficit in 1974. This would be the equivalent of returning to the meat consumption level of ten years ago.

Beyond the economic and health arguments of the food conservationists is the assertion by some that a moral issue is at stake.

"In a world of scarcity," Dr. Brown wrote in his latest book, "By Bread Alone," "if some of us consume more, others of necessity must consume less. The moral issue is raised by the fact that those who are consuming less are not so much the overweight affluent but the already undernourished poor."

A number of religious organizations have urged their followers to observe regular meatless days, a move recalling President Truman's call in 1947 for Americans to go without meat on Tuesdays to conserve food for famine relief.

Most of those calling for reduced meat consumption concede that Government action would be needed, at least in the short run, to assure that the diverted grain gets to hungry countries. Until that happens, many groups are suggesting that Americans send the money saved to private famine relief programs, which would acquire the grain and donate it.

Although corn is not the preferred grain in the most critical countries, the conservationists say genuinely starving people would be unlikely to turn it down.

Supporters of food conservation argue that in many of the regions where corn is grown, the land is good for other crops for which the demand is strong, such as wheat and soybeans.

Dr. Folke Dovring, an agricultural economist at the University of Illinois, has found that many Midwestern farmers could easily switch from corn to a combination of wheat and soybeans and achieve the same or better income.

Because an acre's production of corn sells for more than an acre's worth of wheat, Dr. Dovring said it would be necessary for farmers to plant a second crop on the same land in the same growing season. He said farmers in southern Illinois have found it economically feasible to sow soybeans in the unplowed stubble of a harvested wheat field and reap a crop before the first frost.

One advantage of this alternative is that it requires much less fertilizer. Corn is one of the most fertilizer-demanding of plants. Wheat requires less and soybeans need no nitrogen fertilizer. The release of scarce fertilizer could ease shortages in the poor countries.

"I think it is quite realistic to free agricultural resources this way," Dr. Dovring said.

While there are too few data upon which to project the precise immediate effects of a meat cutback, there is little doubt among agricultural experts that if food production fails to move much ahead of present increases in demand, the wasteful character of dietary habits in affluent countries could become difficult to defend.

6 THE POLITICS OF FOOD

The New York Times / William E. Sauro

President Ford at the United Nations

On Sept. 18, 1974, President Ford called on all countries of the world to join in a "global strategy for food and energy."

"Let us not delude ourselves," he said in his first address to the United Nations General Assembly. "Failure to cooperate on oil and food and inflation could spell disaster for every nation represented in this room."

The President pledged American cooperation with a proposed worldwide system of stockpiling food for emergencies, and he announced that the United States would increase food aid to needy nations and take other measures to help relieve hunger in the world.

Addressing himself sternly to the oil-producing countries, Mr. Ford emphasized the interdependence between the energy and food crises. He challenged the oil producers to "define their policies to meet growing needs" but to do so "without imposing unacceptable burdens on the international monetary and trade system."

"It has not been our policy to use food as a political weapon despite the oil embargo and recent oil price and production decisions," he declared.

He warned that the oil-producing countries, by confronting consumers with restrictions on output, arbitrary pricing and "the prospect of ultimate bank-

ruptcy," would eventually become the victims of their own actions.

On the intertwining of food and energy shortages, he said: "Many developing nations need the food surplus of a few developed nations. And many industrialized nations need the oil production of a few developing nations."

The President exhorted all nations to increase food and energy production substantially and to hold prices to levels that consumers could afford. He warned against "abuse of man's fundamental needs for the sake of narrow national or bloc advantage," and recommended special regard for the world's poorest communities. Declaring that the "United States recognizes the special responsibility we bear as the world's largest food producer," President Ford promised that assistance to agriculture programs in other countries would be stepped up.

On the "worldwide effort to negotiate, establish and maintain an international system of food reserves," President Ford said that in the American view "each nation must determine for itself how it manages its reserves."

Mr. Ford was alluding to proposals from needy countries and from the United Nations Food and Agriculture Organization, a specialized agency, calling for international stockpiling of food.

The American position, as reiterated by President Ford today, stresses readiness to collaborate with a system of emergency food reserves, but insists that in the United States the storing and management of such stocks remain in private hands.

President Ford said that the United States would make comprehensive proposals at the World Food Conference that is to be held in Rome, Nov. 5 to 16. Secretary of State Kissinger is scheduled to address that meeting shortly after it opens.

BOYCE RENSBERGER

On the Linking of Food and Oil

In the last few months [of 1974] the world food crisis has developed from what once seemed to be another exaggerated doomsday forecast to a reality that is gnawing at the bellies of hundreds of thousands of people and threatening to take the lives of millions. Early this summer, when leading agricultural experts began reporting the first signs of an imminent crisis that they said could reach disastrous proportions before the year was out, The New York Times began a series of articles exploring the situation.

Now that Times reporters have pursued the topic in hundreds of interviews with scientists and economists around the world, patterns of consensus have begun to emerge. This is an interim report on a continuing inquiry.

The most basic conclusion that can be drawn from the investigation to date is that among the experts there is virtually unanimous agreement that a serious world food crisis has indeed begun. There is even agreement on this point by some government leaders.

President Ford acknowledged as much in his address before the United Nations yesterday [Sept. 18, 1974]. He called the situation a "crisis" and said a "global strategy" to deal with it was "urgently needed."

There is, however, disagreement among world food specialists on how long the crisis might persist. Many experts say it is only a temporary phenomenon brought on chiefly by a fertilizer shortage that will be over within four to six years. Others contend it is the beginning of what could be decades of unrelenting misery for much of the world.

257

There has been almost total agreement that the most severe impact in the immediate future will be in India, the world's second most populous country, where millions may face starvation in the next few months. The latest wheat crop there has been harvested and has fallen below expectation by an amount equivalent to the food needs of 50-million people for a full year.

Many authorities say that without wide international aid beginning soon, the present Indian food shortage could develop into a famine vastly exceeding in scale anything in sub-Saharan Africa or in India of years past.

The New York Times/William E. Sauro

President Ford making his first address to the United Nations General Assembly linking the food and energy crises.

"The situation around the world is very bad; in India I would say it is grave," said Dr. Norman E. Borlaug, the Nobel Prize-winning scientist who has played a major role in guiding India's agricultural development in recent years.

Dr. Borlaug was the developer of high-yielding, fertilizer-dependent wheat varieties that made India self-sufficient in wheat until recently.

Another important conclusion shared by many is that, because of the increasingly intertwined economies of all countries and because of global resource scarcities, repercussions from an Indian famine would be felt throughout the world.

It is recognized generally that the world's nearly four billion people now draw upon a common pool of food-producing resources, including land, fertilizer, energy, machinery, pesticides and global distribution systems. A change in farm policy—a subject once considered an internal affair of any country—in the Soviet Union, for example, led to the large purchase of American grain in 1972 and contributed significantly to the surge in American food prices.

Indian farmers, to cite another example, were short of fertilizer not only because of the Arab policies that reduced production of oil, from which much fertilizer is made, but also because the United States restricted the export of fertilizer, which was wanted by American farmers.

Until recent years the links between energy and food had largely been taken for granted. When fossil fuels were being mined and pumped in ample quantities, the prices of petroleum-based fertilizer or fuel for farm machinery were low.

With the coming of the energy shortage and oil price rises, competition from other energy uses cut deeply into supplies available for agriculture.

In his United Nations address, President Ford clearly extended the food-energy link from economic and technological bases to the realm of global politics.

Recognizing that the United States is the world's largest supplier of food, or as some put it, "We are the Arabs of the food business," Mr. Ford drew parallels between this country's responsibility on world food supplies and the Arabs' position on world energy supplies.

The link is likely to be of significance as various countries prepare for the United Nations-sponsored World Food Conference in Rome in November.

Among the prime topics for debate at the conference is the establishment and funding of a proposed World Food Authority. This body would, among other things, sponsor efforts to increase food production and administer emergency food reserves to rescue famine victims.

The proposal calls for the new agency to spend as much as $5-billion a year to stimulate agriculture development in poor countries. Supporters of the proposal are looking to the Arab countries and the United States for substantial shares of the money and to the United States for a sizable contribution to a reserve food supply.

By linking the food and energy questions politically and pledging American cooperation, Mr. Ford would appear to be adding pressure on the Arab countries to respond in similar fashion. Mr. Ford gave no specifics. He said these would be presented at the conference in November.

By then, however, the crises in India and Bangladesh may have reached disastrous proportions.

JUAN DE ONIS | # Oil Money and the Middle East

Beirut

The countries of the Middle East and North Africa have a potential for food production that many agricultural experts believe could make a substantial contribution to meeting the world's food needs.

But the region, stretching from Morocco eastward to Iran, more than 4,000 miles, and from Turkey on the edge of Europe in the north to the Sudan, in the heart of Africa, in the south, is an over-all importer of food.

It is costing the region well over $1-billion a year to import wheat, rice, sugar, meat and vegetable oil. These staples are often sold at low, subsidized prices to hold down their cost for a rapidly growing population of 200 million.

Despite the vast deserts that cover much of the region, it has enough good land, water, raw materials for fertilizers and money from oil exports to be self-sufficient if scientific farming was adopted.

"The rate of development and of adoption of agricultural technology new to the Middle East is susceptible to acceleration sufficient to bring about a virtual agricultural revolution within a generation," according to a study prepared in 1971 by the Rand Corporation and Resources for the Future, Inc.

There is a growing awareness, primarily in the oil-exporting countries, of the importance of assured food supplies. Since the Arab-Israeli war in Oct. 1973, the Arab governments have been paying more attention to food requirements in the light of worldwide shortages, inflated prices and threats of retaliation for the higher oil prices imposed by the exporting countries.

The supposed vulnerability of the oil countries as food importers is not taken very seriously in the region. The financial power of the big exporters, such as Saudi Arabia, Iran, Kuwait, Iraq or Libya, is so great that they command whatever supplies are in world trade.

"If there are shortages, they will just buy the rice out of the mouth of the poor people in Bangladesh," an agricultural expert with a private American foundation said.

But the cost of food is a serious concern, particularly in countries with large populations like Iran, Egypt, Turkey and Algeria.

Turkey, after a mediocre harvest in 1974 of less than 10 million tons of wheat, will have to import more than a million tons. This will cost more than $200-million at present prices.

Egypt, which has a chronic wheat deficit, is reportedly shopping for more than a million tons. Iran has been in the market for 400,000 tons. Syria had a good crop and could export wheat. But the Government has decided to build up reserves and is filling new grain elevators against a possible bad crop next year or higher world prices.

In the sugar market, Iran has reportedly paid more than $900 a ton to meet consumer demand. The cost to the Government, more than 40 cents a pound, is four times the subsidized price paid by Iranian consumers.

Nutritional conditions vary widely in North Africa and the Middle East. Countries like the Sudan and Yemen are rated by the United Nations as among the poorest in the world with average per capita annual income of $100 to $200.

In the same area are countries like Kuwait, with a population of 800,000 and a national income of $8-billion or about $10,000 a person.

The Egyptian peasant and his family, often working one acre of land, have a subsistence diet.

In many areas of Saudi Arabia, Jordan, Syria, western Turkey and parts of Iran, nomadic herdsmen follow the open range to feed and water their flocks of sheep.

But with a diet based on bread, beans, milk and cheese

from sheep and goats, olives, dates and occasional mutton, the level of nutrition in the region is generally well above that in most of southern Asia. Starvation is rare.

In most countries of the area, food policy is designed to assure adequate supplies in urban areas at subsidized prices pegged to the wage levels of industrial workers and government employes.

For the immediate future, all indications are for greater food-import demand as the new wealth in the region is reflected in consumption.

For instance, Iran is importing a million sheep carcasses from Australia. Saudi Arabia is increasing imports of live sheep from East Africa and ordering more cattle feed from abroad for local stock.

The critical food imports are wheat, sugar and, to a lesser extent, rice.

When the United States and other producers had large surplus stocks of grain, the wheat-deficit countries of this region, including Egypt, Morocco, Jordan, the Sudan and to some extent Turkey obtained their import needs in bad crop years on long-term credit, often with payment in local currencies.

These easy terms encouraged these countries to produce higher-priced export crops, such as cotton, on land that could have been used for food crops. Low domestic prices for grains discouraged the adoption of more productive wheat-growing methods, requiring machinery and fertilizer.

In general, there was not much capital available in the region for agricultural development. Economic planners showed a clear preference for industrial investment with whatever capital was available.

Now, the region is moving rapidly into massive accumulation of capital in the oil exporting countries, but the sources of cheap food from outside the region have dried up and food imports cost more.

In this situation, in which self-reliance in food is seen in terms of political and economic security, agricultural experts in the region, including advisers from the Rockefeller and Ford Foundations, survey the possibilities of raising food output with cautious hope.

The New York Times/Juan de Onis

Wheat being harvested in Turkey, one of the countries where, many agricultural specialists believe, there is enough good land for self-sufficiency in food production.

There will be more money for agriculture and livestock herding, which are the main economic activity of North Africa and the Middle East. More than 60 per cent of the people depend on farming and herding.

Nearly all the development plans in the region, particularly in the oil-exporting countries, allocate more money to agriculture, rural development and industries related to agriculture.

The easing of financial limitations opens up a possibility of moving faster on major projects to use land and water, to develop fertilizer potential, to manufacture farm machinery and to provide credit and technical assistance to farmers.

In Arab governmental meetings, the Sudan and Syria have been identified as priority areas for agricultural investment.

In the Sudan, a lack of roads and railroad transportation to ports has limited development of well-watered areas for grain, sorghum and livestock.

It is estimated that sorghum production in the Sudan, which was two million tons in 1971, could with adequate transportation be expanded to meet the feed needs of sheep in Saudi Arabia, Jordan and Syria, where overgrazing is a major problem.

In Syria, the main potential is in wheat production, which is generally low-yield there due to erratic rainfall and primitive agricultural practices.

Two great river systems, which have been centers of agriculture since the dawn of history, feed into the North African and Middle East region.

One is the Nile, now regulated in its flow north through Egypt by the Aswan High Dam. There are six million to seven million acres of irrigated land along the Nile and its delta. This, apart from oasis wells, is the only watered land for Egypt's growing population, now estimated to be approaching 40 million.

Under the pressure of population growth, estimated to be 2.6 per cent annually, experts of the Food and Agriculture Organization say that Egypt could raise food production by better water management and by planting two and three crops a year on the same land with more fertilizer.

A large nitrogen fertilizer plant near Alexandria is one of the first projects being financed with Arab oil money and European technology.

Throughout the region, the oil countries, which in most cases have been flaring billions of cubic feet of natural gas in connection with oil production, are beginning or expanding fertilizer projects.

The other great river system is the Euphrates-Tigris, which comes down from the snow-capped mountains of Turkey into the Mesopotamian Plain of Syria and Iraq.

The Euphrates, a torrential seasonal river, was harnessed this year by the Keban Dam in Turkey and the Tabqa Dam in Syria. These dams will provide water for irrigation. Turkey made water from her dam available to Iraq this summer to meet a drop in water levels. In exchange, Iraq sold oil to Turkey on credit.

Water control in Iraq's Mesopotamian region is essential for production in the seven million acres under irrigation because of high salinity in the soil. The salinity must be washed out by fresh water to support crops.

The Rand Corporation study said that Iraq's farming area could be greatly expanded—and yields sharply increased—if proper drainage systems were installed. This is a long-term project costing more than $1-billion.

Under irrigated conditions, farmers in Egypt, Iran and Turkey have obtained wheat yields comparable to the best in the world with the new high-yielding "dwarf" varieties requiring abundant water and fertilizer.

But expansion of irrigated areas takes enormous capital and much time. The United Nations and private foundation experts in the region rule out any "miracle-seed" solution to the food problems.

The experts agree that the major breakthrough in grain production and livestock raising must come in the relatively low rainfall areas extending from the southern Mediterranean to the Anatolian plain, the Syrian steppe and the Iranian plateau.

This would require, the experts say, the introduction of techniques developed in the states of Oregon and Washington, where wheat yield is three or four times higher than in Turkey or Syria under similar conditions of rainfall.

Advisers from Oregon State University and the Rockefeller Foundation, who have been working with the Turkish Ministry of Agriculture since 1969, have adapted the techniques to local conditions in field trials. Tests began this fall in village demonstration plots.

The method involves more work in soil preparation to retain moisture and in eliminating weeds, requiring herbicides or repeated weeding. On extensive plots, this requires farm machinery. The farmers must also run the risk of planting early, before the first heavy fall rain, and must be able to invest in substantial amounts of fertilizer.

If successful, the farmers' yield and income would increase from 50 to 100 per cent. If extended across the 16 million acres in nonirrigated wheat in Turkey, production would not only meet domestic demand of about 11 million tons, but would also make Turkey an exporter.

Since the advisory program began, Turkey has had six

Ministers of Agriculture in five years and a consequent lack of policy continuity.

"Until agriculture is given a higher priority in national policy, the problem of productivity is not going to be licked," a United Nations expert said. "There is no new land to bring into production and the population is growing 3 percent a year. There is not much time left."

LESLIE H. GELB

On the Eve of the World Food Conference

When Secretary of State Kissinger steps before the World Food Conference in Rome on Nov. 5, 1974, he will be addressing many who now believe that mankind's biggest challenge is not so much to avert a nuclear holocaust as to assure economic survival.

Mr. Kissinger is expected to propose meeting the challenge by increasing world food production and by establishing a world food council responsible to the Secretary General of the United Nations.

In a late draft of his speech, obtained by The New York Times, Mr. Kissinger recommends limiting the council's authority primarily to overseeing the activities of four groups of technical experts who would deal, respectively, with food aid, trade, production and reserves.

Administration officials are divided over whether Mr. Kissinger's speech will generate action to help assure survival and whether it will stress sufficiently the idea that scarce resources should be used as more than an instrument of national policy.

At issue is whether the speech confronts this new reality: that food and fuel are changing the shape of world politics just as surely as nuclear power did in the nineteen-fifties and industrial potential in the nineteen-sixties. In a time of scarce resources and almost inescapable economic interdependence, power is regarded here as stemming from self-sufficiency.

Throughout the Ford Administration, but especially in the Department of Agriculture, the view is expressed that world leadership must be exercised by promoting increased food production.

Some officials, particularly those working closely with Mr. Kissinger, hope that pledges in Rome of sizable but unspecified American contributions to a joint effort, coupled with appeals to other countries to do their share, will lead the delegates into careful consideration of food prospects in coming decades.

But others, consisting of officials who have worked on the food problem for years, emphasize the advantages of American self-sufficiency, which, they emphasize, requires self-sacrifice.

The late draft of the Kissinger speech is divided into three sections. The beginning sketches the magnitude of world food shortages and describes in somber terms a world caught by inflation, soaring fuel prices, diminishing resources and continuing population growth.

Then the draft proceeds to outline steps that it says the United States is prepared to take and what the United States expects others to do. These include:

• A pledge, originally given by President Ford, of a major increase in American food aid. No figure however, is specified.

• A call for "nationally held" food reserves, without indicating whether these reserves would be stored by governments, private traders or farmers, or how they would be controlled.

• A commitment to increase American food production as much as possible.

• A promise to help others increase their food production by making American technology "available." No dollar level is mentioned.

• A call to improve the distribution of food from producer countries to recipient nations. No note is taken, however, of the problem of distributing food within countries to the needy.

• A call for "have" nations besides the United States (the oil-producing nations are not singled out, however) to make greater contributions.

The concluding section of the speech provides a detailed description of a "network of new entities" to manage food issues under the umbrella of the world food council.

Administration officials acknowledged that the new groups are intended to bypass the existing Food and Agriculture Organization of the United Nations. There is widespread agreement within the Administration that this organization has been ineffective.

A number of Administration food experts argued in interviews that the Kissinger speech was vague and tentative because Washington really had no policy on food.

"My great concern," one official said, "is that he has come up with watered-down proposals emerging out of interdepartmental battles."

Defenders of the late draft maintained that its purpose and the purpose of the Rome conference were to initiate thinking about the food problem in global terms and to set directions for future negotiations.

It is this theme of facing immediately the prospects of future scarcities while some countries monopolize resources that seemed to dominate interviews not only with American officials but with foreign diplomats as well.

In the nineteen-fifties, when nuclear capability was the currency of power, the world was divided between pro-Moscow and pro-Washington nations. The issue was protection.

In the nineteen-sixties, when industrial capacity was a prime measure of strength, the United States, the Soviet Union, Western Europe, Japan and China, because of her potential, held the world focus. Many less developed nations sacrificed agricultural programs to build industry.

In the nineteen-seventies control of scarce resources has emerged as the new barometer of power. The pivotal points have become North America (Canada as well as the United States, because of riches in food and fuel), the Soviet Union, the oil-producing nations, particularly of the Middle East, and again China. In the eyes of many officials, the issue is now survival.

President Valéry Giscard d'Estaing of France spoke directly of this recently.

"Europe is in the decline," he said, "a decline in population and an impoverishment in resources. It is going down in relation to others who are going up. The Europe we have to build now is a Europe of penury."

How Europe, the United States and others are adjusting to these new realities was discussed by officials and diplomats in terms of the following questions:

First, how are the politics of food and fuel linked, beyond the connection discussed by President Ford before the United Nations General Assembly?

Second, can food be used as a "weapon" in international diplomacy, as suggested recently by Secretary of Agriculture Earl L. Butz and in the past by Mr. Kissinger?

Third, what are the connections between international food politics and domestic politics, not only in terms of inflation but also with respect to the psychology of dependence on food aid?

And fourth, what are the positions likely to be taken at Rome and afterward by the United States and other involved nations?

Officials familiar with the speech by President Ford at the United Nations on Oct. 8 stressed that its main aim was to link food and fuel rhetorically to underline world economic interdependence and to bring about self-restraint on prices on the part of the oil producers in return for self-sacrifice in food aid by the food producers.

Officials agreed, however, that while higher fuel prices drove up the prices of fertilizer and transportation—thus increasing the price of food—inflation in food prices was basically caused by the gap between the demand for food and the supply.

Beyond this, officials seemed to disagree on economic issues. For example, Assistant Secretary of Agriculture Clayton Yeutter said that "food is not like oil; the market is noncompetitive on fuel and competitive on food."

But Assistant Secretary of State Thomas O. Enders said that "the food producers' monopoly exceeds the oil producers' monopoly, and this will increase over time, unlike the oil situation."

Just as Washington seems to want to join food and fuel in the name of international responsibility, the oil-producing nations and the less developed nations are trying to sever the connection.

At the United Nations General Assembly meeting recently,

most nations followed the lead of Algeria, according to diplomats, in distinguishing between food and fuel in the name of a new international economic order.

These nations tend to speak of food aid as a matter of human rights, the diplomats said, but they have applied practically no pressure on the oil producers to lower prices. Instead, the diplomats said, they tend to applaud the redistribution of wealth.

Whether food and fuel are knotted or separated diplomatically may well depend, in the judgment of Administration officials, on how the food producers use their scarce resources.

"I don't see us under any circumstances," said Mr. Yeutter, "withholding food for any political reason. That simply would not be acceptable to the American people."

"Food is a way of meeting people's needs," he continued, "and if it is given and sold in the right way, without political strings, it helps people and contributes to good relations with the United States."

Mr. Enders took a somewhat different perspective.

"Food is not a weapon in any immediate bargaining sense," he said. "Over time, certainly, being self-sufficient or being an exporter of food will be an underlying element in the world power balance."

"Food will give us influence," Mr. Enders concluded, "because decisions in other nations will depend on what we do. You can't limit the definition of power to withholding or retaliation."

However "food power" may be defined in the Administration, food has become an important instrument of American foreign policy. As Congress continues to cut deeply into traditional forms of military and economic aid, food aid becomes an increasingly important substitute for the Administration.

In 1973, for example, South Vietnam and Cambodia received about 70 per cent of all American food loans, advanced in an effort to offset other aid funds cut by Congress.

The recent shelving of the new foreign aid bill, which contained substantial funds for Egypt, Syria and Jordan, has increased the pressure within the Administration for large food loans to those countries.

For 1974, planners of United States food programs said they were operating under priorities set by the White House that would again see the bulk of American food aid going to Indochina for budget support and to the Middle East as a diplomatic maneuver.

Aides of Mr. Kissinger acknowledged that foreign policy objectives continued to have the highest priority in the allocation of food aid. They insisted, however, that the Secretary also continued to argue for expanding the purely humanitarian uses of the program for the hungriest countries.

"One thing you can't overlook," a White House official said, "is how all of this food aid being funneled by the United States, Canada, Australia, Western Europe and the Soviet Union affects the domestic politics of the giver and the receiver."

At one extreme of receivers is India. A foreign diplomat said:

"The primary campaign theme for Indira Gandhi in the sixties was India's drive for food self-sufficiency. 'No more American food aid' became the symbol of the Congress party. Self-sufficiency meant more than freedom; it meant that India could finally take care of itself.

"And it worked for several years, to the point where India became a food exporter. But for the last two years it has been clear that India would need aid, but refused to ask for it. India resented this dependence, and asking for food aid anew would have had horrendous political overtones in India. It would have signified total failure on Madame Gandhi's part."

At the other extreme, diplomats said, are a number of African states that do not even tell their own people they are getting food aid.

"It would be an admission that they couldn't take care of their own people," a diplomat explained, "so they keep the aid quiet and it doesn't become a political issue."

For the food givers, and particularly for the United States, officials said, the effect of food aid on the budget, rather than crop availability, is and will be the governing factor.

"We've got the grain," an Administration budget officer pointed out, "and whether we sell it for hard cash or give it away on concessionary terms, it will raise prices at home."

"What troubles us," he continued, "is that if we export it as food aid, it has to come out of the Federal budget, and we are operating under strict instructions to hold the line on the budget."

Many officials who were interviewed stressed that at the top levels of the Administration there was so much concern about inflation, budget ceilings and balance of payments problems that a long-term food policy could not be fixed.

Many officials could not agree on exactly what decision President Ford had made before he delivered his United Nations pledge of a "major increase" in food aid.

Several State Department officials maintained that Mr. Ford had accepted Mr. Kissinger's recommendation to increase the dollar level of food aid under Public Law 480—better known as the "Food for Peace" program—from about $900-million to about $1.5-billion, with the possibility of going even higher if future American crop reports were good.

A high Agriculture Department official said that the President had decided to use $1.3-billion as a "working guideline."

Officials in the Office of Management and Budget insisted, however, that Mr. Ford had merely decided that there would be an increase, but that the exact amounts would be determined on a quarterly basis.

The Administration seems to be reaching agreement on the issue of reserve stocks, however, and is said to hope to exercise leadership in this field in Rome. As announced by Dr. Butz, the Administration believes that worldwide stocks should be on the order of 30 to 60 million tons of grain. Ten million tons of this grain, officials said, would be earmarked for food aid and emergency relief.

There also is agreement that these stocks should be "nationally held" and not controlled by an international authority.

A number of middle-level governmental food experts contend, however, that this new consensus on reserves is totally inadequate. One argued that "even 60 million tons is not nearly enough, and that many of us said it should be at least 90 million tons."

"When you look at India's needs alone," he continued, "10 million tons for emergencies is pitifully low."

Another Administration expert maintained that "nationally held" reserves would never work because "it's a cover for putting the decision in the hands of farmers and private traders, and they have little incentive to hold stocks."

The position of the Soviet Union is likely to be similar to the American stance in emphasizing increased production as the answer to the food question. A senior Soviet diplomat said in an interview that "we do not believe there is a serious food problem in the world; it is a mismanagement problem."

"Look at China," he said. "They're a nation of 800 million people and they are managing to feed themselves."

The positions in Rome of the less developed countries are expected to vary, but most seem to support proposals for large reserves, paid for by others, and a development fund— all with national contributions submerged in an international framework.

West Europeans and Japanese have told American officials that they would like to see the United States Government once again become the principal grain-holder for the world. They have been told by American officials that there is no chance of that.

7 THE 1974 WORLD FOOD CONFERENCE

United Press International

A Running Account
From Rome

WILLIAM ROBBINS | November 5

Secretary of State Kissinger proposed to the World Food
Conference today the establishment of three new international bodies to coordinate efforts to avert spreading famine
and renewed international tensions.

In his speech, delivered at the opening assembly of the
conference, Mr. Kissinger said: "We must act now and we
must act together to regain control over our shared destiny.
If we do not act boldly, disaster will result from a failure of
will."

Ending on a more hopeful note, he said: "Today we must
proclaim a bold objective—that within a decade no child will
go to bed hungry, that no family will fear for its next day's
bread, and that no human being's future and capacities will
be stunted by malnutrition."

In laying out the program proposed by the United States,
Secretary Kissinger divided the approach into these parts:
- Actions by the traditional food-exporting nations to increase their production.
- Aid programs to help developing nations increase their productive capacities.
- Efforts to improve distribution to food-deficit countries
and help them finance their imports.
- Measures to enhance the quality of food, particularly that
obtained by the "poorest and most vulnerable groups."
- A reserve system to insure against food emergencies,
coupled with an information system to warn against impending disasters.

To pursue these efforts Mr. Kissinger proposed the estab-

279

lishment of the three new international bodies—an "exporters planning group," a "food production and investment coordinating group" and a "reserves coordinating group."

He also proposed, as a means of improving nutrition through food of higher quality, the establishment of a "global nutrition surveillance system" by the World Health Organization, the Food and Agriculture Organization and the United Nations Children's Fund.

However, Mr. Kissinger omitted a proposal contained in an earlier draft of his speech calling for a world food council to oversee action under the proposals. Instead, he noted only that "a number of suggestions have been made for a central body to fuse our efforts and provide leadership."

"The United States is open-minded about such an institution," he said.

Edwin M. Martin, special assistant to the Secretary of State and deputy chief of the United States delegation at the conference, said that Mr. Kissinger had dropped the specific proposal for fear that debate over it might divert attention from the basic issues of food.

In its over-all impact, Mr. Kissinger's speech was less a clarion call for dramatic response to immediate needs than a measured, somber accounting of the scope of the task, stressing long-term goals and international cooperation.

While he pledged that "we will do everything humanly possible to assure that our future contribution will be responsive to the growing needs," the Secretary gave no figures on the prospective size of food aid from the United States in the period immediately ahead.

Secretary Kissinger, standing before a broad blue backdrop emblazoned with the white emblem of the United Nations, delivered his address in a low monotone to a hushed audience of more than 1,000 delegates filling a cavernous hall of the Palace of Congresses.

He spoke after Secretary General Waldheim had opened the conference with a speech calling for urgent measures to increase food production in the developing countries. Mr. Waldheim also emphasized that sufficient food stocks must be established on an international basis to meet emergencies.

Mr. Kissinger drew restrained applause at the end of his

address, in keeping with the somber tone of his message and reflecting, on the part of some delegates, especially from the neediest nations, disappointment that the United States was not disclosing specific large increases in aid.

However, Mr. Kissinger did offer some figures. He said the Ford Administration was requesting an increase of $350-million in development assistance in its current budget and said that the United States was willing to contribute $65-million for nutrition research and special nutrition-aid programs under his proposal for improving food quality.

In his address, the Secretary laid special emphasis on co-operation by the oil-producing countries in all the aid programs. In this respect also, the speech as delivered differed from an early draft, in which the oil exporters were not specifically pointed to.

"The oil exporters have a special responsibility in this regard," Mr. Kissinger said. "Many of them have incomes far in excess of that needed to balance their international payments or to finance their economic development." He continued:

"The continuing massive transfer of wealth and the resulting impetus to worldwide inflation have shattered the ability of the developing countries to purchase food, fertilizer and other goods.

"The United States recommends that the traditional donors and the new financial powers participating in the coordinating group for food production and investment make a major effort to provide the food and funds required. Ways must be found to move more of the surplus oil revenue into long-term lending or grants to the poorer countries."

Mr. Kissinger noted that at present there was a 2.5 per cent gap between what developing nations produce and what they need. By 1985, he said, the total food imports they will need will rise from 25 million tons to 85 million tons.

The traditional exporting nations should follow the United States' example and adopt policies to promote all-out food production, he asserted.

But the United States proposals on development assistance, food aid and grain reserves were what the delegates were waiting most eagerly to hear.

For development, Mr. Kissinger proposed efforts that

would increase the growth rate in food production from 2.5 per cent a year to 3.5 per cent. He noted that while the developing countries had 35 per cent more land in grain production than the developed nations, they produce 20 per cent less.

In this effort, he proposed increased research and investment. He said the United States would triple its own contribution to international research centers and to research by American universities on the agricultural problems of developing nations.

Mr. Kissinger recommended that the World Bank join with the Food and Agriculture Organization and the United Nations Development Program to convene his proposed "coordinating group for food production and investment" this year. This effort, he said, should bring together "both traditional donors and new financial powers," that is, the oil-producing countries.

He did not suggest a financing goal. Other interested persons have suggested development funds as high as $5-billion a year.

On this point, Mr. Martin explained that the United States felt such a figure had been "pulled out of the air" and had no way of knowing whether that amount could be used efficiently.

Secretary Kissinger said that while the developing countries should be aided with food and funds, they should also be helped to help themselves, particularly through trade. He noted that the United States trade bill made provision for preference to imports from such countries.

On food reserves, he said: "A worldwide reserve of as much as 60 million tons of food above present carryover levels may be needed to assure adequate food security."

He proposed international agreements on each nation's responsibilities for reserves and guidelines should be drawn on their management. The agreement should include an information system for the sharing of data on stockpiles and crop prospects, he said.

He also suggested a sanction against countries that refuse to cooperate in dealing with food emergencies, as the Soviet

Union has done in the past, although he did not mention any specific country.

Mr. Kissinger did not touch on the question of how the United States might manage its own reserves. Secretary of Agriculture Earl L. Butz has said that the responsibility should be left with the commercial trade. Other observers have contended that such a system would be too uncertain.

A high United States official attending the conference said today that the United States would "handle whatever reserve responsibility is assigned to us." If the volume proves too great for the trade to handle, he said, then the Government itself might have to manage part of the stockpile, although the Administration prefers to avoid that cost.

Another high-level official who was traveling with Mr. Kissinger and was familiar with details of the preparation of the speech, said the United States was hopeful of being more generous than the speech indicated. He said it was hoped to increase both the dollar amount of food aid and the actual volume.

Because of inflation and uncertain supplies, however, decisions will continue to be made on a quarterly basis, he said.

CLYDE H. FARNSWORTH | *November 6*

Suggestions that people in rich countries eat less to free food for the third of the world struggling for existence have begun to emerge as one of the key issues at the World Food Conference here.

Church and voluntary charitable organizations from Canada are urging that the conference include in its final declaration a statement that the affluent nations intend to trim their diets.

Meanwhile, Canada pledged today a 20 per cent increase in her food aid to hungry nations, a move that was viewed as an effort to put pressure on other countries with food surpluses for similar pledges.

The question of eating less sparked an exchange during the

day at a strategy session of the American delegation between Senator Mark O. Hatfield, Republican of Oregon, and Secretary of Agriculture Earl L. Butz.

Senator Hatfield argued that reduced consumption, particularly of meat, could help meet the food shortage in South Asia and the sub-Saharan countries of Africa.

Dr. Butz countered with the argument that the grain component of meat could not be transferred directly into food aid because the animal forage was not usable in that way. He asserted also that even if the food released were edible by humans, it could not be transferred immediately because someone has to pay for it.

The point of view expressed by the Secretary has been disputed by others here as well. For example, Barbara Ward, the social scientist, has said that the money saved from eating less should be spent buying grain to ship to hungry nations.

Lester R. Brown, a senior fellow of the Overseas Development Council in Washington and a former Agriculture Department adviser, said grain sorghum, originally taken over to North America from Africa in the food stores of the slave ships, has been used as a food in India since 1970. Sorghum, high in nutrients, feeds cattle in the United States.

Asserting that it takes up to eight pounds of grain to produce one pound of meat, Mr. Brown estimated that a 5 per cent reduction in meat consumption in the United States would free 6 million tons of grain. This, he said, is equivalent to 60 per cent of the present food gap of 10 million tons in the part of the world on the brink of starvation.

He and other experts have also cited health reasons for eating less meat. The American Heart Association has recommended a one-third cut in meat consumption.

Commenting on demands for eating less, Edwin M. Martin, deputy chief of the American delegation, said that high beef prices in the United States had already reduced consumption of meat and released feed grain for other purposes. He said American cattle raisers were complaining loudly that they could not make a living at today's prices and had been destroying their livestock rather than take the animals to market.

Christian Bonnet, the French Farm Minister, when asked

what his food-loving country thought of the ideas to reduce consumption, said, "They are intellectually seductive, but totally impractical at the present time."

Many experts here said that they thought one result of the conference could be to spur voluntary reductions in food consumption, even if governments did not actively support such action.

Church and other groups in the United States, it was noted, have already called on members to eat less meat. Students at Yale, for instance, have asked the university administration to omit one meal a week, and the idea was said to be catching on at Harvard. Nearly 2,200 Yale students joined a campus fast yesterday to mark the opening of the food conference here.

"I think the people of the United States would like to do something moral for a change after Vietnam and Watergate," said Mr. Brown.

After World War II President Truman closed the distilleries in the United States for three months to free grain for a hungry Europe. Today Americans are consuming a ton of grain a year each, or its equivalent in meat, compared with only a half ton in Mr. Truman's day. Indians today consume 400 pounds a year.

"Voluntary reductions are possible," says Susan Sechler, co-director of the Agribusiness Accountability Project, a Washington-based public interest research organization, "and there should also be a government policy to put pressure on the food business to discourage wasteful consumption."

Her group is one of many organizations represented at this conference in the hope of goading governments into action.

CLYDE H. FARNSWORTH | *November 7*

Major grain-producing nations—including the United States, the Soviet Union and China—have agreed to consider a program to limit their foreign sales in an effort to free grain supplies for emergency aid to hungry people.

American sources said that a secret meeting of the producing nations had been held here yesterday, bringing China and the Soviet Union together for the first time to discuss cooperative action for dealing with the world food crisis.

The nations attending the meeting discussed the mechanics of the proposed program of emergency aid for the 500 million people facing starvation or malnutrition in the next eight months, the sources said.

The move represented a major breakthrough at the World Food Conference, where 130 nations have gathered to organize systems for increasing food production and building emergency stocks to insure, as Secretary of State Kissinger put it, that within a decade "no child will go to bed hungry."

Policy differences between rich and poor countries had led to procedural delays at the conference that threatened to hold up the start of the mobilization efforts in the war against hunger. A.H. Boerma, the Dutch director general of the United Nations Food and Agriculture Organization, afraid that the conference would drift from its objectives because of bickering, organized the meeting of the producing states to deal with the problems of the next eight months, which are considered critical.

He produced a paper for the heads of the delegations of the United States, the Soviet Union, China, the European Common Market, Canada, Australia and Argentina. It showed the latest F.A.O. estimates as of Oct. 15 of the grain shortage facing countries mainly in South Asia and the sub-Saharan region of Africa.

The total shortage in these countries is from 7 million to 11 million tons. At the current price of roughly $200 a ton, the value of the grain that is needed is about $2-billion.

Mr. Boerma broke down the needs as follows: India, 3.4 million to 7.4 million tons; Bangladesh, 1.9 million; Sri Lanka, 200,000; Tanzania, 500,000; Pakistan, 1 million, and 20 other countries, mainly in Africa, a total of 1.3 million.

The reason for the wide gap in estimates for India is that officials in New Delhi have been reluctant to acknowledge the magnitude of their difficulties.

Information on exactly what occurred at yesterday's meeting was hard to obtain. Some participants refused all comment.

The Chinese were represented by their head of delegation, Hao Chung-shih, the Agriculture Minister, who said at a plenary session of the conference today that his country had become self-sufficient in food.

He reported that China had imported $2-billion of grain, mostly wheat, over the last three years and had exported $2-billion of grain, mainly rice, over the same period.

China's rice exports are largely to third-world countries.

"Our contribution to solving the world food problem is yet very small, Mr. Hao said, adding:

"It is our hope that, along with the development of our industry and agriculture, we shall be able gradually to change this state of affairs."

The head of the Soviet delegation, Nikolai N. Rodionov, a Deputy Foreign Minister, has not yet spoken before the plenary session of the three-day-old conference, which runs through next week. The Soviet Union is represented at the conference even though it is not a member of the sponsoring Food and Agriculture Organization.

Edwin M. Martin, deputy chief of the United States delegation, said the Boerma group of producing nations had had a luncheon meeting yesterday and had agreed to meet again next Wednesday.

Mr. Martin said the position of the United States, as the world's biggest grain exporter, was that "we will agree to consider" export rationing.

A major question involves working out a way to spread the financial cost of the emergency program. Participation of the Russians and Chinese would mean that for the first time their countries would be sharing some of the financial responsibility for global programs, which up to now they have avoided.

If the emergency effort goes into effect, it would probably mean less grain for such countries as Britain, Japan, West Germany and Italy. These four account for 36 per cent of all the grain bought in international commerce.

Agriculture Secretary Earl L. Butz, chief of the American delegation, and Mr. Martin sat in for the United States at yesterday's meeting.

Tonight, under pressure from Senator Dick Clark, Democrat of Iowa, Secretary Butz sent a cablegram to President Ford asking whether the United States would revise one of its positions at this conference.

The position, which has come under some attack here, was to make no firm commitment on additional food aid this year. Senator Clark proposed at an American delegation meeting tonight that the United States double its spending on food aid to needy nations under Public Law 480 from $175-million budgeted this year to $350-million.

The United States has budgeted altogether nearly $1-billion for food-aid programs this year, but only 20 per cent has been destined for the hungry nations. Most of the other aid is to support American foreign policy.

Much has gone to South Vietnam and Cambodia. This year Chile, Jordan, Syria and Egypt are due to get larger shares of the Public Law 480 spending.

Secretary Butz is leaving here Saturday for Egypt and Syria. In Cairo he is expected to sign an agreement to give 200,000 tons of grain to Egypt.

WILLIAM ROBBINS | *November 8*

The United States expects to double its food assistance to hungry nations for humanitarian purposes, increasing the total in that category from the present one million tons to two million tons a year, according to key members of the American delegation at the World Food Conference here.

The delegation cabled President Ford today for permission to declare the United States intention publicly.

The move was confirmed in an interview by Secretary of Agriculture Earl L. Butz, who has been meeting privately with top representatives of other nations on the urgent problem of aid to prevent famine, as well as on other subjects related to the conference.

"If the immediate world hunger problem is going to be solved, it is going to be solved by the nations that have the grain—and some way has to be found to solve this critical problem," Dr. Butz said. "The grain has to be found in the

United States, Canada, Argentina, Australia and the European Economic Community."

The delegation's cable to the President followed insistence by some members of the large Congressional group here, led by Senator Dick Clark, Democrat of Iowa, that some such move should be made.

The United Nations Food and Agriculture Organization estimates that South Asia and the sub-Saharan region of Africa face a grain shortage during 1975 of seven million to 11 million tons.

A member of the American delegation disclosed today that a possible new source of food aid to ease that shortage had been identified at a meeting of the grain-producing nations. It is Canadian wheat—possibly as much as three million tons.

Senator Clark had proposed at a delegation meeting last night, according to sources who were present, that United States food aid for humanitarian purposes be increased from a budget level of $175-million to $350-million, enough to provide approximately a million tons of grain. Secretary of State Kissinger had offered a budget increase figure of $50-million.

Authority for such aid as grants is contained in Public Law 480, which provides for the so-called Food for Peace program. The same law provides for other food aid in the form of long-term credits, which accounts for the largest part of the food assistance volume.

"We're probably going to ship that much more anyway," Dr. Butz said, referring to the proposed increase. He acknowledged that the whole food-aid program was now running at a rate 1.5 million tons above the 3.3 million provided last year, but he said there was no assurance it would continue all year at the same rate.

"But then again, we don't say it won't," he said.

One delegation source said that it was not hard to persuade Dr. Butz to support the request to Mr. Ford.

"It's what he [Dr. Butz] has really wanted to do all along," the source said. "The question whether we make the increase public seemed academic. Our food aid is actually running at a rate of 1.5 million tons over last year, anyway."

Another official here had said that the Administration was

making decisions on a quarter-by-quarter basis and intended to refrain from volume projections because of possible impact on grain prices.

But previous refusal of the United States to disclose specifics of its proposed food aid had threatened to detract from the list of proposals made by Secretary Kissinger in a speech here Tuesday, the opening day of the conference, for long-range measures to help food-short developing nations.

Delegation sources said that the aid increase would be in both grants and long-term credits.

A second private meeting of leading grain-producing countries, called by Dr. Butz, included representatives of Australia, Canada and the European Economic Community, or Common Market, besides the United States. The participants from the other countries were not identified, but they were said to be high-level officials.

The meeting was held yesterday afternoon, following a meeting of delegates from the same countries and other exporters and major importers, called by A.H. Boerma, director general of the Food and Agriculture Organization.

At yesterday's meeting, as in a private session Tuesday, the subject was how to reserve enough of the world's short grain supply to meet the needs of the so-called "M.S.A.'s"—the most-seriously affected nations—whose food deficit was estimated at seven to 11 million tons.

On this question, the delegates generally were said to have pleaded that they would have to await instructions from home, but some clarifications of their grain positions were said to have emerged.

The Canadian representative reportedly said that early snow and frosts had cut his country's wheat harvest to the extent that Canada was left with substantially less than the 11 million tons of wheat she had hoped to export.

The delegate estimated that Canada had been left with three million tons of wheat damaged by early snow and frost and thus unfit for milling. But observers noted that such wheat, while unacceptable to buyers from developed countries who had contracted for high-quality grain, was suitable for chapattis, the flat wheat cakes popular in India, the country that has been hardest hit by food shortages.

The principal problem, the observers said, was how to finance aid shipments of this grain.

The Common Market was said to have 6.5 million tons of wheat for export, most of it committed. Australia was said to have reported that all her wheat crop was committed. Her delegate said, however, that he would ask whether some commitments might be released.

The United States has about 28 million tons of wheat for export. All but about seven million tons of it is already committed to foreign buyers. Of the seven million most is said to be "morally committed" to countries such as Japan that have agreed to exercise restraint and to space out their purchases.

But the United States is convinced that many sales contracts on the books will never be executed, delegation sources said.

Secretary Butz, emphasizing the importance of the opportunities he has had here for contacts with top food officials of other countries, said that he had discussed the commitment volume with Pierre Lardinois, Agriculture Minister of the Common Market, and Joseph Ertl, Agricultural Minister of West Germany.

He said both had promised to discuss the matters with their importers and try to shrink the volume booked.

The United States is trying to get many of the hungry countries to accept rice, of which the United States has a record crop, in the preferential-sales portion of food aid. But despite easy credit, many of those countries consider the rice too expensive.

Mr. Boerma said in an interview that he had received no reaction thus far to his request to the major exporters and importers to find ways to reserve grain for the needy. He had proposed a total of 10 million tons.

"I just want to make sure that we don't come up to the end of the year without supplies and have people wringing their hands and saying 'I'm sorry but we've run out of grain,' while we watch millions of people starve—on television," he said.

"I told them, 'I don't know whether you can bear the responsibility for determining who is going to live and who's going to die.' "

In other developments today, the Soviet Union made its

official statement to the conference in a speech notably devoid of anticapitalist rhetoric, although it blamed much of the present food problem on other "social and economic structures" and cited its own agricultural progress since the Bolshevik revolution of 1917.

The Soviet chief of delegation, Nikolai N. Rodionov, who is a Deputy Foreign Minister, promised: "We will make constructive contributions to any solutions and to progressive actions."

But Mr. Rodionov said he saw no need for pessimism. He said that Soviet specialists contended that the world had enough land to feed 40 billion people, more than 10 times its present population.

CLYDE H. FARNSWORTH | *November 9*

The United States delegation, under pressure from Congressional advisers, proposed a resolution today at the World Food Conference urging that the nonagricultural use of fertilizer be reduced to ease a critical shortage in hungry South Asia.

About 15 per cent of the fertilizer consumed in the United States is used for such purposes as the improvement of suburban lawns, cemeteries and golf courses.

That 15 per cent would have been enough to add two million to three million tons to the wheat crop of India this year, specialists at the food conference reported.

More than 2,000 delegates at the conference took a morning recess today for an audience with Pope Paul VI at the Vatican. In an address, he called for urgent action to deal with starvation, but took exception to pleas for population control that had been heard here.

"It is inadmissible that those who have control of the wealth and resources of mankind should try to resolve the problems of hunger by forbidding the poor to be born," the Pope said.

The American proposal on fertilizer was made at the urging

of Senator Hubert H. Humphrey, Democrat of Minnesota, who pressed the delegation chief, Secretary of Agriculture Earl L. Butz, into action at an American strategy session last night.

Dr. Butz has been opposed to making any call for restraint, either at this conference or in the United States itself. He had argued that the fertilizer scarcity was temporary—the Agriculture Department believes there will be a surplus again within three years—and that Americans should be allowed to do as they please.

American delegation officers said they were uncertain whether today's proposal, if not accepted by the conference of 130 nations, would be followed up by any voluntary rationing or allocation program in the United States.

It was too early for formal comment on the surprise American move. Officials from developing countries generally seemed to favor it. Analysts said it would probably be difficult for rich countries to oppose it.

The resolution, while carrying no legal sanction, nevertheless would serve to focus a policy of moral dissuasion on the body politic of the rich countries. This could have an important effect in getting the fertilizer where it is needed.

One ton of fertilizer can produce 10 to 15 additional tons of grain in India, says an American agricultural expert, Lester R. Brown, who spent six months living in an Indian village.

In the United States, where fertilizer is often used to the saturation point, efficiency declines as more and more is applied. There is a point of diminishing returns, just as with an individual who eats two sandwiches and then is not so hungry for the third.

Mr. Brown estimates that one ton of fertilizer produces only five additional tons of grain in the United States.

The total shortage of food, mainly in South Asia and sub-Sahara Africa, was estimated by the Food and Agriculture Organization of the United Nations, the sponsoring body of this conference, at between seven million and 11 million tons of grain.

This could mean starvation or malnutrition for half a billion people over the next eight months—a period that is considered critical.

A major task of this conference will be to organize a relief effort to avoid such a catastrophe.

The United States intends to double its humanitarian food aid this year. Together with other food-exporting countries, the United States is considering rationing grain sales to more affluent countries to free supplies for hungry nations.

Statistics on chemical fertilizers show that world use has increased sharply since World War II. The combined use of nitrogen, phosphate and potash was less than 10 million metric tons in 1938. The figure was 78 million metric tons last year and is expected to top 80 million this year.

One metric ton equals 2,204 pounds.

Last year and this year, shortages and high prices of natural gas and naphtha, critical raw materials in making nitrogen fertilizer, developed in many nations.

WILLIAM ROBBINS | *November 10*

Delegates to the World Food Conference have completed preliminary work on an international early warning system for commodities that could help smooth out wide fluctuations in prices and help ease impending crises in years of short crops.

The system would call for all governments to report regularly on "crop and livestock conditions and other relevant aspects of their food supply-and-demand situation affecting world food security," under a resolution debated by a conference committee last week.

All nations participating in the conference, including China and the Soviet Union, have members on the committee.

Delegations now have begun a review of revised language on the proposed system, designed to meet reservations and questions raised by several countries — including China's fears of violations of individual states' sovereign rights.

The information system is part of a larger world food security plan that would include an international grain reserve system.

But the information system alone, if adopted in its present

form, would be a significant step toward breaking through the type of secrecy that exacerbated the worldwide impact on supplies and prices of the 1972 Soviet grain deal with the United States.

Because Soviet cooperation is considered highly important, observers consider initial expressions of interest in the information system by the Soviet delegation to be encouraging.

"They asked all the right questions," said an American participant in the negotiations.

Much of the rest of the world has grown highly sensitive to Soviet operations in grain markets since Soviet traders moved secretly into the American market in 1972 and, dealing individually with six large grain corporations, bought up about one-fourth of the United States wheat crop.

Those transactions, coupled with heavy buying by other importing nations, sharply reduced world stockpiles. The depletion of those supplies and short crops in wide areas in 1972 and 1974, caused an upward price spiral that has not yet been ended.

A 1973 information-exchange agreement between the United States and the Soviet Union did not prevent a repetition of secret trading of the same sort, which led recently to White House action that first blocked and then cut back two large purchases by Soviet traders as world supplies tightened.

The Soviet Union can have a heavy impact on world markets both because of wide fluctuations in its own harvests and because of its state-controlled buying operations. In addition, Western leaders note that buying decisions of state-controlled trading agencies are less subject to changes in prices and supplies than are those of private traders.

"Without adequate information, the two systems just don't mesh," Secretary of Agriculture Earl L. Butz said recently.

During Dr. Butz's stay in Rome as head of the United States delegation, he has had at least one meeting on the subject with the head of the Soviet delegation, Nikolai Rodionov, Soviet Deputy Foreign Minister. In an interview this week, Dr. Butz said:

"I made the point that if they are going to be a part of the community of nations, they must share the responsibility. I tried to explain to him that, in the absence of information, they must expect the rest of the world to build defenses against them."

Just such a defense was proposed here last Tuesday in an address by Secretary of State Kissinger. Although the Secretary did not mention the Soviet Union by name, he proposed a sanction against countries that failed to cooperate. Preference in distribution of international reserves, he said, should be given to cooperating nations.

The original draft proposal on the early warning system for commodities included, besides a call for information on crop and livestock conditions, a provision seeking to expand international systems for collection of data and urging aid by United Nations organizations in the development of such systems.

It also contained a provision "recognizing the important role of a comprehensive, timely and adequate flow of information on stocks, prices, export availabilities, import requirements, agricultural input supplies, weather conditions and forecasts, plant diseases, pests and other relevant matters."

The members of the Soviet delegation seemed concerned about the practical details, an American observer noted. Their questions dealt with what sort of international agency might be used, how it would be staffed, how costs would be shared, what the budget impact might be and whether confidential data could be protected.

Most countries want the job to be done by an existing international organization rather than through some new structure. What agency that might be is not an idle question because the Soviet Union is not a member of the Food and Agriculture Organization, one of the agencies suggested for the role.

However, the Soviet Union is a member of the International Wheat Council, an agency created many years ago to handle the now-moribund international wheat agreement that still has a data-gathering and analytical staff. The United States favors expansion of that council function to handle the proposed early warning system for commodities.

The Soviet questions were among 47 statements made by various nations to propose amendments as the committee worked, word by word and comma by comma, through a resolution to set up the information system.

The members of the Chinese delegation, aside from raising questions about national sovereignty, gave no clue whether they might decide to join in the plan, once they got instructions from home.

However, interest shown by several East European countries, including Hungary and Bulgaria, was considered encouraging for the success of the system that will eventually be worked out, but a strongly negative reaction came from Poland.

WILLIAM ROBBINS | *November 11*

Half of the additional food supplies needed to stave off widespread famine will have to be found in the United States, an official of the World Food Conference secretariat said today.

"It has to come from the United States—nobody else has it," the official said, speaking on the basis of surveys made in preparation for the conference.

The United States delegation planned to meet privately tomorrow with other grain producers to try to determine where the needed food might be found.

By the time of that meeting, the Americans expect to have a reply from President Ford on their request for permission to announce that the United States will provide a million tons more of food assistance than was provided last year, an American official said.

The conference secretariat and the United Nations Food and Agriculture organization have determined that 8 million to 10 million tons of additional food aid will be needed this year.

Four to five million tons will have to come from the United States, the secretariat aide said. He said that about a million tons more might come from Canada. Any additional grain would have to come from the European Economic Community, Australia or Argentina.

The identification of possible aid sources was one of a number of developments today, including the following:

Five countries—Bangladesh, India, Pakistan, Sri Lanka and Indonesia — planned to call tomorrow for food grants totaling 10 million tons to meet the present emergency and for additional tonnage to be made available on long-term credit.

Some oil-exporting countries, led by Algeria, Iran and Venezuela, prepared a resolution calling for creation of an agency. to channel agricultural aid to the poorer countries. The agency would include representatives of donor countries, oil producers and aid recipients.

Senator Dick Clark, Democrat of Iowa, said he would introduce legislation in Congress to carry out the intent of an American resolution offered Friday calling for restraints on nonagricultural uses of fertilizer.

President Luis Echeverria Alvarez of Mexico, the first head of state to address the conference, reiterated a Mexican proposal for a world food and agricultural research bank and, at a news conference, said his country had begun discussions with Venezuela on creation of a separate fund for Latin America if the conference failed to act.

The secretariat's attempt to identify possible sources of emergency grain dealt only with availability, not with financing arrangements. Besides seeking funds from the traditional donor nations, the secretariat and the Food and Agriculture Organization are expected to turn to the oil countries.

The four to five million tons of grain reportedly needed from the United States does not take into acount the one million tons of American aid yet to be announced.

Much of any additional aid would be expected to come from the 28 million tons of wheat that the United States has for export. All but seven million tons of that has been committed to foreign buyers, United States officials have said.

But the secretariat aide said it was believed that the United States, through its continuing review of sales contracts, might find some that were not true commitments and some involving tonnage that might be deferred until after next June, when new wheat harvests start coming in.

It is thought that other countries, similarly committed,

might find additional grain available through the same process.

The imminent threat of famine is increasingly overtaking the emphasis on long-term solutions that were given priority in the original planning of the World Food Conference.

Among the resolutions drafted to deal with the long-term questions is a proposal for a food aid fund equal to the immediate relief sought by the five needy countries.

For that fund of 10 million tons a year, the secretariat has also identified possible sources of supplies. Again the United States would be the major supplier, followed by Western Europe, Canada and Australia.

The United States would probably have to supply 5 million to 5.5 million tons. Canada has already pledged a million tons a year for the next three years, and Australia said she would give 550,000 to 600,000 tons a year. The European Economic Community is considered a possible source for 2 to 2.5 million tons.

These supplies fall short of the 10 million tons sought, but it is thought that the rest could be obtained from smaller producers, primarily Argentina.

In his address, President Echeverria laid much of the blame both for the food crisis and for inflation on the more affluent countries.

"The rise in prices, the confrontation of markets, and the crisis of raw materials cannot be attributed to the third world," he said. "In the final analysis, this situation has been determined and brought about by the inability of the great industrial nations to submit their production model to a system of international solidarity and shared development and interdependence based on equity and justice."

Of the food crisis, President Echeverria said:

"The famine that today is paralyzing the activities of entire nations has been manufactured with the same detachment as that employed in the construction of the atomic bomb.

"The progressive transformation of cereals and grains into meat that makes overconsumption of meat in certain affluent areas of the world possible destroys the possibility of a sufficient amount of protein in other parts of the world."

His charge was similar to a growing demand being heard during the conference for more restraint in developed nations on meat consumption.

CLYDE H. FARNSWORTH | *November 12*

"Pan" sounds like the French, Italian, Spanish and Japanese words for bread. In Greek mythology Pan is the god of the pastures, patron of the shepherds. In English pan is a kitchen vessel or what the critics do when they don't like a play.

Pan is something else again at the World Food Conference—a feisty eight-page daily tabloid newspaper published to keep the delegates on their toes, so that this meeting of 130 nations will be a springboard for action to help people who are starving.

With a life no longer than the 12-day conference, which closes at the end of this week, Pan is irreverent, cynical, spunky and professional, put out by a dozen part-time and full-time journalists.

"OK, says Dr. K, we'll play, you pay," the paper said in a headline after Secretary of State Kissinger addressed the conference last Tuesday, proposing new programs for augmenting food production while stressing that other nations had to help pay the bill.

The delegates are put on notice to stay awake. Pan's photographers stalk the meeting rooms snapping pictures of anyone dozing and rush them into print.

The "thought for today" column shows a starving child with the caption: "Remember, they can't eat your words." The tubs of pasta sent out for the delegates' lunch are shown along with officials gorging on the stuff. On page 1 a reader crying in the wilderness calls for a one-day fast.

Pan introduced a "fat tax." A scale was prominently displayed at the meeting hall and delegates were urged to weigh themselves and pay $3 into a famine-relief fund for each pound they were overweight.

The paper focuses on immediate issues—the dispute in the

United States delegation over whether to increase food aid this year; the problem of fertilizers and pesticides; farm incentives, and starvation in Bangladash.

"We know we're successful because we get criticism from both sides, those who think we're too radical and others who see us as too conservative and Western-oriented," says Robin Sharp, one of the reporters and London representative of Oxfam, a committee for famine relief. He used to work for the Australian Broadcasting Commission in Washington.

Five thousand copies are printed daily in the plant of The Rome Daily American under a standard commercial contract. And if delegates skip some of the speeches, they cannot afford to miss Pan, whether they like the paper or not.

Jamshid Amouzegar, Interior Minister of Iran, said he liked its sense of humor and impartiality. A senior official of the Zambian delegation said it was "bright, lively and punchy." A.H. Boerma, Director General of the United Nations Food and Agriculture Organization, termed the paper "amusing and interesting, if a bit unpredictable."

Less impressed is Glen Leet, president of the Community Development Foundation of New York, one of the hundreds of representatives of nongovernmental organizations sent here as observers. He objects because Pan is not a "good news" newspaper.

"We are concerned that if only news of conflict comes from Rome that people will lose heart at the prospects for international cooperation and will withhold the support and cooperation so essential to protect millions of people from starvation," he said.

Criticism of Pan has come from other sources. It was disclosed that the Soviet delegation had lodged a protest with the information secretary calling for the closing of Pan on the ground that it was not an official publication.

The paper had strongly criticized a Soviet statement that world agricultural systems could support 30 billion to 40 billion people. "Some have brought food, if not enough; some have brought money, if not enough," said Pan. "The Soviet Union has brought cynicism and a bellyful of it."

The conference is being run by the Food and Agriculture Organization, but there is no United Nations money in Pan.

Oxfam Christian Aid, another charitable organization, and Friends of the Earth, the San Francisco-based environmental group, are providing the $40,000 for production costs of the paper's one English-language edition.

The reporters, most of them British and most on vacation from their papers in London, are paid about $100 each.

WILLIAM ROBBINS | *November 13*

Representatives of most of the world's major grain-producing and grain-importing nations reported here today that they could not yet determine where enough grain might be found to avert famine in the five most seriously threatened countries.

They made this report at a meeting with Addeke H. Boerma, director general of the United Nations Food and Agriculture Organization, which is sponsoring the 130-nation World Food Conference here.

However, the Canadian Minister of Agriculture, Eugene Whelan, was quoted as having said that at least one million tons of the total of seven million to 11 million tons that the F.A.O. estimates is needed by the five countries could be supplied by Canada if financing were available.

The five countries are Bangladesh, India, Pakistan, Sri Lanka and Tanzania.

In addition to Canada, six countries—Argentina, Australia, China, India, Japan and the United States—were represented at the food-aid meeting, which took the form of a working luncheon. Also attending were delegates to the Rome conference from the International Wheat Council, the United Nations World Food Program and the International Bank for Reconstruction and Development.

The Soviet Union, which is a major grain producer and frequently a heavy importer as well, was absent today, although it was represented at the first meeting of the group, last week.

The group agreed to meet again with Mr. Boerma on Nov. 29, about two weeks after the expected close of the world conference.

The group's response was greeted gloomily by many here who had hoped for a more immediate and positive response to urgent pleas for commitments to rush food aid to the hungry.

Similar gloom among advisory groups here followed a briefing for reporters tonight, at which Senator Robert Dole, Republican of Kansas, appeared with the two officials of the United States Administration who are leaders of the American delegation.

Senator Dole proposed placing before Congress the delegation's request for permission to announce a million-ton increase in humanitarian food aid by the United States. This would double the American commitment.

The request to President Ford had been made in a cablegram signed by Secretary of Agriculture Earl L. Butz, chairman of the American delegation, and Edwin M. Martin, deputy chairman, who is also a special assistant to Secretary of State Kissinger. They acted upon the urging of many members of a large Congressional advisory group here.

Mr. Martin said tonight that no response to the message had been received.

In other comments, Mr. Martin said that the United States was "strongly supporting" a resolution calling for donor countries to work out a long-term 10-million-ton-a-year food-aid program.

He also said the United States found a proposal by Arab countries for a new agency for agricultural development and food aid "extremely interesting," if it meant that "substantial new money" for aid would become available. He was clearly alluding to possible contributions from the oil-producing countries.

At Mr. Boerma's meeting on food aid, several countries, including the United States, were said to have questioned the accuracy and the basis of the seven-million-to-11-million ton estimate of the Food and Agriculture Organization of the needs of the five most seriously threatened countries. The F.A.O. has also estimated an additional need of about a million tons for 15 to 20 other countries.

The United States estimates the total need for the five for this crop year at 10.5 million tons. The United States is said to have reported that six million of that has already been met, with the rest "in sight" if financing can be found.

The most optimistic response at the meeting was said to be that of Canada. Mr. Whelan, the Canadian Minister, said at a news conference for Canadian correspondents that not only could Canada make the grain available, but she would also share proportionately in the financing.

Earlier today at the food conference, Senator George McGovern, Democrat of South Dakota, proposed world cutbacks in defense spending to make money available for food aid. A similar proposal has been made by Peru and supported by the Vatican.

WILLIAM ROBBINS | *November 15*

President Ford refused today to permit the American delegation at the World Food Conference to commit the United States to a million-ton increase in emergency food aid to nations threatened with famine.

The decision, announced by the Secretary of Agriculture, Earl L. Butz, at a news conference, overshadowed other developments on a day in which substantial progress was reported on plans for more food for the future. They included the shaping of resolutions on an international grain reserve and long-term internationally financed aid.

In explaining President Ford's decision, Dr. Butz said the increase "would have a bullish effect on the market." He cited budget constraints, tight supplies and the possible impact on American consumer prices, already sharply inflated.

Another reason, given privately, is that the Administration is unwilling to commit itself for fear that if prices do rise, budgeted funds would buy less grain than the commitment would call for. Decisions on food aid have been made on a quarterly basis to maintain flexibility even though shipments have been at a rate that would produce a 1.5-million-ton increase, Administration sources say.

Commodity experts here question the idea of an impact on

grain markets. "The traders have already discounted it," a source close to the Administration said of the purchasing. "They know as well as anybody that the Government is already doing it."

Last Friday the American delegation requested President Ford to give it permission to announce that the United States would increase its aid for humanitarian purposes from one million to two million tons.

The request followed a meeting at which major grain-producing nations were presented with a report estimating that South Asia and the sub-Sahara region of Africa face a grain shortage of seven to 11 million tons in the next year.

Dr. Butz, at his news conference, charged that three Democratic Senators attending the conference, acting "for partisan political gain," had placed the United States in a defensive position by pressing Mr. Ford to announce an increase in humanitarian aid. Of the Senators who led the initiative the only one whose name he mentioned was Hubert H. Humphrey of Minnesota. The others were Dick Clark of Iowa and George McGovern of South Dakota.

Referring to their public statements, Dr. Butz asserted: "These things have placed the United States in a position of seeming reluctant to go along with food aid. Nothing could be further from the truth."

Though the Secretary acknowledged signing the cablegram requesting permission to announce an increase, he said he was only passing along the Senators' position which they had expressed in private meetings and then in public statements. However, a copy of the message obtained by The New York Times makes it seem that the proposal was the sense of the American delegation.

"Suggest minimum one-million-ton increase current fiscal year 1975," the cable said. It expressed the belief that such an increase was feasible both in terms of budget considerations and "in terms of the supply situation."

"Belief here is that shipment of 4.3 million tons will likely develop anyway," it said, "and announcement here would be extremely constructive at this time in view of Canadian and Australian announcements:"

American shipments last year totaled 3.3-million tons. The

Canadians have pledged a million tons a year over the next three years and Australia has pledged a fixed proportion of gross national product.

In announcing the American position, Dr. Butz detailed the history of the United States food aid to developing countries and noted that it had given 46 per cent of such assistance worldwide since 1962. He also said that more wheat and rice were scheduled for food aid this year than last, with lower shipments of livestock feed. Now, he said, "you need food for people rather than for animals."

"We are indeed shipping more food to the critical areas of the world," he added, citing commitments already made to Bangladesh this year totaling 250,000 tons.

In a recent interview Dr. Butz said that the United States would probably increase shipments this fiscal year as much as the cablegram proposed.

With the American statement the focus of the 12-day conference, which ends tomorrow, shifted from the issue of immediate relief for countries threatened with famine, which had overwhelmed attention, to the long-term problems that the United States delegation has insisted are its primary concern.

"The immediate problem of world hunger is not going to be solved by this conference," Secretary Butz, who is the delegation chairman, had said. "Somehow, we have to find a way to solve this critical problem. But it has to be found where the supplies are—in the United States, Canada, Argentina, Australia and the European Economic Community."

He and his principal aides have been conferring privately with ministers from the other major grain producers on steps to solve the immediate problem, among other subjects.

His assessment appeared to many to be confirmed Wednesday when a meeting of major producers and importers with A.H. Boerma, Director General of the United Nations Food and Agriculture Organization, failed to identify sources for the 7 million to 11 million tons of grain that the F.A.O. estimates are needed by five most seriously threatened countries—Bangladesh, India, Pakistan, Sri Lanka and Tanzania.

Another such meeting is scheduled here Nov. 29. An Administration source said the United States questioned the F.A.O. estimate and expected to tell Mr. Boerma that the five-million-ton-need estimated by the United States will be no problem if financing can be obtained.

Others here have not been willing to accept the United States position on conference priorities. Sayed A. Marei, secretary general of the conference, said this week that pledges for immediate relief would be a measure of its success, and, breaking a diplomatic silence, called on the United States to pledge an increase.

Senator Clark, at a news conference with Mr. McGovern and Mr. Humphrey, expressed the urgency felt by many delegates and observers: "It would be unfortunate to say we are concerned about future generations but not interested here in the half-billion that may die now."

However, Sartaj Aziz, deputy secretary general of the conference, took an optimistic view, saying: "If the position is unchanged it doesn't mean it gets worse. This may not be the last word because the meeting scheduled for Nov. 29 is due to take up this question." He also said he could see that there might be "all kinds of domestic reasons" for the American stand.

Other reactions were mixed.

The Pakistani Agriculture Minister, Khuda Buksh Bucha, said: "I hope it won't have a negative effect on the conference. Perhaps this is internal politics. I think that the American decision to contribute with other donor countries toward a 10-million-ton-a-year goal in food aid is a major achievement of this conference. The United States will be a major contributor."

Joseph Mungai, Agriculture Minister of Tanzania, said: "It is a disappointing outcome in that quite a number of countries were banking on these food supplies."

Some progress in committees working on plans for food for the future were detailed by Richard E. Bell, a Deputy Assistant Secretary of Agriculture, who accompanied Dr. Butz at the news conference. Work is "essentially completed," he said, on an early-warning system to provide information that could help avert serious crises or deal with them expeditiously, on the international grain-reserve plan and on the 10-million-ton-a-year food aid plan.

All such plans are embodied in resolutions, with details to be worked out by negotiating groups.

Mr. Bell said he was encouraged by a statement made in committee sessions that Moscow would be willing to consider an information system.

While noting that the 10-million-ton goal was a substantial increase over present levels, he said it was "feasible provided there are new donors."

In another committee, a proposal by Arab countries for an agricultural development fund has been put in the form of a resolution calling for voluntary participation. The United States usually prefers bilateral aid rather than submerging its help in multilateral funds.

The White House press secretary, Ron Nessen, said today that it would not be proper to say that President Ford had "turned down" the request by the United States delegation to increase American food aid by a million tons.

At a White House briefing he said that the United States would honor the commitment by Secretary of State Kissinger, who pledged increased food contributions in the current fiscal year despite adverse weather.

Mr. Nessen, who said that the United States could not be more specific about the amount of assistance until more information was obtained about crop levels, explained that the Administration feared it would compound inflationary problems if it committed itself to a figure.

To avoid adding to inflationary pressures, Mr. Nessen said, commitments will be made on a quarterly basis and will depend on the most up-to-date crop reports.

The United States will do everything it can to insure larger contributions in the future, he added.

Senator Clark, an Iowan, issued a statement saying that the White House decision "means that we as a nation are unwilling to put forward any meaningful additional assistance to meet the immediate problem of world famine."

"The White House is wrong in defending its refusal to approve the proposal on grounds that the purchase of an additional one million tons would drive prices higher and cause inflation," he added. "In fact, the President just approved a sale of grain to the Soviet Union which was more than twice as large, and it caused no increase in prices."

Meanwhile, at a news conference Secretary of State Kissinger said that he expected that before the year was over the United States would increase not only the dollar amount but also the quantity of food aid it would provide to hungry nations.

He expressed regret that the question of emergency food assistance had come up during a conference that the United States had proposed to deal with long-range solutions to food-supply problems.

WILLIAM ROBBINS | *November 16*

A new United Nations agency to supervise programs to give the world, and particularly the less-developed nations, more and better food, was approved by the World Food Conference here today.

The new organization, to be called the World Food Council, will have a secretariat in Rome, associated with the Food and Agriculture Organization, but will report to the United Nations in New York.

Though it requires endorsement of the parent organizations, that action is expected to be a formality, considering the worldwide representation at the conference here.

The new structure represents a key accomplishment of the conference, whose plans it is to help carry out. It was the result of an intricate compromise between underdeveloped and developed nations that was reached in the final session of this 11-day meeting of 130 nations.

Edwin M. Martin, deputy chairman of the American delegation, said that the United States was pleased with the results of the conference.

"This conference was not called to get food to people tomorrow but to lay out a plan of action to prevent the crisis that we have now from recurring," Mr. Martin said.

His apparent allusion was to President Ford's refusal to

commit the United States to a million-ton increase in emergency food aid. However, Mr. Martin acknowledged publicly
what others have said privately, that "we will probably be
giving that much" in additional food aid, but added, "It
would not be useful to announce a figure."

As the delegates gathered here Nov. 5, many hoped that
pledges of immediate aid for some 460 million people imper-
iled by hunger would be made while they worked on long-
term food-supply problems.

Those hopes for immediate pledges during the conference
faded, but before the delegates closed their sessions today
they gave the projected council a number of new programs to
supervise and coordinate, with details and machinery to be
worked out later. The major plans were the following:

• An agricultural development fund, originally proposed by
several Arab nations, including major oil producers, but later
sponsored by many other nations.

• A fertilizer-aid program, with help for increased supplies
for developing nations as well as for new and improved
plants.

• A pesticide-aid program, with research into residual effects
and other environmental questions.

• An irrigation, drainage and flood-control program to aid
developing countries.

• Expansion of agricultural research and training and
methods of disseminating findings among powers.

• A nutrition-aid program, including special feeding for malnourished children and studies on fortification of staple
foods with vitamins.

• Recognition of women's role in agriculture and food, their
right to equality and the special nutritional needs of mothers.

• A call for "achievement of a desirable balance between
population and the food supply."

Earlier in the session, the conference completed work on a
10-million-ton-a-year food aid program for developing
nations, an internationally coordinated system of national
grain reserves, and an early-warning system of data-sharing to
help alert the world to any climatic or other threats to food
supplies or sudden surges in demand.

In another action, the developed nations effectively resisted

demands of the underdeveloped nations for trade preferences, saying that the conference was not a forum for trade
negotiations. Instead the conference adopted a resolution
that requests improved treatment of exports from the poorer
countries.

The compromise reached today on a World Food Council
ended a deadlock between developed and underdeveloped
countries over what sort of follow-up mechanism should be
created to supervise and coordinate food-aid and development programs.

The United States and other developed countries had
wanted a coordinating body to be created and controlled by
the United Nations Economic and Social Council. The underdeveloped countries had wanted establishment and control
by the United Nations General Assembly of whatever body
was created.

The major powers have more influence on the Economic
and Social Council, where representation is on a regional
basis, than in the General Assembly, where each nation has
one vote and the developed countries are outnumbered.

Had the meeting ended in a deadlock, the developed
countries would have automatically won their point, because
the conference must report to the Economic and Social
Council. Apparently, however, no one wanted that kind of
result.

A strong influence on the outcome, according to some delegates, was the Soviet Union's support for those who wanted
the Economic and Social Council to be the umbrella organization.

The solution gave recognition to the positions of both
sides.

Under the agreement, the new World Food Council will be
established by the General Assembly as a United Nations
body reporting to the Assembly through the Economic and
Social Council.

Members of the group will be officials of ministerial or
other high level who will meet from time to time, but the
everyday work will be done by the staff of the secretariat in
Rome.

The secretariat's staff and budget will be drawn from the

Food and Agriculture Organization, but it will be independent of that agency.

The new World Food Council will be responsible for coordinating work of all United Nations agencies now dealing with food.

Mr. Martin emphasized, however, that the new body would not have the power to order action but would have a coordinating role and the responsibility for reporting to the United Nations on needed actions.

The conference also recommended creation of two subsidiary units — a world food security council and a food aid committee, which would take over responsibility for the present World Food Program and coordinate both bilateral and multilateral aid operations.

In one of its final actions tonight, the conference adopted a carefully worded declaration that a committee had spent the entire time of the conference in drafting.

It calls on all governments to "accept the removal of the scourge of hunger and malnutrition as the objective of the international community as a whole," asks "all governments able" to "substantially increase their agricultural aid" and urges all to "reduce to a minimum the waste of food and of agricultural resources."

CLYDE H. FARNSWORTH | *November 17*

Sayed Ahmed Marei of Egypt, secretary general of the World Food Conference, said today that "I am absolutely certain" the Arabs will contribute "millions, no, hundreds of millions of dollars" to an agricultural development fund for third world countries that oil-producing nations have just proposed.

His comment to newsmen shortly after the two-week food conference ended was one sign of the pressure on the oil producers to contribute more to development of the poorer nations.

The fund they proposed at the 130-nation conference was

seen as a response to such demands. The increases in oil prices have aggravated the problems of growth, development and food supply for many of the underdeveloped nations.

"Despite our resolutions, a large number of people face starvation," said Mr. Marei.

"The proof of what we say here must be seen in acts and facts," said the chief of the Algerian delegation, Layah Yaker.

Many delegates, after agreeing yesterday on the creation of a World Food Council within the United Nations to co-ordinate the fight against hunger, said that probably the main achievement of the conference was to focus public attention on global resources and their utilization.

It has been estimated here that half a billion people face starvation or malnutrition in the next eight months if they do not receive food aid. Such starvation could become a recurrent disaster, specialists warned, if resources are not used more effectively.

Defensive comments from many officials of oil-producing nations at the conference indicated the extent of the pressures on them.

"You can't put the blame for the food crisis on the oil countries," said Interior Minister Jamshid Amouzegar of Iran. "The food crisis has its roots in unfair policies of the developed countries, the enormous grain purchases of the Soviet Union and the population explosion."

He said that Iran was "prepared to give—and give more—provided we do not replace the traditional donors' contributions," that is, those of the Western countries.

Secretary of State Kissinger, in a speech last week in Chicago, called for increased Western cooperation to deal with the repercussions of oil-price increases.

"A major responsibility," he said of aid contributions, "must rest with those oil producers whose actions aggravated the problems of the developing countries and who because of their new-found wealth now have greatly increased resources for assistance."

The deputy chief of the Saudi Arabian delegation here, Taher Obaid, retorted: "We are not rich. Richness comes from structures, which we don't have. We import everything from needles and thread to automobiles at inflated prices. We have a continent to develop and services to improve."

Saudi Arabia said that she was already giving 6 per cent of her gross national product in aid. For Iran the figure, according to Mr. Amouzegar, is 7 per cent. Abdullah al-Quandi, a Foreign Ministry official in the Kuwaiti delegation, said that his nation had set aside 8 per cent of her gross national product for aid projects.

"We have contributed more than our share," said Mr. Quandi. "That is not talk but a fact. We were acting even before this conference was organized."

The Western nations give well under 1 per cent of what is, however, an immensely larger over-all gross product.

Before the fund is established, Secretary General Waldheim of the United Nations must be satisfied that there is enough money earmarked for it. Contributions to the fund are voluntary, and so far there have been no firm commitments to the fund.

The United States and West Germany felt that there were sufficient existing international aid groups.

"We have adequate outlets for our money," said the deputy leader of the American delegation, Edwin M. Martin. While they did not seek to block the proposed fund, the industrial countries indicated that they would not be the first contributors.

Summing Up

CLYDE H. FARNSWORTH | *The Struggle Behind the Facade*

They were not selecting a candidate, but discussing hunger in the world and what to do about it. Yet at times the World Food Conference in Rome assumed some of the character of an American political convention.

There were 1,250 delegates representing 130 countries and 165 delegates representing 47 United Nations agencies. There were spokesmen for four liberation movements and 300 non-governmental organizations. Almost all of them had interests to defend and ideas to promote, and the result was politics.

There were the old rich, like the United States and the European Common Market states, aid givers for years; the United States alone has provided $25-billion since World War II. They were prevailed upon to give more.

There were the new rich, the oil producers, whose net income this year will top $50-billion. They were urged to share their wealth.

There were the Communist antagonists, China and Russia, who sat down together and with other major producers and consumers of grain, urgency prevailing over normality. That group will meet again Nov. 29 in an effort to aid the half billion people facing starvation or malnutrition in the next eight months.

And there were the poor. Thirty-two of the most seriously affected states, mainly in South Asia and sub-Saharan Africa, caucused to find the most effective way to make their case for more food aid now and greater security in the future.

As happens in more conventional politics, there were some incongruous combinations. The hungry poor are part of a group of uncommitted nations—and so are the oil exporting states. The latter remain members despite their new affluence.

The convention air was pointed up by the presence of a score of American Congressmen and by the frenzied lobbying of the nongovernmental organizations, most of them charitable, voluntary agencies in the rich countries. The American Senators were making politics, but they also took some constructive action.

Because the leaders of the American delegation were taking what he thought was unusually cautious approach to new ideas, Senator Hubert Humphrey, Democrat of Minnesota, said at one of the delegation briefings:

"We seem to be taking the position that this is somebody else's show in which we are the reluctant participants. . . . Why can't we make a few decisions without referring everything back to Washington?"

That afternoon Edwin M. Martin, the deputy delegation leader, announced a decision by the United States to accept a 10-million-ton annual food aid goal of donor nations.

Among the nonaligned nations, there was much politicking over the conference leadership role between Algeria and Mexico. Mexico won, sealing the victory with an address by its President, Luis Echeverria Alvarez. But while he was castigating the rich nations for multiple variants of colonial subjugation, he himself was the target of leaflets branding him as the C.I.A.-Rockefeller imperialist cover for slave labor. .

Politics does not proceed without food and drink, even here. President Echeverria made a bid for leadership among the conference gourmandisers in a caviar reception on a Rome roof garden. An even more lavish reception was hosted by Saudi Arabia. The United States delegation sought to set a tone of austerity. The word went out that there would be no American receptions.

As at an American political convention, currents of antagonism ran beneath surface cooperation. Two officials, Sayed Ahmed Marei, an Egyptian agrarian reformer who was secretary general of the conference, and A.H. Boerma, who is Dutch and is Secretary General of the United Nations Food and Agriculture Organization, had the responsibility of organizing the meeting and conciliating between competing interest groups. But they had their own problems. Mr. Marei was generally identified with the needy nations of the under-developed world, Mr. Boerma was criticized for being too Western-oriented. As it turned out, Mr. Marei's deputy, Sartaj Aziz, a Pakistani, was credited with a major behind-the-scenes role with bringing some of the factions together.

There was some open carping. The representative of Senegal, for instance, said of S.A. Jabati of Sierra Leone, chairman of one of the conference committees, that Mr. Jabati had been "high-handed" in the way he had "shut the mouth" of various delegates.

The accusation may or may not have been justified, but there was no shortage of words at the conference. Some of the talk was pure self-service, some bombast, but some could turn out to have real meaning as the world struggles to deal with an awesome problem. Governments all over the world will be deciding in the coming months whether they were just words or expressions of national will.

WILLIAM ROBBINS | *Plans for the Future*

Delegates to the World Food Conference convened here Nov. 5 to try to shape a broad international plan for eradicating hunger. By adjournment yesterday [Nov. 17], they had produced a number of resolutions containing the outline of systems that might eventually achieve that goal if developed and fully put into operation.

Many had hoped, however, that the delegates could do something to meet the immediate needs of the vast numbers of people who, it is feared, may die of starvation or malnutrition before any long-term plans to aid them can be put into final form.

While such problems were not solved, the representatives of the major food-exporting countries, who met during the conference with Addeke H. Boerma, director general of the Food and Agriculture Organization, are due to meet here again on Nov. 29 at his request. As a result of the food conference, the participants in the new meeting may have a clearer picture of how great the immediate problem is and how much food could be made available to meet it.

One of the complications here was that the preparations for the food conference did not reflect the parallel deterioration in the world food situation.

The committee structures for the conference were fashioned to deal with long-term problems, and plans made in the form of draft resolutions by preparatory groups continued to follow the aims suggested by the organizers even as crop prospects worsened.

The change in world food conditions came between September, 1973, when Secretary of State Kissinger proposed the food conference in a speech at the United Nations, and Nov. 5, when the delegates met in the Palace of Congresses on the outskirts of Rome under auspices of the Food and Agriculture Organization, a United Nations agency.

Many countries faced the threat of famine as a result of widespread weather disasters, among them drought, floods, inopportune rains that delayed plantings or early snows and frost that damaged crops.

While the framework of the food conference remained unchanged, the threat of widespread famine heightened the sense of urgency about the work of the delegates here. National leaders who spoke at the meeting were not prevented by the long-term focus of the agenda from announcing to the world what they intended to do about the immediate threat.

Attention centered on opening day on Secretary Kissinger, who delivered what was considered to be the keynote speech.

There were widespread hopes that he would announce a large increase in aid from the United States and that his speech would start a wave of pledges that might meet the needs of the most seriously threatened countries— Bangladesh, India, Pakistan, Sri Lanka and Tanzania. Primary concern had shifted to these nations from the sub-Saharan regions of Africa, where a season of rains has eased the disastrous effects of a long drought.

Hopes for such a United States pledge flourished even though there had been clear signals that no such move would be forthcoming at the conference.

Mr. Kissinger gave none. But expectations rose after several Senators persuaded Secretary of Agriculture Earl L. Butz, the leader of the American delegation, to send a message to President Ford asking for permission to commit the United States to increase its emergency food aid to nations threatened with famine from one million tons to two million.

But even as they waited for a reply—which was eventually negative—the delegates were working to shape programs based on the hopes they had brought here.

Aside from the primary hope of famine-threatened countries like Bangladesh for immediate relief, their delegates and others came here with a variety of goals, not all of which could be met because of basic conflicts.

Nearly all the developing countries wanted more help in programs for development of agricultural resources, such as improvement of irrigation systems, and increased supplies of fertilizer and pesticides, products that were in nearly as short supply as food.

Many wanted pledges of food assistance until those development projects could begin to raise food output.

But some, like Liberia, were not even agreed on that. James T. Philips, Jr., Liberia's Minister of Agriculture said he thought any aid should be given in cash on the ground that shipment of free or low-priced foreign commodities tended to stifle production in recipient countries.

"Agricultural development responds to price incentives," he said.

Many other developing countries wanted preferential treatment for their exports.

Major donors among the developed countries wanted assurance from poorer nations that they would give greater emphasis to agriculture in their efforts to become more nearly self-supporting.

In particular, the United States, which has long been the major source of food assistance for distressed countries, wanted other governments, especially those of the newly rich oil-producing countries, to provide more help.

The delegates adopted resolutions calling for a 10-million-ton-a-year food aid program and envisioning an international grain reserve system, with supplies to be built up by cooperating nations in years of plenty to guard against future emergencies. They also approved a proposal for an early warning system to provide for the sharing of information on crops, supplies and any major projected changes in demand.

For the longer term, they agreed on a resolution calling for an agricultural development fund, an idea proposed by a group including oil-producing nations, and they approved programs for irrigation, fertilizer, pesticides and nutrition assistance.

But all these are mere outlines on paper until specific action is taken to put them into operation. There were few specifics beyond the 10-million-ton figure for the food aid plan.

Edwin M. Martin, deputy chief of the American delegation, observed as the conference closed that the success of that plan would depend on whether some new donors of cash or supplies would come forward.

Noting that no cash donations had been pledged, he said he could give no assurance that the United States would participate without some indication of large new sources of money. This was a clear allusion to the oil producers.

"We already have adequate outlets for our money," he said. "We are not looking for new places to spend it."

For all of these resolutions, it is generally agreed, success will depend on negotiations still to be conducted and machinery still to be established.

Responsibility for that is to be placed on the World Food Council, a new agency to be set up by the United Nations General Assembly, and a consultative group on food investment and production, which is to negotiate details of the food-aid system, including national responsibilities.

The new food council is to be responsible for coordinating the work of the new programs proposed here as well as that of existing institutions, such as the World Food Program and the United Nations Development Fund. But, Mr. Martin said, "it is a coordinating body without teeth."

Despite all the uncertainties, delegates were generally pleased by what they had started.

Summing up today, Mr. Boerma, the Food and Agriculture Organization's director, remarked to his own council: "I regard the results for the long term as extremely promising."

But he added: "There is still a very grave problem affecting the food supply of millions of people over the next few months."

8 SURVIVAL

BOYCE RENSBERGER | # The Will to Cooperate

In the months since agricultural experts first forecast the famine that is now causing deaths in India, leaders in many fields have come to regard the present world food situation not merely as an acute crisis but as the beginning of a chronic global condition that calls for fundamental changes in the way people live and governments cooperate.

In the view of many experts, events of 1973 and 1974, such as the Arabs' oil embargo and the huge Soviet grain purchases, have rapidly thrust the world into an era in which there are scarcities in a number of resources, scarcities that would otherwise have come only one at a time over a period of many years.

It is clear, however, that there exists a wealth of potential solutions to almost every problem in the food situation. Some are sweeping proposals requiring concerted international action; others are small, concrete measures that could be adopted by peasant farmers.

The limiting factor, virtually all those consulted agree, is the strength of will of leaders in government and finance to make food production and distribution matters of high national and international priority.

Many experts share deep misgivings over whether the world's leaders, relying on traditional political and economic relations among countries, can soon come to grips with the situation peacefully. They feel that the crisis could spawn crippling divisions at a time when global interdependence and cooperation are becoming crucial to peace, economic stability and improved living conditions for all mankind.

There is even concern for the welfare of the United States if the world's food resources, substantially in the hands of Americans, should be withheld from other countries in the way oil-producing countries withhold their resources. The United States controls a larger share of the world's exportable food than the Arab countries' share of oil.

The United States depends on many smaller countries for supplies of several vital minerals. Some experts suggest that a selfish American policy on food resources, including fertilizer, might backfire by setting a pattern that could place this country at the mercy of those countries should they decide to use their resources as weapons.

Another factor, the experts feel, is the economic viability of foreign countries that may purchase American exports. Food shortages could lead to such economic deterioration within some countries that they could not continue as or become customers of the United States. The effect on the American balance of payments and the stability of the dollar could be serious.

Agricultural economists say that the single most severe effect in the United States of a failure to enlarge the global food supply rapidly would be continuing high rates of inflation.

Many economists agree that rising food prices are a major factor in American inflation. They say the prices are rising largely because American consumers are now competing with the Soviet Union and other countries for very limited supplies.

A crop failure in Siberia or in India sends foreign buyers to the United States grain market to compete directly with American bakers, cattlemen and other food processors. Expanding the food supply by improving agriculture in other countries would be one way to fight inflation not only in the United States but everywhere.

In the view of Dr. Jean Mayer, the Harvard nutritionist and chairman of a nongovernmental group of delegates to the World Food Conference, "this is a very critical period in the history of man.

"What we do now," he has said, "in the face of this situation with all its ramifications, can influence the quality of life everywhere for a long time to come. The influence can be good or bad."

For all the apocalyptic talk, experts on the world food situation are not forecasting perpetual famine anywhere, at least for the foreseeable future. For one thing, food supply depends on weather. This year it has been bad for much of the world. Next year it may be good and some countries that now have shortages may even grow a surplus of food.

What most of the leading authorities do foresee is a marginal situation extending for some years, with the duration depending on what remedial actions are taken. One year there may be enough food to go around; the next there may not be.

Because reserves of food upon which to call in time of scarcity are now so low—the lowest in a 20-year period that has seen world population grow by a billion—outbreaks of famine may come more frequently than in the past. Regions that have suffered continuing malnutrition may become larger and the depth of deprivation may grow.

Small fluctuations in rain or fertilizer supply or moderate epidemics of crop diseases that once would not have seemed serious on an international scale now may be enough to depress food production below the thin margin of reserves.

Just to maintain present barely adequate levels of per-capita food production requires the world's farmers to increase output by about 2 per cent a year, the rate of population growth. Over the long run, this is being done but in any single year the actual production may be above or below the required level.

One solution to this uncertainty is at least as old as the Biblical Joseph's granary—the practice of storing grain from a surplus year to be eaten in a deficit year. Indeed, agricultural societies everywhere have successfully used such a system on local scales until population growth made the demand for food so high that surpluses could not be set aside even in good years.

Another factor affecting food supplies has been the trend in affluent societies toward consumption of meat grown on grain. Dr. Georg Borgstrom of Michigan State University estimates, for example, that the world's cattle consume as much food as would 8.7 billion people. As meat-eating affluence spreads, the demand for primary food products grows much faster than does the population.

To meet the deficits of recent decades many countries have turned to importing food from the handful of countries blessed with good land, stable climates and a long history of scientific, high-technology farming that are still capable of producing surpluses. These are primarily the United States, Canada, Australia and Argentina.

This practice worked for a decade or so, until the surpluses of even those countries were nearly eaten up. This is where the world stands now.

"If we're going to tackle this problem, the first thing to do is separate the short-term situation—the starvation in India right now—from the long-range solution—making each country as nearly self-sufficient as possible," said James P. Grant, president of the Overseas Development Council, a private American consultative group.

This view is widely shared by other food authorities who feel there has been confusion leading some to believe that the experts are suggesting that the United States should continue forever to rescue India and other hungry countries with unending food aid.

The consensus among those consulted is that even if there were not political obstacles to this, it would simply not be possible in practical terms. American agriculture is abundant, but not that abundant. There is virtual unanimity that, over the long run, the main solution is to intensify and expand agriculture within the poorer countries and to lower the rates of population growth there.

Short Term Solution A Humanitarian Matter

The short-term situation, on the other hand, is essentially a humanitarian matter. If substantial food aid is not provided soon, the famine that has already taken hundreds and perhaps thousands of lives in India may claim millions in 1975. Also the drought in sub-Sahara Africa, now abated with a season of good rains, may resume, requiring further food aid there.

At present the country most able to end the Indian famine is the United States. Despite the drought during 1974 in the American Midwest and West, which affected corn and soybeans, the wheat crop was good. Even so, political considerations have weighed at least as heavily as humanitarian sentiments.

Many world agricultural experts feel that the United States has not made a large enough commitment of food aid to India and fear that it may take a disastrous famine there—"beamed into our living rooms every night like the Vietnam war," in the words of one—to stimulate action on the scale that is needed.

Dr. Sterling Wortman, a plant breeder and vice president of the Rockefeller Foundation, a major benefactor of agricultural research around the world, said he hoped that mass starvation could be averted but noted that "the disappearance of the surpluses could be the most important single, favorable event of recent years if it results in widespread attention to agriculture, plus effective action."

Many authorities also urged that a second step, after direct food aid now, would be the supplying to India of fertilizer and fuel for irrigation pumps. If the food shortage there is to be remedied, Indian farmers must have more fertilizer and fuel to raise the next crops.

If Indian farmers can get fertilizer and fuel for their pumps, they will have a good chance of producing enough food in the next crop seasons to overcome most of their own deficits. Mr. Grant suggested that it might be necessary for American farmers to share some of their fertilizer with Indian farmers.

Instead of using a pound of fertilizer in the nearly saturated soils of the United States where it might raise food production by only two or three pounds, the same pound could be used in the nutrient-starved soils of India to yield three times as much food. Thus, a slight reduction in American productivity might readily be translated into a major increase in Asian productivity.

Beyond rescuing the people suffering now, the next needed step is the establishment of a world grain reserve that would share among all countries the burden of preventing future famines.

Some American interests, including grain traders who make their money on fluctuations in the market prices, oppose a world reserve on the ground that it will tend to stabilize prices by absorbing surpluses and releasing grain when scarcity might otherwise drive the price up. Many American farmers fear that prices will be stabilized at the low end of the range.

It is generally agreed that a world grain reserve should be organized in such a way as to maintain the confidence of farmers that they will not suffer.

Longer-Term Goal: Improved Farming

Compared with the short-term solutions of food and fertilizer äid and a world grain reserve, the long-term solutions considered necessary appear substantially more difficult. The goal can be stated simply: improve farming in the poor countries.

One of the most consistent comments by agricultural scientists who have visited many hungry countries is that the low productivity of farming in them does not result from any innate backwardness of individual farmers but the lack of government support for programs to make the latest methods and equipment available. "I have a lot of respect for the small farmer," said Norman E. Borlaug, a wheat scientist who spends most of his time consulting with farmers and government leaders around the world. "Almost invariably, when you look at what he's doing with his land, you find he's producing the maximum under the situation he has to work with. The thing is that he usually doesn't have much to work with."

In a handful of countries governments have made concerted efforts to tell farmers about new methods and to set up rural credit mechanisms through which poor farmers may borrow money to buy fertilizer or equipment. Food production has grown impressively.

Even in India, for example, farmers in the Punjab were able, with strong government support, to adopt new high-yielding varieties of wheat at a rate faster than American farmers adopted hybrid corn, the classic success story of United States farming.

In most poor countries, however, farming has long been considered an unglamorous activity warranting only low priority in national development efforts.

One effect of the present food crisis, many experts say, is that governments are beginning to realize that they must play a stronger role in encouraging their own countries' agricultural development. Closely related is the emerging view that it is not necessary, or often even desirable, to try to install American-style, large-scale machinery-intensive farming methods in countries now depending on small labor-intensive farming.

Scientific farming practices can be employed on tiny farms of only an acre or two on which all the work is done by one family with no tractors.

Labor is what most poor countries have plenty of, and agricultural scientists are now adapting many techniques to make use of it. Where this has been done, as in Taiwan and South Korea, small farmers are enjoying rising standards of living and are beginning to have the money to spend on modest consumer goods such as shoes, pots and pans and bicycles.

The stimulus for small industries in small towns is growing and, some economists say, this more modest route of development is making more solid gains than did the showy steel mills and skyscraper hotels that once symbolized prosperity in poor countries.

In Dr. Wortman's view there are four prerequisites that must be met before farmers can change to new, higher yielding systems:

• There must be new techniques or materials that are demonstrably superior. These include the new seed varieties with higher yield and resistance to disease, fertilizer and methods of using it, irrigation methods and systems for multiple cropping or intercropping. All of these are produced by scientists in research centers needing money.

• Farmers must be able to acquire the necessary materials when and where they need them and at prices they can afford. This often calls for a credit system so that a farmer can borrow money against the prospect of a higher yield.

• The farmers must be shown how to make use of the new materials and methods. This education, or "extension" system, many experts point out, must be in the hands of people who themselves are skilled farmers and can command the respect of the unlettered farmers.

• The farmer must be assured of selling his products at a price that will pay back his investment in expensive fertilizer and other materials and give him a profit. This may require government regulation of marketing and distribution systems.

Many agricultural scientists feel that if these requirements are met, it should be possible to more than double food production in underdeveloped countries using technology that is now available.

A key problem over the long run is the rate of population growth. While agricultural progress over the last 10 or 15 years has been spectacular, the growth in population has largely wiped it out.

Whether fertility can be controlled in time to avert chronic widespread famine is a matter of wide debate. There is general agreement that while a rising standard of living based on agricultural advances tends to reduce the birth rate, the effect probably is not rapid enough in the more populous countries to control numbers before famines exact devastating tolls.

Most authorities generally regard Africa and Latin America as relatively less difficult problem areas because of their lower population densities and the existence of much unexploited potential farmland. In fact, there is talk that if the Arab countries could be persuaded to invest in what is now largely unused land in Argentina, the potential is there for vastly increased, high-technology wheat production.

India however, is regarded as a very different situation. The population is already high and growing fast. Almost all suitable land is under the plow. Some experts say privately that they do not see how vast long-term suffering and social chaos can be avoided in India before agriculture is improved sufficiently and population is controlled.

While it may be possible to itemize the major areas of needed long-term action in only four categories, none of the experts pretends the job of feeding mankind adequately will be simple or easy. It is an almost overwhelmingly complex matter with direct links to the energy crisis, inflation and the vagaries of international politics.

Nevertheless, some steps toward solutions recommended by food experts are not beyond the abilities of individuals, including both American consumers and peasant farmers.

Because the production of meat, particularly beef, requires so much grain, Americans are being asked to reduce their meat consumption. Every pound of beef represents eight to ten pounds of grain, enough to feed an Indian adult for a week.

In many poor countries as much as half the grain that is grown is lost to rodents and insects through improper storage. It has been suggested that if, instead of heaping it in the corner, farmers would store their grain in old oil drums or in baskets propped up on stilts, much more could be saved for human consumption.

To conserve badly needed fertilizer for export to poor farmers, it has been suggested that Americans forgo or cut back on fertilizer lawns, golf courses and cemeteries. In fact, some activist groups are recommending that homeowners raise vegetable gardens, which would require little or no fertilizer, instead of grass.

Few food experts believe it will be possible to continue very long on the present course, with the rich countries monopolizing food resources with their meat-heavy diets and thick crops of suburban grass that never feed a cow.

To increase food supplies only at the present slow rate, behind demand and with no emergency supply, is to invite repeated disasters.

Many of the experts think that the resources exist to feed every person well but only if they are shared. There is evidence that if they are shared, the rate of population growth will decline. There is also evidence that when they are not shared, the social and economic effects within and among countries may be profoundly disrupting.

At risk is not only the agony of lingering death for millions, mostly children, but the character of the world left for the survivors.

POSTSCRIPT

No miracles were expected from the World Food Conference in Rome, and none came to pass.

That international meeting, like many preceding it and others still to come, brought into play sharply different national viewpoints imposing real constraints on optimal solutions. Out of the conference came resolutions calling for expanded food aid and the creation of a World Food Council, a new United Nations agency. But the commitments on help for the hungry were vague and, as an American delegate observed, the council emerged as a "coordinating body without teeth."

Even so, the year 1974 may come to be seen as a major turning point in mankind's efforts to banish the age-old scourge of hunger. In a remarkable and telling way, many factors—notably the acute fuel shortages resulting from Middle East embargoes, bad weather, and rising demands for grain coupled with a disturbing decline in world food reserves in relation to population—produced an issue that captured the attention of world leaders and ordinary citizens alike and underlined the interdependence of the world's peoples.

Farmers dependent on chemical fertilizer and fuel to drive farm machines, whether in Asia, Africa, the United States or elsewhere, were affected by the reduced flow of oil and the prices that had to be paid for what flowed. Efforts to improve living standards in the Soviet Union had a direct impact on the food budgets of American families. Nor was the rest of the world immune to the hunger produced by the shifting monsoon pattern in India or the advancing desert in the Sahel.

Such links in the complex global food system suggest that the most rational approaches call for joint and cooperative actions dealing with the system as a whole. Only small beginnings have been made in that direction, however, and the most realistic hopes seem to lie in increasing food outputs in each country to levels as near self-sufficiency as possible.

For 200 years nations have been preoccupied with an industrial revolution that in many places has obscured the bedrock importance of agriculture as the sustaining base of man's well-being. With food production becoming more critical, self-preservation underscores the need for governments throughout the world to devote more attention to agriculture and population-resources balances as critical components of national policy.

Crises have their ups and downs, and before long bumper or even record crops here and there could make the world food crisis seem like an exaggerated peril. But the race between food production and rising population will be far from over. The margin of safety, should one develop, is not likely to grow large again for some years. As reflected in this volume, the condition is chronic, not transient.

The situation is not hopeless. Much can be done to cope with the problem. But to do so effectively will require much effort, much skill and much good-will—on a continuing basis.